On Time, On Target

Taken just a week after discharge in January 1946, I was twenty-one, and the war was over. I looked forward to a peaceful if uncertain future after three years of the horrors of war.

ON TIME ON TARGET

The World War II Memoir
of a Paratrooper in the
82d Airborne

John D. McKenzie

PRESIDIO

Published by Presidio Press, Inc.
505 B San Marin Drive, Suite 160
Novato, CA 94945-1340

Library of Congress Cataloging-in-Publication Data

McKenzie, John D.
   On time, on target : The World War II Memoir of a
   Paratrooper in the 82d Airborne / by John D. McKenzie.
      p. cm.
   Includes bibliographical references.
   ISBN 0-89141-714-1
     1. McKenzie, John D. 2. World War, 1939–1945—
Campaigns—Western Front. 3. World War, 1939–1945—
Personal narratives, American. 4. Soldiers—United States—
Biography. 5. United States. Army—Biography. 6. United
States. Army. Parachute Field Artillery Battalion, 456th—
History. I. Title.
D756.M42 2000
940.54'1273—dc21
    99-058260

All photos from the author's collection unless noted.
Maps by Aegis Consulting Group

Printed in the United States of America

Contents

Preface

The viewpoints expressed in this book are those of an enlisted soldier, not a commissioned officer or a general. I was a "grunt," one of those on the sharp edge of war who actually carried out orders and did the fighting. I define "grunts" as those soldiers below the rank of major whose main goal was to carry out the strategies and tactics designed by those above them to defeat the enemy. The army did its best not to enlist mental incompetents or psychopaths. By eliminating those groups, the range of intellectual ability of those who served in the army varied as widely as it could within the general U.S. population. Ours was a citizen's war and, with reasonable exceptions, most of those who were physically and mentally able to fight were called upon to serve. During World War II more than 16,300,000 men and women served in the U.S. armed forces. Of those, 1,078,162 (6.6 percent) became casualties, of which 407,316 (2.5 percent) died. Casualty rates in combat units like the 82d Airborne Division, in which I served, were much higher. When I returned to the states I set out to obtain a good education—financially aided by the GI Bill—a fine wife and family, and a good and satisfying life. I was one of many who marched into the maw of war and escaped. Many others did not.

Throughout my forty-year business career I enjoyed studying history. After my retirement at age sixty-six in 1990 I decided to do the concentrated study and research necessary to write historical works. My first book, *Uncertain Glory: Lee's Generalship Re-Examined,* was published in 1996. This book, my war memoir, is quite different. It is written from two perspectives: that of one who actually experienced the violent combat described and that of a historian.

I was a typical college boy, an eighteen-year-old engineering student at Purdue University, when I was drawn into the chaos of World War II in May 1943. There followed 959 days of high adventure, horror, and boredom.

Although I consider the war to have been the most exciting, adventurous, and exhilarating time of my life, writing this book has been difficult for me for several reasons. First, I am an introspective, private person who finds it difficult to disclose to others my personal feelings to the degree necessary. Second, I lost a score or more of friends and comrades to death, wounds, and the unknown. For some time after my return home I suffered from a case of survivor guilt. A litany of subconscious thoughts drove this, including such ideas as: Why did I live and they die? They were certainly no better or worse than I. And, finally, Maybe they died *because they were my friends,* or their association with me brought them death. That last, most terrible of thoughts is clearly nonsense, but the subconscious mind does not recognize it as such. One of the problems with this kind of guilt is that those around me could not even begin to understand it, so there was no easy way to talk it out with someone and bring it to a conclusion.

To allow me to continue to function well as a human being, my mind erased my memory bank of most of the names and some of the dates, while leaving a pretty clear memory of events. I was able to recall only a handful of names of men with whom I had served when I first began work on this book. Then, in April 1997, I read the combat log of my wartime battery commander, Lt. Col. Herman L. Alley (Retired), who was then a captain. It is a complete record of events described in stark, clear, telegraphic prose, and it served as a great refresher for my memory. Captain Alley transcribed his log in 1996 from notes he made contemporaneously with those terrible events from 1942 through 1945. It is a sober and sometimes somber statement because most of the soldiers who are specifically noted by name had something bad happen to them: they were killed, wounded, captured, tried by a court-martial, or punished for misconduct. I feel fortunate to have appeared in it only once. In a very few instances my memories are at odds with Captain Alley's log. When I concluded that my memory was faulty, I corrected my statements. However, when I remained convinced my memories were correct, I stayed with them, using my own recollections as my main source.

When I first read that log and the rosters that Captain Alley attached listing the men who served with me at various stages of the war, I experienced a deep depression that soon receded. I think finishing the book has proven to be cathartic for me. I hope that it will bring an end to my more than fifty years of guilt feelings. Much more important, I hope that this book will serve as a lasting memorial to my lost comrades and be of value to others.

My decision to write this book resulted from two recent occurrences. In June 1994, the fiftieth anniversary of the Normandy invasion, my son Dave suggested that I write of my war experiences, pointing out that it would be interesting to him, to his sister Anne, and to my grandchildren, John III and Jaime. It was a suggestion with which I could not argue, but I still had the problem of recovering the memories that I had suppressed.

In April 1995 I had my right hip replaced. I spent months recuperating in the hospital and at home. There was little that I could do, so I spent much of the time trying to discover if I could recall my wartime experiences. As these attempts to remember went forward, I found myself bombarded with memories of those times over fifty years earlier. I concluded that I could write an outline and tentatively decided to attempt the book.

The outline became a good preliminary basis of my story. I found my memory of events improved substantially as I began to expand it. Place names and dates were difficult for me to remember, so I used works written by others to refresh my memory. As I attacked each chapter, I found that my memory of those long ago events improved. It was almost like a dam breaking, flooding my mind with great quantities of knowledge every time I approached a new part of the book.

The 456th Parachute Field Artillery Battalion (PFAB) was part of the 505th Parachute Regimental Combat Team. The team was made up of the 505th Parachute Infantry Regiment (PIR) and other engineer, tank, and support troops—about five thousand men. The 456th followed the 505th throughout the European campaign. For the most part, we went where the 505th went. Additionally, as a field artillery forward observer, I spent most of my time in combat with elements of the 505th.

I want to emphasize that this is *my* personal story. I was not a combat infantryman. Although I was often with them and observed many of the things these men did, they were much braver than I. From time to time I report what happened to my comrades while I was not present. I base my narrative of those events on contemporary reports by those who were there. I hope that my story can serve as one representation of the multitude of other stories that will never be told.

My aim in describing what happened in those tumultuous years is to bring the reader into the action. I want the reader to join me in feeling the cold, seeing the blood, picking up the dead body of a good and valued friend, escaping capture by the dreaded SS, jumping out of an airplane, rolling in the mud, liberating a concentration camp, and even using an army field latrine. I also want the reader to feel the exhilaration of staying alive after fully expecting to die. I not only describe my battles and other experiences, I express my feelings about the things that were happening around me and how much I think the conditions of humanity have improved for the better since 1945.

It is worth noting that I use "army time" throughout the book. The army day starts at just after midnight (0001), goes through noon (1200), and ends at 2400. Thus, 1500 is the same as 3 P.M.

Since this book is also meant as a memorial to those men, living and dead, who served with me, I have used real names whenever possible. In a few instances I report something that might be considered disparaging to a comrade. I have no interest in opening old wounds or causing grief for anyone, so in those cases I have changed the name or otherwise concealed the individual's identity. If I have placed anyone in the wrong place at the wrong time, misrepresented someone's place in an action, given credit or blame to the wrong person, or left anyone out, the errors are mine alone. Any such errors are inadvertent; and I sincerely apologize for any that appear herein.

I want to acknowledge the assistance of Betty, my wife of fifty-two years, who has supported me in every possible way while writing this book, including accepting the unenviable task of proofreading it several times.

Alan T. Nolan, a noted Civil War historian and friend who helped me write a Civil War history book, encouraged me to write of my World War II experiences, as did my son, John D. "Dave" McKenzie Jr., M.D. Dave helped me overcome the subliminal emotional problems the war caused. He also read the manuscript and made many helpful suggestions.

My daughter, Anne McKenzie Nickolson, carefully edited my writing and pointed out areas where military terms garbled the common sense ideas I was trying to describe. Her editing and encouragement helped me finish the book.

John A. Price, a retired Colorado district court judge and my comrade in the 456th PFAB, helped jog my memory where it was weak and clarified my recollections of times, places, and the order of things. In addition, thanks to contacts John maintained over the years, I was able to meet with Richard W. Mote, who served as a gun mechanic in Battery A. Richard contributed some useful notes on our fighting in Normandy. John also led me to Captain Alley and his above-mentioned combat log, and to Mrs. Starlyn Jorgensen, whose late father served with me in the 456th, although I do not recall him. Star shared with me a scrapbook she has compiled on the battalion's wartime service. It includes records and articles written by members, newspaper and magazine clippings, and documents she obtained from the National Archives. It, too, served as an excellent source of information, and filled in many gaps in my memory.

Samuel "Sam" Kennison, M.D., is a friend, neighbor, and retired psychiatrist. When I began to write this book I had a strong desire to learn why I had trouble recalling my more difficult experiences. Sam, who is interested in the subject, worked with soldiers with emotional problems during and after World War II and explained how repression works in the human mind. Sam has been very helpful in allowing me to understand my own case and those of many others.

Charles "Chuck" Everill, a good friend and business associate, also has been most helpful. A former newspaper editor, Chuck read my first draft and made many suggestions on word usage and areas needing expansion and clarification.

William Hanchett—an emeritus professor of history at San Diego State University and a leading expert on the Lincoln assassination and the Civil War—and I became friends because of our mutual interest in that conflict. After reading a draft of this book, Professor Hanchett became enthusiastic about it as a "window into the times of World War II" and gave me much-needed encouragement.

Tom Hanchett proofread a final draft of the manuscript and made a number of useful suggestions.

Working with the editors and staff of Presidio Press in the production of this book has been my pleasure. My goal was to publish the best book I could, and their changes and suggestions helped meet this goal. I particularly wish to acknowledge the contributions of Bob Kane (a retired colonel), E. J. McCarthy and Lynn Dragonette. Dale Wilson, an independent copy-editor employed by Presidio, edited the work well, correcting some errors and pointing out areas that need expansion, shortening, or correction. Kit Bonn did an excellent job in making my rough maps understandable. Everyone exhibited a most professional manner.

My heartfelt thanks to all!

1

From College Sophomore to Airborne Trooper

My war began on 12 May 1943 and lasted for 959 days. This may not seem to be a very long time, but it included parachute jumps, four major battles, and the loss of many friends. After spending time training in England, I fought from Normandy to Berlin.

I was born in Los Angeles, California, on 24 June 1924, the only child of Mildred and Henry McKenzie. My father held management positions and remained employed throughout the Great Depression. We were not wealthy, but his continuous employment at a good salary for those times allowed us to live comfortably. The depression extended from 1929 to 1936, and it was terrible for many American families. I recall my mother buying weekly bags of groceries for some neighbors, and every night we connected a long extension cord to our next-door neighbor's house so they could have light in the evenings. The utility company had turned off their power when they were unable to pay their bills.

Throughout much of World War II, my mother worked almost daily as a volunteer with the United Service Organization (USO) in Hollywood. Most of the time she was the volunteer manager of movie studio tours, and as such she guided many thousands of servicemen and -women through the major Hollywood studios. Many well-known movie actors and actresses would not allow service personnel on their sets unless Mildred McKenzie was with them. Both of my parents' kindness to others served as an early lesson in altruism that has influenced my life.

My father's work caused us to move frequently. As a result, I attended numerous schools and met many diverse people in California, Tennessee, Massachusetts, and Ohio. My parents allowed me a great deal of independence. Beginning at age twelve, I traveled alone by train to spend each of the next three summers with relatives at Lake Tahoe, California. My parents also allowed me to spend a week alone in New York City so I could attend the 1939 World's Fair at age fifteen.

Although my father did not attend college, he became an efficient business executive through diligent self-education. One of his major goals in life was to see me graduate from college, and on the day of my birth he began saving money for that purpose. He always challenged me intellectually and urged all forms of learning upon me, particularly mathematics and related technical subjects. My parents were loving and set rules for my behavior; for the most part, I followed them. Mine was a very happy childhood.

World War II began for America on 7 December 1941 with the surprise Japanese attack on the U.S. Pacific Fleet at Pearl Harbor. With the start of the war, everyone at my high school in Wyoming, Ohio, became active in paper and metal drives to support the war effort and prepared packages to be shipped overseas to soldiers and sailors.

After graduating from high school at seventeen, I entered Purdue University to study engineering. There I was required to join the field artillery Reserve Officer Training Corps (ROTC) program, which later affected my army career. Soon after arriving at Purdue, I registered for the draft. However, rather than be pulled out of school in the middle of a semester, I accepted an opportunity to join the army with an induction date two weeks after my freshman year ended. Living in five states, traveling alone on many occasions, and completing a year at an engineering university gave me a level of sophistication, self-reliance, and confidence that was rare among eighteen year olds. Nevertheless, I was still just a kid of eighteen.

By May 1943, my parents had moved back to California, where my father managed a war plant that produced armored amphibious vehicles. After the school year ended in April, I traveled by train to Los Angeles to be inducted. I entered the service at Fort MacArthur in San Pedro, California, on 12 May 1943, after spending a week visiting with my parents. After passing the physical examination and other tests, I was assigned to field artillery basic training at Fort

Bragg, North Carolina. Like everyone else, I was by then only a number; mine was Army Serial Number 15,312,751.

My view of army service was simple: it would be a great adventure. Like most of my teenage peers, I had little fear of dying because I thought I was immortal. We all thought we had the best army in the world because it had never been beaten. We were convinced that our generals and other leaders were the best in the world and that they would protect our lives no matter how difficult the situation in which we might find ourselves. Most of us were convinced that God was on our side, so we had little to worry about. Teens my age were making fewer sacrifices than did older men who had to leave their wives and children to serve their country.

In 1943 the full extent of the Nazi evil, along with the malice and madness of Adolf Hitler, were still not clearly recognized. We knew that the Gestapo killed Germans who were in opposition to the state, but we were unaware of the systematic elimination of huge populations of Jews, Gypsies, ethnic Russians, and others the Nazis had singled out for extermination. Genocide was a seldom-used word, even in technical circles, and it was unknown to the general population at the time.

After a week at Fort MacArthur and a weekend pass we were loaded into Pullman cars for the five-day trip to Fort Bragg. Most of the troops I was with had never ventured away from home before, and homesickness quickly became the prevailing disorder on that train.

My initial field artillery basic training consisted of instruction in close-order drill and physical development, with lots of marching and running and some camping out in the swamps and woods that were the major topographical features at sprawling Fort Bragg. On 24 June, after forty-three days of service, I passed my nineteenth birthday like any other day: marching and drilling. After six weeks of boring instruction I was selected for Morse code training because I had done well on the IQ tests. The Morse code training was too tedious and repetitive to suit my taste. I really hated it.

One Sunday afternoon I went to the post exchange (PX) and had a malted milk drink. The next morning I felt very ill and went on sick call. The doctor who saw me said I was fine and accused me of "goofing off." Never in my army days did I malinger, so I was really offended. He ordered me back to my unit, and soon I was too sick to care what he thought.

About an hour after I got back and after considerable verbal abuse from the cadre, I passed out. I awakened two days later in the post hospital. I later learned that seven soldiers had drunk milk products at the PX at about 1300 that Sunday, and two died. It took four weeks for sulfa drugs and other treatment to get the bacteria out of my system. During much of this time I was well enough to act as a volunteer orderly in the gastrointestinal ward, which had one influx after another of various intestinal illnesses. My stay there convinced me that going back to an army hospital for any reason was something I should avoid at almost any cost.

I was given a two-week convalescent furlough upon my release from the hospital. To make it to my parents' home in California and back in time, I had to fly. The army ran the only airline we could use, and its service was unscheduled to say the least. I was taken to the airport at Fort Bragg, and there I was listed as a no-priority passenger, which meant that almost anyone could "bump" me along the way to Los Angeles. The planes used were C-47s, the military version of the Douglas DC-3 twin-engine transport. They were used as troop carriers and glider tow planes by the airborne divisions. The aircraft proved so reliable that they continued in military and commercial service for many decades. After waiting a few hours I was informed that there was a plane going to Memphis with an available seat, so I took it. I waited for two hours in Memphis before being told I could fly to Oklahoma City. This process continued with stops in Denver and Phoenix, and I finally arrived in Los Angeles two days after leaving Fort Bragg.

I had a wonderful ten-day visit with my parents. My mother included me on one of her USO tours of a Hollywood studio. I recall the three of us going to the Lawry's prime rib restaurant in Beverly Hills, which was owned by a Mr. Frank who was a friend of my father. Mr. Frank welcomed me and treated us very well, although prime rib was off the menu because of meat rationing; they served turkey instead.

On the way back to Fort Bragg I had a priority since there was a specified reporting date in my orders. Nevertheless, the trip still took two days with six stops. Although much more primitive than today, air travel was still the best form of transportation available. We sat in uncomfortable metal seats along the sides of the plane, often with piles of cargo strapped down in the middle of the compartment. No drink or food was served. The difference between flying in those Spartan army transports and today's luxurious jet airliners is so great that it is difficult to believe how much of an advance has taken place. Those pitiful army airline services were a first attempt at moving masses of people and supplies by air and one of the precursors to modern commercial aviation.

I had to start over when I went back to the code school. Before I became ill, my closest friend was William Wallace, who had also completed his freshman year at Purdue. Bill was very bright, but my illness separated us. I never saw him again although I looked for him at Purdue when I returned there after the war ended. I hope Bill survived the war, but I cannot be sure. Bill was the first on my list of friends lost to death, wounds, or the unknown.

The way those huge training camps worked was to organize a cadre of experienced soldiers who served as teachers and administrators. The new soldiers, or trainees as they were known, were assigned to areas of specialization in companies of about two hundred men. A captain who was assisted by two lieutenants commanded each company, and a sergeant commanded each barracks of about forty-eight men. The company commander and his subordinates were in charge of discipline, keeping records, and training. This form of organization made for a two-caste society with the trainees being the lowest of the low. We had no privileges, and with rare exceptions were confined to the post all of the time.

One Saturday morning in early August I was summoned to the orderly room. Thinking this could only mean trouble, I was pleasantly surprised when I saw my father in the company commander's office. I have no idea how he managed to save enough gasoline coupons to allow him to drive from California to North Carolina. Although he said he was on business, I am sure his main purpose was to see me. My father was a good manager and salesman, and somehow he talked the captain into giving me a pass from 1200 Saturday to 1800 Sunday. He had rented two rooms in a Fayetteville tourist home, and it was a great pleasure for me to sleep in a good bed with real sheets (two things in which the army never believed). We visited and had three good meals together. Our parting had a strange finality to it since we both knew I would soon be going overseas. Fortunately, we both lived to see each other again a little over two years later.

Although I became reasonably proficient in hearing, transcribing, and sending dashes and dots, what I really learned was that I wanted to find something—anything!—else to do. After seven weeks of code school which completed my basic training, I was sent to Fort Meade, Maryland, to wait for assignment to the European theater of operations (ETO). Not many things are worse for a soldier than being in the army when it really has nothing for him to do. The discipline was not bad, what made this time intolerable was the dullness of having no useful duties. I did get several weekend passes to visit Washington, but the USO facilities—the only sleeping quarters I could find there—were depressingly similar to the barracks at Fort Meade.

By that time, January 1944, the powerful German army had tasted its first severe defeats. The Russians had driven the Germans farther back from the gates of Moscow and destroyed nearly an entire field army at Stalingrad. The Western Allies had driven the Germans out of North Africa and Sicily and invaded the Italian mainland, driving the German armies north to a point just south of Rome. The Italians had surrendered to the Allies, abandoning their Axis partner, Nazi Germany. Stalin was demanding that the Western Allies support the Russian war effort by invading France and establishing a second front in Europe. We all knew that such an invasion was inevitable in 1944, and we also knew we would be part of it somehow. The only things we did not know were where and when the invasion would occur.

All of us hoped to be assigned to a unit in an organized and well-trained division where we could get to know the men beside whom we would have to fight. However, in January we were assigned to a replacement artillery battery. This ad hoc unit was to be shipped in parts from Fort Dix, New Jersey, to somewhere in the United Kingdom. Individuals then would be assigned to combat units as replacements for casualties after the invasion. The unit consisted of eight hundred men under a captain and two lieutenants. Its leadership was so weak that I was made an acting corporal. The only real benefit to this was that I no longer had to peel potatoes on kitchen police (KP).

In late January we boarded a liberty ship, which was a really poor excuse for transportation. The North Atlantic in the dead of winter is a most unpleasant place in which to take a trip by ship. We were in a large convoy, and on the two of thirteen days when we were not in a storm, it was fun to watch the destroyers and corvettes weaving among the ships at high speed to protect us from submarines. Our convoy was lucky: only a single German torpedo struck one of the forty ships in it. The ship survived and limped into port. Still, the incident was enough to tell all of us we were in a very serious situation. We knew that survival was unlikely if anyone ended up in the freezing ocean. As we proceeded through one raging storm after another, almost everyone I knew became deathly seasick. Maneuvering on the icy deck was especially difficult. Somehow I escaped the seasickness, but three less fortunate men on board died from it. The situation was not helped by the fact that the ship was British. Our hosts served us their usual fare of boiled, dried codfish three times a day as our main source of nourishment. The ship's captain reported our progress toward Europe every day, and the storms were so bad that on one day we actually *lost* twenty-four miles.

Our ship landed at Liverpool on 10 February 1944 and we boarded a train that took us to Wales. I was one of the first hundred men to go to a new camp to set it up. Here began what seemed at the time one of the worst six weeks of my existence. After being dropped off at Cardiff, we were trucked west to nearby Barry on the coast. A few miles inland from Barry was a low, swampy meadow in a vale just below a beautiful manor house. Someone said it was a golf course, which it may well have been in a peacetime summer, but that February it was a cold swamp. We were given a hundred eight-man tents and ordered to build a camp there.

No one knew how to put up the tents, but we all learned quickly enough. If we had not, we might have died from exposure. We had no transits or other surveying instruments but I had taken a surveying course at Purdue, so I made a primitive transit from wood scraps and a few nails. Using that, a compass, some string, and a hundred-yard tape, the three officers and I laid out a tent city for eight hundred soldiers. Our methods were similar to those used by the Roman army two thousand years earlier. Water squished under our feet when we walked, and any hole we dug would instantly fill with water. The temperature was constantly between thirty-two and forty degrees Fahrenheit, and the relative humidity was 100 percent. Sanitary facilities were miserable, and conditions were ripe for many unpleasant diseases. We had no doctor or medical facilities of our own, although there were hospitals available for us in Cardiff.

What made our situation worse was the isolation. We seemed to have been forgotten by the U.S. Army, and the British authorities probably did not even know we were there. We managed to get food from somewhere, and we all became sick. Dysentery was the most unpopular and frequent disorder. We were never quite sick enough to die or go to the hospital, instead we just stayed in our bunks until the illness passed, trotting to the latrine whenever necessary. I had dysentery several times. At night, with no flashlights or other lighting but with extreme urgency, dysentery makes for a terrible mess in the morning. When we weren't sick we stood guard in cold, tin sentry shacks. In most cases, this meant we did not even have an opportunity to march a route and get some exercise. What we were guarding or why anyone would want it was a puzzle we never figured out.

In mid-March some officers from the 456th Parachute Field Artillery Battalion (PFAB) visited our artillery replacement camp looking for volunteers. They had just arrived in England from the Anzio beachhead in Italy, where the battalion had suffered heavy casualties. They explained that the 82d Airborne Division, of which they were a part, would spearhead the invasion of France and would no doubt see heavy fighting. If we volunteered, we had to agree to complete a parachute jump school that the division planned to organize. If they were given time, the parachute training would come before the invasion; if not, it would come afterward. They emphasized the fact that the 82d was an assault division and that its mission would be to help establish a beachhead. Once this was accomplished, it would return to England to prepare for another assault. They said everyone would be granted furloughs after the division's return from France.

After being an abused orphan in Wales for six long weeks, it took me about ten seconds to decide to join the 456th. It is a decision I have never regretted. Although the offer sounded dangerous, the alternative idea of joining an unknown outfit as a casualty replacement (cannon fodder) did not appeal to me as being very safe either. Having the opportunity to train with the men I was going to fight beside appealed to me. Being in an elite outfit meant that someone might care for me, and I might care for it.

Those of us who volunteered were trucked to Market Harborough, a pleasant little English midland town southeast of Leicester. Even in war, the English countryside is beautiful in the spring, with an abundance of bright flowers and flowering trees. The 456th was billeted in a country manor just north of town. It was truly beautiful, although anything would have been wonderful to me after our situation in Wales. My quarters were in the mews (stables), and with their brick floors, solid walls, and nearby sanitary facilities and baths, it was like heaven on earth.

Somehow the paratroopers never learned I knew Morse code—or maybe they simply weren't interested in this skill. Anyway, I never volunteered the information. Basic intelligence was in relatively short supply and thus a valuable commodity. Being an ex-college boy, they saw some in me. They were also impressed with my surveying training, ability to read maps well, and interest in making some kind of a positive contribution. I was assigned as an acting reconnaissance corporal, and promised I would gain that rank permanently if I demonstrated an ability to carry out my assigned duties. Those were twofold: become a qualified member of an artillery observation team that would help to direct fire against the enemy, and help scout out the various positions that elements of the battalion would occupy and place them accurately on a map.

Two general attributes were considered essential for a paratrooper to function efficiently and stay alive: an excellent state of physical fitness and the development of heightened mental alertness. The former was easy to accomplish because we ran in formation for two hours and did two more hours of calisthenics each day. The second point meant anticipating everything and being surprised by nothing, a skill that was much more difficult to learn. Many kinds of combat exercises and training—in large or small groups, by night or day, under live fire, when fresh or tired—helped to increase our alertness. Being aware of everything around us and remaining constantly alert to possible threats from all directions was emphasized to us trainees. We were placed in many scary simulated combat situations, and soon the tendency to be paralyzed by fear and indecision began to disappear. It was replaced by the confidence we needed to react properly to most surprises. One of the things they tried to instill in us was to reach a calm and measured decision of what to do quickly, no matter how threatening the situation we faced. The degree to which the officers and noncoms were able to accomplish this directly affected our ability to survive later.

Everyone knew we were training for the invasion of France. The battalion, however, had a fundamental problem concerning its equipment. The 456th was equipped with twelve light 75mm pack howitzers. Originally designed to be carried by mules over difficult terrain, the weapons had been adapted for delivery by parachute. Each artillery piece, with its ammunition and other equipment, was dropped in about twenty bundles. The weapon was then assembled on the ground. After being dropped and assembled, several leather straps were attached to the howitzer, and a crew of about twelve troopers pulled it from place to place. We spent many hours pulling our howitzers at the double time in training.

We quickly discovered that if any of a howitzer's important parts—the barrel or the right wheel, for instance—was not recovered after the drop, the weapon was useless. Since the drop into France would most likely be at night, the question was whether enough complete guns and men could be assembled to form an effective artillery unit. Furthermore, at that time most of the men in Battery A had not yet undergone basic parachute training. These factors led to the decision to bring us ashore by sea on the third day of the invasion.

Although we were not qualified as paratroopers, we were still issued jump boots. My shoe size is 12½ AA—a size that is difficult to find most anywhere. I made a serious mistake when I disposed of a properly sized pair of army boots. The closest sized jump boots they were able to come up with for me was 11D. They were short and uncomfortable but there was nothing I could do about it. I wound up

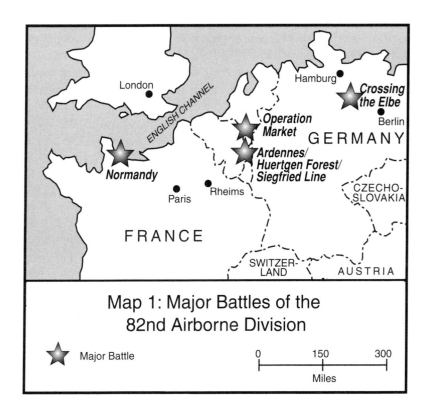

London

Hamburg

*Crossing
the Elbe*

Berlin

ENGLISH CHANNEL

*Operation
Market*

GERMANY

*Ardennes/
Huertgen Forest/
Siegfried Line*

Normandy

CZECHO-
SLOVAKIA

Paris

Rheims

FRANCE

SWITZER-
LAND

AUSTRIA

Map 1: Major Battles of the 82nd Airborne Division

Major Battle

0   150   300

Miles

training and going into Normandy with sore feet. My problems with jump boots plagued me throughout my service.

By mid-May we were as ready to invade France as we would ever be, and my corporal rank was made permanent. Most of the division was trucked to airfields in southern England from which they would take off for France, while we were moved to a restricted camp, Saint Mary's Hill Camp No. 3, in Wales. Security was tight—a double row of barbed-wire fences surrounded the invasion force camps with a four-yard space between them. We stood guard inside the fence and military police (MPs) stood guard outside. The compound thus was more like a prison than an army camp. When we arrived on 25 May, no one had any idea how soon we would be going or where the invasion would occur. Most of us remained in this prison arrangement for ten days, with no facilities for running or other physical exercise beyond calisthenics. At no time were we given any details of the invasion plan or the part we would play in it. To say there was tension would be an understatement.

On 29 May, Battery A's vehicles, howitzers, and ammunition were loaded on ship number 212, the *Excelsior,* at Rothgate Docks in Cardiff. I was among the troopers who went along to load the guns and vehicles; the rest of the battery boarded on 3 June. Already on board was a regiment from another infantry division. These men had not yet been told what their destination was. The *Excelsior* sailed for France at 1715 on Monday, 5 June.

2

Chaos at Normandy

There were about one hundred fifteen officers and men from Battery A on board the *Excelsior* when it set sail from Cardiff. We knew we were part of the invasion force but, like the infantrymen already on board, we had not yet been told where or when the assault on the Germans defending the French coast would take place. Captain Alley, who was informed, briefed the officers, and we told the enlisted men what we knew. The ship anchored in Bristol Channel at about midnight.

D day was 6 June. That evening, the ship's bulletin boards had several copies of General Eisenhower's speech in which he said the invasion had begun and that its initial steps had been successful. Some heard the speech on radios. We read this announcement with great interest. We later learned that General Eisenhower had also prepared a speech announcing the invasion's failure. Fortunately he never had to deliver it. We received no meaningful information about our 82d Airborne Division comrades other than that they needed our artillery support. The *Excelsior* sailed from its Bristol anchorage just before midnight as part of a large convoy.

On our way to France, German Stuka dive-bombers thrice attacked our convoy, and most of them were shot down. We saw one naval escort vessel hit but the bomb glanced off its deck and exploded in the water. There appeared to be no serious damage but scattered bomb fragments must have caused casualties. By dawn on 8 June we were all dressed with full packs and equipment, including life preservers. The ship weighed anchor at dawn and began to move toward the beach. It was a beautiful, sunny morning and the sea was a rich turquoise blue. As we moved in, the water changed to light green and then a sandy darker shade. We anchored again where a sailor said we had ten to fifteen feet of water beneath our keel. Toward the east and the open sea, the sky was clear and bright blue. To the west, the sky over the beach was dull and full of dust and smoke.

Our ship arrived off Utah Beach at 0815, one of a huge number of other ships, all waiting to unload men, equipment, and supplies. Warships were firing at targets ashore, and we cringed as their shells passed overhead. The bigger shells from battleships and cruisers sounded like boxcars flying through the air. German shells were falling at random among the ships, and we saw a Landing Ship Tank (LST) hit a mine off to our right. The explosion tore a huge rent in the LST's side and it settled to the bottom, a few feet of water lapping at the vehicles on deck. Ours was the first unit to disembark from the *Excelsior,* and at about 1400 Captain Alley's party of about sixty-five men scrambled down nets into an awaiting landing craft. They hit the sandy bottom well offshore and we could see them wading through four-foot-deep water to the beach. There were waves but they did not seem too high. Those of us still on board were pleased that no shells landed near our comrades. They moved quickly across the beach to a transit area at Houdienville.

Many Allied planes were overhead at all times, protecting the hundreds of ships from any brave German pilots who might dare try to attack them. Barrage balloons were rigged on many ships to impede low-level attacks. I remained with 1st Lt. Henry J. Aust's party of about fifty-five men along with the battery's guns, vehicles, supplies, and ammunition. We were scheduled to follow Captain Alley's party later on the eighth, but the beach master said the beach was too crowded with equipment and ordered us to remain aboard until the next morning.

Meanwhile, our advance party ran out of food when we did not arrive with the equipment and supplies as planned. Captain Alley and our supply sergeant, SSgt. John J. Donohue, stopped a truck and persuaded the driver to throw off several cases of rations. A passing brigadier general from another division questioned the propriety of this act. Captain Alley explained his plight and the general moved on without taking any action.

It required several landing craft to ferry the rest of Battery A's men and equipment to the beach. The boats could hold a howitzer along with its prime mover (a six-by-six truck loaded with ammunition) and a jeep, or a combination of four to six other vehicles. After some of us scrambled down the nets to handle them, the vehicles had to be swung down into the landing craft using the ship's crane. It was hard labor for the few men left on the ship. Several of us loaded three or more craft before going ashore ourselves. It was a choppy trip mainly because the boats were not very seaworthy. Some men were seasick, something I again avoided.

The craft I was aboard grounded quite near the beach. The water was only a little over a foot deep so, rather than having to manhandle it, the jeep I was in drove onto the beach without even getting us wet. Others were not so lucky and got soaked.

The beach looked like an enormous junkyard with many burned-out trucks, tanks, and other vehicles. Sunken ships and landing craft littered the shoreline. Most of the bodies of soldiers who had been killed during the assault landing had been removed, but the amount of wreckage was unbelievable. Several heavy enemy guns located farther up the Normandy coast continued to fire on Utah Beach. Fortunately, no German artillery observers were in a position close enough to direct their fire accurately. This random shelling covered a fairly large area and did little damage. However, an occasional shell came down on troops or equipment. Statistically, the shells were of little danger to individual soldiers, but those few men who were killed or hurt were just as dead or maimed whether they were intentional targets or the victims of random hits. A shell fell every fifteen minutes or so, and they were a great nuisance. The shelling was motivation for us to get off the beach as quickly as we could and leave it behind us. The weather had turned from clear to cloudy with intermittent rain. This allowed German bombers to fly in the relative safety of the clouds and drop bombs randomly upon the beach area, including us.

The rest of the 82d troopers had been fighting for three days without adequate artillery or armored support so we were sorely needed. Nevertheless, the crowded beach and delays prevented our rushing to their aid as quickly as we wanted. As we landed, we

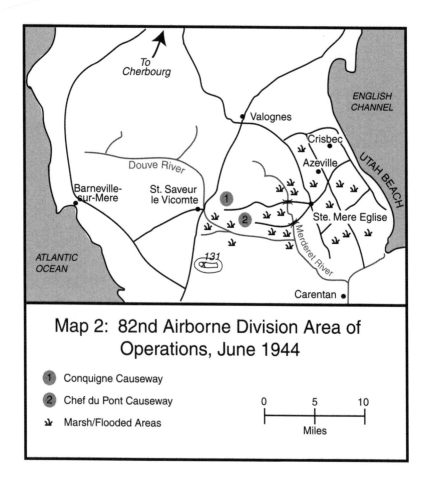

Map 2: 82nd Airborne Division Area of Operations, June 1944

moved to a transit area just behind the beach until we were all as-sembled. Then we moved to join Captain Alley's party, which had marched a mile inland the day before. Just before dark, a German bomber dropped cluster bomblets a hundred yards in front of our position. Someone shouted "Gas!" when he smelled the acrid smoke and we almost had a panic as men rushed to put on gas masks. Although it proved to be a false alarm, we kept our gas masks near us from then on.

We learned later that the troops who came ashore on Omaha Beach to the east suffered many more casualties and met much greater German resistance. The critical situation at Omaha Beach on D day brought the invasion much closer to failure than anyone realized. At no later time was there to be such a threat of failure.

The 82d Airborne had not fared very well, either. When the division jumped just after 0100 on 6 June there were banks of clouds over the drop zones. Because of this, some pilots made the drops blindly from the unusually high altitude of about two thousand feet. Other pilots flew too low and troopers jumped from unsafe altitudes. Instead of each of its three parachute infantry regiments remaining concentrated after being dropped in three carefully designated drop zones, the division's ten thousand troopers were scattered over an area measuring twenty miles by forty miles. Only about 30 percent of the men landed where they were supposed to, and the division suffered many casualties. Those who landed far away from their drop zones tried to make their way back to the airhead, doing as much damage to the Germans along the way as they could. Wandering groups of paratroopers held up many of the German reinforcements and confused their high command as to where the main landings were. Although not planned this way, the division had accomplished its primary mission by preventing the enemy from reinforcing the strong defensive positions in the heights above Utah Beach. A second objective was to trap German defenders along the beach, making a gigantic sandwich with them in the middle and Allied troops on both sides. This objective was only partially accomplished, and a few German defenders escaped. Although capture of both causeways across the flooded Merderet River was a specified objective for D-plus-l, the paratroopers captured neither.

If they were given the time to bring up and concentrate strong units to reinforce their positions, the Germans could turn the flooded Merderet into a strong defensive line. Therefore, quickly capturing the causeways across the Merderet was essential. However, using infantry alone without artillery and armor support proved futile. We were one of four of the division's artillery battalions being rushed to support a new effort to cross the Merderet. Also, tanks and artillery units assigned to the 90th Division were rushing toward positions from which they could support the planned 82d assault on the causeways. The Germans in the area were, at least temporarily, weaker in manpower, but they had the advantage of being on the defensive, and they had some armor to augment their defenses. At the same time the American army was trying to bring more forces to bear, the German command was racing to bring in more defenders.

On the afternoon of 6 June, the 325th Glider Infantry Regiment (GIR) landed in the area on both sides of the road leading to our first position. Although the landings were successful from a tactical standpoint, many gliders had been wrecked when they landed, causing some casualties. The fields between our position and the road leading from the coast were littered with gliders, most still intact. The Germans had driven a number of poles—known as "Rommel's asparagus"—into open fields where they thought Allied gliders might land. Some had explosives attached to them. For the most part, too few of these poles had been placed to be very effective, but they did cause a few losses. Once again, statistical chance and randomness seemed to be the rule.

Frequently, we saw the dreaded red German signs reading: "ACHTUNG MINEN" (Attention Mines). Mines had already been cleared from along the fringes of the road and in our position, but the signs were effective in preventing soldiers from wandering, something most soldiers have a tendency to do. Of all the dangers soldiers faced, I think I shared the general feeling that mines were the worst. They were hidden, unexpected, insidious, and often caused dreadful wounds. Another disturbing distraction along the way to our assembly area was the intermittent line of jeeps and ambulances moving in the opposite direction. Each jeep had one or two stretchers laid crosswise over the hood and the backseat, and these were occupied by wounded soldiers being moved from a field hospital back to the ships for evacuation to better medical facilities aboard ship or in England.

The ten-mile drive to the assembly area took more than two hours. We learned why as we approached Sainte-Mère-Église, where we were directed to our assembly area. We were one of a number of units in line in the column, so every time the leading unit reached the dispersion area the whole column stopped—sometimes for a half-hour—while the lead unit moved toward its designated position. We finally reached the head of the column and were ordered to move to our assigned area. There we set up and dug in our artillery pieces. The battalion had only ten of its twelve pack howitzers in position. About this time we learned that our two missing howitzers, along with about twenty men from our battalion who were to operate them, had been dropped with the 505th PIR on D day. One gun was recovered on D day and saw action immediately; the other was complete except for the breechblock, which had been lost, thus making the gun useless. The parachute party lost one man killed and one officer slightly wounded.

In the late afternoon on 9 June, 1st Lt. Richard A. Ross led a party of four, of which I was a member, to establish an observation post while our battery was setting up. Just before we left battalion headquarters, Brig. Gen. James M. Gavin came to determine when the battalion would be ready to support his planned attack. The general was a tall, thin, handsome man whose nickname was "Slim Jim." We had all been issued jumpsuits impregnated with a compound to protect us from mustard gas, which Allied intelligence predicted the Germans would use to resist the invasion. This treatment eliminated any airflow through the fabric and made the jumpsuits very hot and almost impossible to clean. They were also stiff, uncomfortable, and smelled bad. In fact, we had orders not to wash our jumpsuits since that would neutralize the protection against poison gas. However, after no signs of gas other than our false alarm, almost everyone decided that washing those smelly, hot uniforms was worth the risk.

Gavin was a "spit-and-polish" West Pointer but this day he looked more like a ragamuffin. He had a dent in his dirty helmet—he had apparently rolled in the mud several times when he landed—and his normally shiny boots were muddy and had cuts in them. His messy condition had no effect on his efficiency and determination to take the causeways. I stood on the edge of the group to whom he was speaking. He was very happy to see us, and he pointed out that he and his men had been under German artillery fire for three days without the ability to call for a response from the unit dedicated to their support. He now instructed us that if the Germans fired ten rounds at us, we were to fire a hundred back at them. After it was decided that we could begin providing fire support by 1700, my group trotted off toward its assigned post a mile or two toward the front. As we moved forward we came upon a dead German in the path. He was the first dead man we had seen up close. Fifty yards farther on we came upon twelve dead American paratroopers lying along a path that closely followed a hedgerow. They were parachute infantrymen, probably members of a patrol that had walked into an ambush in the difficult hedgerow country. Of all the things I remember about Normandy, the odor of the dead, both men and farm animals, is most deeply etched in my memory. The stench became overwhelming and brought the war very close to each of us. Although the odor would not hurt us, the message of death was threatening because one could easily imagine his own body giving off a similar odor. The stench clung to everything, and there was no way for us to escape it.

The pattern of hedgerows, each eight to fifteen feet high, made it impossible to see very far. Before our party arrived, the 505th had advanced to the flooded Merderet River and established a small foothold on the opposite side that included a small hamlet called The Station. The 505th needed to enlarge its foothold and capture another hamlet, Le Ham. The bridgehead needed to be enlarged until it had two crossings leading to it, one near Le Ham on the other side of the Conquigne causeway and another at a causeway to our left, called Chef du Pont. Once the bridgehead was enlarged to the point that it included three miles of land on the other side of the Merderet, it would form the jumping-off place for an attack westward to seal off the Cotentin Peninsula.

Our observation party advanced to a hedgerow at the edge of the flooded Merderet from which we could see the German positions between the Conquigne and Chef du Pont causeways along the far bank. The infantrymen, who were holding the position for us, had been told not to fire their rifles from this position unless fired upon in order to preserve it as a good observation post. We climbed about ten feet up to the top of the hedgerow. From there we could see the Conquigne causeway a few hundred yards to our right and the Chef du Pont causeway about two miles to our left. We had been warned not to call for artillery fire across the river south or west of the Chef du Pont causeway because a thousand or more parachute infantrymen were surrounded by Germans in that area.

Although we were ready to direct fire within a few minutes of arriving, we were told to wait because tanks and some of the needed additional artillery pieces were still held up on the road from the beach. We were told the attack would probably be made during the night or at dawn. This gave our four-man group time to do some housework. Lieutenant Ross sent our driver and me back to headquarters to lay another telephone line to duplicate the one we had laid on the way out to ensure we would have communication with the guns if a line were broken at a critical time. We were also to pick up our jeep with all our personal belongings and drive it back to a thicket of trees about a hundred yards behind our observation post. The lieutenant and the sergeant would begin to dig foxholes while we were away. On the way back, we came upon a graves registration team picking up the twelve dead paratroopers. It was a really depressing sight for both the driver and me. We each wondered how soon we might get the same morbid and final attention. The lone dead German still lay undisturbed but his face had bloated and he was in an advanced state of decay thanks to the warm sun.

We drove back with all our stuff, a three days' supply of K rations, and our battery commander, Captain Alley, who wanted to look over our position. When he finished, he said he would walk back to the battery alone, following our phone lines. As we drove out of the battery area, I noticed that Captain Alley was holding his binoculars in his hand and frequently raised them to his eyes, looking at something. I was worried that he saw some threat that I could not see, such as an enemy soldier, and I asked him what he was searching for so I could help. He said he had broken his glasses just before we left England and the binoculars helped him see distant objects. I was impressed that he did not use this problem as an excuse to stay in England but instead came over with us.

When we returned to our post we finished digging our foxholes, a job that took almost two hours. Three infantrymen had joined us to provide additional security and to act as couriers to maintain contact with a nearby infantry battalion headquarters. By this time it was dark and we were exhausted. We ate our K rations, a can of deviled ham, some cookies, a candy bar, and an envelope of concentrated coffee that we mixed with cold water. We spent a restless night with one of the four of us taking a turn staying awake, guarding our puny position against German patrols. How a German patrol would make it three hundred yards across open water and find us in the dark was a good question, but we were taking no chances.

At about 2130 an infantry courier awakened us and said the attack to capture Le Ham would begin at 2230. We were ordered to direct fire into the area immediately west of Le Ham at 2215 and keep it up for fifteen minutes. All artillery units in the vicinity were to participate. From 2215 to 2230 a dozen tanks and as many as six artillery battalions with as many as twelve guns each threw everything they had at the German positions. By the light of star shells and flares from our post we could see that the fire was on target and seemed to be very effective. We could not understand how any German could survive the furious barrage. We watched as paratroopers from the 505th PIR and glider infantrymen from the 325th GIR crossed the Conquigne causeway and charged into the front and flank of the Le Ham position. The Germans recovered and resisted the attack strongly but our armor destroyed two enemy tanks in Le Ham and the Germans evacuated their positions.

Shortly before dawn the enemy mounted a vicious counterattack that our infantrymen turned back with great difficulty with the help of artillery fire. Six of our tanks made it across to the bridgehead, which was becoming more secure by the minute. Throughout the day reinforcements crossed the causeway, and by evening no possible German counterattack could have eliminated our bridgehead. A few miles to the southeast, other troopers from the 82d captured the Chef du Pont causeway across the Merderet and relieved a group of our troopers who had been trapped on the other side of the river since D day. The way was now clear to extend the bridgehead deeper into the Cotentin Peninsula.

Just before dark we had our own immediate and personal problems. The Germans had evidently seen reflections from our binoculars or something else that gave us away and correctly identified our position as the one being used for artillery direction. The enemy pounded us with heavy rifle, mortar, and artillery fire for several minutes. The former was ineffective but a shell landed very close to us. A metal fragment hit my steel helmet and bounced harmlessly away, leaving a gash on it. I still remember the sound and shock. One of the infantrymen assigned to guard us was hit in the chest by a shell fragment, piercing his lung. Air and blood bubbled from the wound as he tried to breathe, but it must have been fairly shallow because he seemed to be losing little blood and there was no exit wound. We contacted headquarters by telephone and were told one of us should drive the man back to the field hospital while the rest continued to observe the enemy. We expected things to calm down soon after dark. We were also ordered to move our position about two hundred yards to the north and not to take any chance of exposing ourselves before morning, when the infantry would probably need our supporting fire again. This order meant that another set of foxholes had to be dug. Each hole was four to six feet deep and a little larger than the size of the occupant lying down. The ground was very hard.

Lieutenant Ross showed me the route on a map and ordered me to drive the wounded man back to the field hospital in the gathering darkness. We put a compression bandage on his wound and loaded him into the backseat of the jeep after giving him a shot of morphine to ease his pain. We had seen the field hospital just off the road we had used earlier to get to Sainte-Mère-Église. The lieutenant made sure I knew the password for the day and off I went. Afraid my passenger might die any minute, I drove recklessly in an effort to make it to the main road before complete darkness fell. Twenty minutes later, I drove into the field hospital's reception area.

It was overloaded with wounded American and German soldiers who had been brought back from the day's heavy fighting. It was impossible for the overworked hospital staff to treat every soldier as soon as he was brought in, so I helped take our friend into the triage tent. There I learned what triage meant. The wounded were divided into three categories: the lightly wounded who could wait for treatment, those who were so badly wounded that they had no chance of survival, and those who were wounded seriously enough to need immediate attention but had a good chance for full recovery. Priority treatment was given to the badly wounded who had the best chance of recovery. Next to be treated were those whose wounds were likely to be fatal. The lightly wounded were treated last. Our friend's wound, although not as severe as we had feared, was serious enough for him to receive immediate treatment. When he entered the tent for treatment I went back to the jeep and left.

I liberated some C rations from a depot near the field hospital. C rations were real food: canned stew, Spam, and fruit, among other things. They were much better than our K rations, so I took them and drove back to battery headquarters. I was challenged in the dark three times along the way. It seemed to me that I came close to being shot each time since every rear-echelon military policeman was convinced that the area around him was crawling with Germans. Captain Alley ordered me to stay at headquarters that night and not risk going forward into really dangerous territory in total darkness. He allowed me to call Lieutenant Ross and tell him our infantry friend would most likely recover, that I was okay, and that I would return shortly after first light. I slept in a foxhole that had belonged to a comrade in Battery A who had been wounded.

The next day we crossed the causeway into Le Ham amid even more bodies and carnage than we had seen thus far. As we crossed the causeway, we saw German tanks up close for the first time. We had all heard of the gigantic Tiger tanks and lived under the misapprehension that every German tank we saw was a Tiger. These were much smaller, less powerful models. Nevertheless, they had a lower profile than our tanks, a huge gun, and wide tracks. Their armor must have been very thick because our tank or antitank shells had made deep gouges in them. Each of the enemy tanks had been hit several times with little effect. Our tank guns and antitank guns were popguns compared to the high-velocity 88mm guns the Germans fired at our comparatively lightly armored tanks. We did not think this was a forecast of good tank actions for our side since we had watched twelve of ours fight two of theirs over the previous two days, with six of ours lost before their two were finally destroyed.

Before we had time to establish another observation post we received orders saying that the 90th Division would relieve us, and that we were to return to the Sainte-Mère-Église area to rest and refit. We were to make the exchange at dusk. After we moved back across the

Merderet, we watched a firefight erupt between the green troops of the 90th and seasoned 4th Division GIs occupying positions next to them. This panic-driven firefight involving rifle, mortar, machine-gun, artillery, and antiaircraft fire lasted for almost four hours before it could be stopped. Both divisions suffered casualties.

Everyone was relieved to have survived those first few days of combat. The past was forgotten and the future was completely discounted. This was an occasion to live solely in the present once we had moved back four miles to relative safety.

Inexhaustible supplies of several local Norman liquors had been found. These consisted of hard cider and calvados, a potent brandy distilled from it. Everyone I knew, both officers and men, proceeded to get very drunk. Personally, I was always what today would be identified as a "nerd." I was more interested in books and museums than bars, and this was my first heavy drinking experience. My headache was unbelievable throughout the next day.

That night, after exchanging many tales, we all fell into a drunken sleep thinking the division would be recalled to England after a few days to prepare for another airborne assault. Unbeknownst to us, there were no immediate plans for such an assault. Our generals had decided to let us stay in Normandy and fight a little longer.

3

The Fight Continues

We were ordered back to the front lines after only one day of rest. The division had gained in manpower strength since our total casualties were more than offset by the return of thousands of the men who had been dropped as far as forty miles from their planned drop zones. The 82d's troopers, along with those of the 101st Airborne Division, had done everything they could to damage the enemy: they shot up trucks, killed German soldiers in rear areas, tore up telephone lines, and attacked supply dumps. Since they were usually near the other ten to twenty members of their jump "stick," these groups of well-trained infantrymen were too tough for most German rear-area troops to handle. Avoiding large concentrations of Germans, they moved mostly at night and then sneaked through the Allied front lines anywhere they could, eventually rejoining the rest of the division. A few lost troopers landed so far away that they were taken to Paris by the French underground. There, they joined the French resistance and fought beside them until the city was liberated later that summer.

The Germans had several batteries of heavy guns at Crisbecq and near Azeville, just inland and a few miles north of Utah Beach. These guns were blindly but sometimes successfully dropping shells on the ships, supply dumps, and troops on the invasion beaches, and the air force's attempts to destroy them with bombs failed because the guns were in well-designed, heavy, concrete fortifications. Other infantry divisions had been unable to break through the German infantry guarding the route to the guns, so on the night of the twelfth part of the 505th Regimental Combat Team (RCT) was assigned the job. This team was made up of two battalions from the 505th PIR, our field artillery battalion, and some tanks that were temporarily assigned to support the team.

In a vicious assault the next day, parachute infantrymen supported by artillery and tanks drove the German defenders from their positions. This allowed the 4th Infantry Division to pass through the 82d and capture the two gun positions. Our supporting tanks performed well against the enemy infantry, and they were fortunate that no German tanks were in the area. Our infantry suffered heavy casualties but the attack eliminated the possibility of enemy artillery causing many additional random casualties on the beach. We abandoned our hopes of returning to England and became convinced we would all die in Normandy. Along with the 101st Airborne Division the 82d had begun to emerge as an elite division capable of doing things other, less well-trained divisions could not accomplish. There were signs that we were becoming the high command's firemen. No one liked this idea since it was not our primary mission and would soon bleed us of our strength and our capability.

It had been estimated that about 30 percent of the division would survive the planned European campaign unhurt. This proved to be an overestimation since our actual casualties were higher than expected. Everyone in the division was fully aware the odds were against him surviving fully intact. In these circumstances, my experience with a large number of soldiers and their death or wounding led me to the belief that the great majority developed a purely fatalistic day-to-day attitude that allowed them to continue to function effectively.

It has been said that there are no atheists in foxholes. In fact, many men did turn to God in those extreme circumstances. Some also felt that a loving God would not place them in these circumstances where random death was everywhere, and the good had as great a chance of dying or being horribly maimed as the bad. Fatalism was a middle ground. Stated simply, fatalism can be defined as accepting whatever happens after taking all the possible positive actions for the benefit of oneself and one's unit. Generally speaking, a soldier in the proximity of extreme danger for the first time relied on religion for support, but after repeatedly seeing the randomness and unfairness of how death and wounding happened around him, this sole dependence on religion ended for most. Religious explanations for what was happening seemed inadequate. Fatalism became a more acceptable psychological mechanism, allowing many to continue to function. This is not to say that men completely abandoned religion, most simply adapted to a new psychological defense against their terrible circumstances.

Looking back from fifty years later as one of the less than 20 percent of the survivors of the 82d who was not killed, wounded, or injured, I accepted fatalism in the midst of that extreme chaos. I now consider this was important to my holding onto my sanity as many of my friends died around me. It has also made me more adaptable to facing and solving the problems of later life. In a positive manner, the whole experience has led me to place much greater importance on good performance, good acts toward others, honesty, morality, and giving my family and associates the best support I can.

On 14 June, the 82d Airborne Division was assigned to rescue the 90th Division, which had been given the mission of attacking across the Cotentin Peninsula. When successful, this move would isolate the German troops that were preventing the U.S. Army from capturing the port of Cherbourg. This huge deepwater port was essential to future planned operations in Europe since it could handle much of the great quantities of supplies needed to support our offensives. The 90th had advanced only about five hundred yards from the positions we had turned over to them on the tenth, suffering heavy casualties in the process. Although later in the war the 90th proved to be an effective division, at that time it was still green, poorly led, and the men had lost their will to fight.

In order for an artillery battalion to function and deliver accurately aimed fire on selected targets, it had to have three efficient elements. First, the guns on the ground had to be located exactly on a map. Second, observers had to be located where they could physically identify enemy targets. Third, the fire-control center, the brains of the battalion, had to have precise maps of the terrain that accurately depicted the positions of the howitzers and their observers, friendly troops, and all likely target areas. In addition, it needed radio and telephone contact with the guns and observers, as well as with important infantry commands in the area. Small spotter planes were also used to direct artillery fire. This was a dangerous job, as was demonstrated on 14 June when the Germans shot down a Piper Cub spotter. We passed the plane's wreckage, which still contained the charred body of an observer from the 82d Airborne Division Artillery headquarters sitting perfectly upright. It was a terrible sight.

We could direct fire most accurately on observed targets. Sometimes, however, it was necessary to call fire on the map coordinates of suspected targets or on targets identified in aerial reconnaissance photos. Ideally, the guns were emplaced about two miles behind the front lines—a compromise between their safety and the need to deliver accurate fire on targets well behind enemy lines.

The U.S. Army in World War II possessed a great capability in its artillery, which was both effective and destructive. Both sides worked hard to find their enemy's artillery and knock it out. Besides using aerial spotters, triangulation of the sound of our guns, and other means, the Germans sent infantry patrols behind our lines at night to try to locate our guns. Once found, they would direct counterbattery fire into the areas they had identified. In Normandy, our guns came under fire many times. There were only two defenses: move them or destroy the German artillery. We tried both but moving them proved consistently to be the better of the two.

In addition to moving to escape counterbattery fire, whenever the front line moved or we were assigned a new area of operation, the entire complex system that made up an artillery battalion had to be torn down and completely reassembled. When I talked to my friends back at the battery location they told a story of frequent frustration and exhaustion. The guns were moved more than twenty-five times during our thirty-three days of combat in Normandy (no one kept an accurate count)—sometimes twice in one day. Each time the guns moved they had to be dug in to protect them from nearby hits by enemy artillery. This required digging a hole about two to three feet deep and fifteen to eighteen feet in diameter, with the dirt mounded up in a berm around it. At each new location surveyors emplaced the guns, plotted their locations on a map, and determined the distances to the observers, the front lines, and to target areas. Sometimes the guns were registered; that is, they fired against known points to check the accuracy of locations depicted on the maps. This complex process had to be done quickly in order to get the guns back into action, requiring great effort by all.

Digging in a gun did not give absolute protection, but it did help protect the gun and its crew from flying shell or bomb fragments. There was no protection from direct hits. In 1997 John Price told me that a German shell landed right next to him in his gun pit at one of the battery's positions in Normandy; fortunately, it did not explode.

After the guns were safely emplaced and ready to fire, everyone had to look to his personal safety. Personal foxholes also had to be dug at each new location. The smarter men dug individual holes but some gunners dug holes that could accommodate up to six men. Although a single enemy shell could kill all the men in a single hole, it was unlikely that six men spread out in individual foxholes would be killed—even if several shells landed nearby. It thus was not long before the practice of digging apartment-sized foxholes was abandoned.

During our short rest I found a use for my two years of high school French: I was able to barter with the farmers, trading cigarettes and other things for liquor. We shared some with our officer, and someone told him I spoke French fluently. When the infantry battalion to which we were attached needed directions and other information about the area, I was asked to translate. I tried to explain that "fluent" was a huge exaggeration, but they asked me to try, so I did. The local French proved very cooperative. They hated the German occupiers, and now they wanted the war to go somewhere—anywhere—else. My rudimentary French allowed us to obtain the information we wanted. The more I used the language, the more proficient I became, and the more I found myself translating and negotiating. Although my French was marginal, most American soldiers had no capability, and the local Frenchmen spoke no English.

On 14 June we began to attack westward toward our objective, Saint-Sauveur-le-Vicomte, five miles away. Saint-Sauveur was a road junction town through which German troops marched on their way to relieve their forces in Cherbourg. The capture of Saint-Sauveur would leave only the coast road open to German troops moving in and out of Cherbourg, and that road could be shelled effectively from the sea. We took Saint-Sauveur on the evening of the sixteenth after two days of hard fighting. That night the 9th Division attacked through our positions against no opposition, and by the twentieth had reached Barneville-sur-Mer on the coast—a move that cut the last road between the main German forces and those now isolated in Cherbourg.

Two weeks of heavy fighting made all of us think more deeply about our individual mortality. For my fellow soldiers and myself, our greatest fear was not death but being seriously wounded. We would have defined a serious wound as one of these: a wound to the head that destroyed or very severely and irreversibly limited intellect, the loss of more than one limb where they joined the body, the loss of genitalia, becoming blind in both eyes, or facial disfigurement. Of course, we did not worry about mental problems caused by the war. Later, however, we were to recognize that these could be as devastating as some of the worst physical wounds.

Being wounded was never considered positive but wounds happened often, resulting in soldiers having strong feelings that some wounds were not a bad alternative. Whenever someone was wounded less seriously we were relieved for him; if it was a bad wound we all shared his devastation. The army's policy was to get wounded men away as soon as possible, both for their own good and to prevent survivors from brooding over their comrades' ill fortune. Unfortunately, this often meant wounded men just disappeared, making us think the worst of every situation since we seldom received any more information about them unless they returned. Many soldiers made pacts with their closest friend that if one of them was badly wounded, the other would kill him; a number of such agreements were acted upon.

I believe the occurrence of self-inflicted wounds was less common in the 82d than in other divisions, but they did occur. This practice did not usually work out to the victim's benefit since self-inflicted wounds tended to be obvious. Mostly, men wounded themselves because they thought the certainty of a controlled wound was a superior choice to waiting for the possibility of random death or a serious wound. I knew of a few men who inflicted wounds on themselves. This usually led to imprisonment or confinement in a mental hospital and a dishonorable discharge; in addition, the man became a pariah. Moreover, it was almost impossible for a man who wounded himself to avoid a serious loss of self-esteem.

During the advance to Saint-Sauveur, our little four-man team followed a simple routine: we directed fire on enemy targets, we dug in frequently, and a few times we came under enemy fire. No one was hurt or even scared in a major way. With Cherbourg sealed off on the twenty-first, the 505th was placed in a defensive position on the line with orders to resist any German forces that might try to break through our lines to supply their troops at Cherbourg. Our team was ordered to stay in the 505th's regimental headquarters and respond to requests to provide artillery fire wherever it was needed. We were located on a wooded hill, designated on our maps as Hill 131 because its summit was 131 meters above sea level.

It had begun to rain on the twentieth, and it rained steadily for four days in a hundred-year storm of near-hurricane strength. The artificial dock (called a Mulberry Harbor) at Gold Beach, one of the British beaches, was practically destroyed; the one at Utah Beach was more sheltered and survived with minor damage. The four days of strong winds and heavy rains made conditions miserable for the troops in the line because foxholes accumulated about a foot of water. Even after frequently bailing out one's hole with a helmet, the bottom was cold, wet, and muddy. Neither the Germans nor we were able to avoid becoming soaked clear through. The weather was too bad for either side to attempt any serious offensive action.

My twentieth birthday was on 24 June, and dawn brought a clear day that promised to be pleasant, warm, and sunny. The problem was that the U.S. Ninth Air Force, which provided our close air support, chose to celebrate my birthday in a really spectacular fashion. A reconnaissance patrol reported to the regimental commander that it looked like the Germans were concentrating a large number of troops and some tanks on another hill a little over a mile south of our position. If the report was true, it could mean that the Germans were planning an attack in hopes of breaking through and getting

supplies and reinforcements to Cherbourg. The 505 PIR commander, Col. William B. Ekmann, decided to summon fighter-bombers
to break up the concentration.

Right away things began to go wrong. We had no direct radio contact with the planes (this did not come until later in the war), so we
would fire a white mortar or artillery smoke shell into the target area
and set off a yellow smoke grenade to mark friendly troop positions.
Unfortunately, Murphy's Law, which decrees that "what can go
wrong will go wrong," was in full control that day. The grenade we
employed, which was labeled yellow smoke, spewed out a white cloud
next to our position. Compounding the problem was the fact that
the shell that was supposed to mark the enemy position proved to
be a dud.

We all looked on as the bird colonel ran with an entrenching
shovel to cover up the source of the white smoke in the center of his
headquarters. But he was too late. Thirteen P-47 fighter-bombers
were circling overhead waiting for proper target identification. Each
had two five-hundred-pound bombs, and we all knew what was coming next. We all dove for our foxholes. It didn't matter that their bot-
toms were wet and muddy, our survival was at stake. Mine had about
six inches of water in it, and I was forced to lie on my back to avoid
drowning. From my worm's eye viewpoint I watched as the planes
dove and dropped their bombs, which fell in a rough grid centered
on the white smoke. I expected each and every clearly visible falling
bomb to join me in my hole.

The noise deafened everyone for hours, and the Germans must
have been laughing their heads off if they really were on the neigh-
boring hill. Amazingly, no one suffered more than temporary deaf-
ness, but everything left above ground was destroyed by flying
bomb fragments: weapons, canteens, supplies, four nearby jeeps,
and all the kitchen equipment. Although this presented some in-
convenience, everyone was satisfied with the result—especially
when we began to recover our hearing a few hours later. With only
a little worse luck this incident could have been one of the worst
fratricidal incidents (soldiers being killed or wounded by "friendly"
forces) of the war. The experience greatly reduced our confidence
in the effectiveness of air strikes against dug-in troops, whether they

happened to be German or American. We continued to be gophers until the end of the war.

Our surviving this horrendous accidental bombing illustrates how randomness and luck dominated our lives. Most soldiers thought luck was their most valuable attribute or commodity. Those who died and those who lived followed no understandable pattern. Many could not believe that God made individual life-and-death choices in battle. In this state of chaos, luck seemed the only arbiter.

Our observer team returned to the battery after the bombing incident. We were pleasantly surprised to find that our first mail since mid-May had come in on 21 June. Corporal Angus J. Young, our mail clerk, gave me five letters: one from my girlfriend Sylvia, and four from my parents. My mother had also sent two "care packages" containing goodies that I shared with the rest of my team. We rested for two days and then went out again.

Not much happened to us in the next week since the infantry battalion to which we were attached was in a defensive position facing south, and there was little action. On 2 July we returned to the battery and bad news. A random German shell had landed in the midst of the battery area the day before. Young, the mail clerk, was eating his supper under a tree near the kitchen when the shell struck, killing him instantly. Three others were wounded, one of whom had to be evacuated. The other wounded were treated by our medics and returned to duty. Angus Young's death hit us all badly. He was popular both because he was friendly and got along well with everyone and because he delivered our cherished mail.

That same afternoon I joined 2d Lt. John S. Osmussen's observation party, which was ordered to return to the 505th's headquarters. The 505th had been ordered to capture Le Haye du Puits, which was just south of the hill on which we had been bombed. Visibility was poor, so most of our artillery fire was directed against suspected enemy locations and at positions identified in the reports of patrols that were sent behind enemy lines at night. After a short bombardment, the attack began at 0630, and within two hours German resistance had been broken. We followed the infantry into Le Haye du Puits and then set up an observation post on the summit of Hill 131.

After the battles around Hill 131, our actions were routine and unexciting until 9 July. On that date, I joined a party led by Lt. For-rest W. Eckert. The four-man party also included Captain Alley's driver, a Greek we all called "Dayman" because his Greek name was too hard to pronounce. Dayman had expressed a burning desire to go out with an observation team to "see some action." We had to lay some telephone wire from the battery area to the command post (CP) of the 505th's 3d Battalion, which we had been assigned to support.

Dayman was scouting about two hundred yards ahead of the rest of us while we laid the wire and dug it in. We came under heavy mortar fire and Dayman was seriously wounded. The rest of us came out frightened but unharmed. We carried Dayman the short distance to the CP and the medics there treated him before he was evacuated. Dayman's wounding brought my list of friends who had been killed, wounded, or lost to the unknown to four.

On 11 July we learned that the 82d would return to England to regroup and train for its next mission. Our initial reaction to the news that we would soon be returning to the comparative peace and safety of England was not to believe it. It seemed to all of us that it was just a cruel joke being played on us by a crazy army. Of course we were all delighted when we packed up our tattered belongings, assembled, and began moving back toward the beaches the next day.

Almost all of the wreckage had been cleaned up at Utah Beach. On the thirteenth we moved out on the manmade dock and boarded the British-crewed LST 309. This meant more meals of boiled fish! At least this time we had canteens and five-gallon water cans full of hard cider or calvados to wash it down. We sailed for England at 1130 on the fourteenth.

As we left Normandy, I had completed my 428th day in the army. Among the many things I learned in thirty-three days of combat was that, in the field, a soldier lived in his own private cocoon. This cocoon served as a barrier to information. When he was deep in his foxhole his cocoon extended only a few inches around him. If he was watching bombs fall, it extended a thousand feet up from the confines of his hole. At night it was limited to a matter of feet but most of the time it extended to the limits of his sight and hearing—but not beyond.

It seemed the army's policy was to tell us nothing, certainly nothing bad. Our battery officers knew a little more than we did but told us only what they had to. Few things broke through our cocoons. Among those that did were things we learned while moving from place to place, rumors, orders, the army newspaper *Stars and Stripes* (which we rarely saw), and letters from home that we received weekly and shared. Army censors limited the information we received from the outside. Compared to what we saw or heard from within our cocoons, this outside information was of little value, although it was appreciated. In discussing this situation with other soldiers, I learned that one's assignment affected the size of one's cocoon. A gunner, who was tied to his artillery piece, had a limited cocoon. On the other hand, a forward observer such as myself had a much greater and more varied view of what was occurring.

After more than fifty years of thinking about it, I have concluded that this sense of living in a cocoon had much to do with the mental health problems soldiers faced during and after their service. Certainly it contributed greatly to combat fatigue. There were two other feelings that were engendered: a sense of individual isolation and the feeling that no one outside really cared what was going on in one's cocoon. When these feelings became a source of continuous worry and brooding or if they could not be rationalized, men cracked under the strain. If a returning soldier could not leave these feelings behind him and readjust to civilian life, he quickly found himself in conflict with his new environment.

The reason we had escaped the front lines and were going back to England to prepare for the next assault was that airborne operations offered an opportunity to attack the enemy in depth. In Normandy, the airborne divisions assaulted the German rear areas, forcing them to fight ten miles or so behind the beaches. Their strong presence helped divert the defenders' attention from the invasion beaches and contributed to the breakdown of the enemy's defenses. The Germans simply could not handle all the attacks they faced in depth, and they soon became too weak to conduct an effective general defense of the coast.

4

Back to England

As we left Normandy at 1130 on 14 July 1944, Bastille Day, the atmosphere on our ship was one of celebration, like we imagined it would be on a cruise ship. We all felt we had cheated death and were glad to be alive. This changed when we reached Southampton at 2030 that same night and discovered that flying bombs the Germans fired from northern France, Belgium, and Holland were striking the area every hour or so.

We called these enemy weapons "buzz bombs." They were small, unmanned airplanes driven by ramjet engines, each carrying a warhead with about a thousand pounds of high explosives. They flew at well over four hundred miles per hour, so they were faster than most Allied fighter planes and antiaircraft guns also found them difficult to track and destroy. They could not be controlled from the ground, so they were targeted against a large general area, such as a city the size of Southampton or London. The Germans simply pointed a buzz bomb toward the target and sent it on its way. A timer turned off the engine at a point calculated to put the bomb over the target area and down it went. They told us that Southampton had been under attack for a week.

We left all of our artillery pieces, trucks, and other heavy equipment in Normandy, so we had only our personal weapons and gear to unload when we arrived. By 0800 we were aboard a train headed north. During our ten hours in Southampton, six buzz bombs fell in the harbor area. This impressed us but did no harm we could see until, just as we were beginning to march to the rail station, one bomb struck a ship and set it afire. Our train pulled into Leicester at 1300 and we made it back to Market Harborough by 1600.

After the mud, rain, noise, danger of combat, and personal exhaustion we experienced in Normandy, my little spot in a stable on a real bed was heaven indeed. We quickly learned to appreciate army food cooked from fresh ingredients more than anyone thought possible after a month of eating mostly field rations. The reputation of army cooks reached an all-time high, at least for a week or two. The occasional meals we ate at a local fish-and-chips shop were even better. Most of us believed fish and chips were the high point of English cooking, although, to be fair, GIs had little chance to experience better fare.

After two days of putting our things back in order, washing everything, and giving the supply sergeant personal lists of things we needed, orders were posted authorizing a week's leave for the battalion, with half the men going the next Monday and the remainder the following week.

Another order stated that after the leaves were completed, those not parachute qualified would be required to go to a two-week jump school beginning as soon as it could be organized, probably in three or four weeks. The alternative to volunteering for jump school was to be returned to one of the replacement camps. We had two days to decide, but after Wales, it was easy for me: I announced my choice ten minutes after reading the order. To my knowledge, no one who had been in Normandy failed to sign up for jump school. The camaraderie, unit loyalty—whether from a general to those below him or from a private to those above him—and pride that came from being in the division were strong motivators to stay, despite the recent demonstrations of combat's horrors. The fact that we had at least a month of assignments that would keep us out of the fighting may also have helped some make the decision. The prospect of going to a replacement unit and then becoming a casualty replacement in an unknown unit was far from attractive. The $50-per-month bonus for being parachute qualified did not hurt either.

When I reported that I wanted to go to jump school, 1st Sgt. Arthur V. Hazlett told me he had been counting on me and added that I would have to take my leave during the second week. In the meantime, he said I would be part of a team touring several replacement camps in Wales and western England to find more qualified volunteer replacements during the next week. The team was made up of three commissioned officers and three noncommissioned officers (NCOs). As a corporal, I was the lowest ranking member of the team. The rationale for including me was that some soldiers might be more comfortable talking to other enlisted men than solely to commissioned officers or more senior NCOs. We were seeking volunteers whose physical and mental abilities were greater than what was required for other army units. An airborne volunteer had to have an IQ about ten points higher than the army minimum, and we sought men whose IQs were fifteen points higher. We also looked for former athletes and men in obviously good physical condition.

One of the many points we stressed in our presentations to prospective volunteers was the importance of individual initiative in the 82d. Based on our experience, we said an army's success depends on two somewhat opposing concepts. On one hand, it must function as a mass unit without allowing individual variations or weaknesses. Thus, men in any unit must have and respect disciplinary factors like obeying orders without hesitation, unit loyalty, keeping commitments, respect for commissioned and noncommissioned officers, acceptance of difficulties, loyalty to and willingness to support their fellows, and physical fitness. On the other hand, the division encouraged independent thinking, contributing new or contrary ideas, and acts of bravery.

All armies and the units in them must reach a compromise between these two disparate factors. The entry requirements for both officers and enlisted men joining the 82d Airborne meant we attracted volunteers with more than the usual number of positive disciplinary factors. The division therefore reached a compromise that accentuated their individuality. Once a trooper completed the physically and mentally challenging jump school, he was a highly self-disciplined soldier. This allowed our leaders to concentrate the majority of our training on individual skills and teamwork at all levels.

Much of the superior efficiency of the 82d and other airborne units can be traced to their focus on platoon, squad, and individual training. When its men are well disciplined and the smaller units perform consistently with excellence, a division becomes a formidable force.

The reason we went to replacement camps for recruits was that there were not enough parachute-qualified graduates of the four-week-long jump school at Fort Benning, Georgia, to replace the troopers the division lost in Normandy. We were able to attract just over three hundred volunteers who met our requirements. Of those, sixty came to our battalion. After a month in combat, this more intellectual and less dangerous task was a rewarding experience. Later, we learned that the division had sent out scores of such recruiting teams, and most had been as successful as we were.

I had a most pleasant surprise when I returned from my recruiting trip. Staff Sergeant Donohue, our supply NCO, had found me a pair of size 12C jump boots. Although they still were not my exact size, they were a great improvement over the size 11D boots I had been wearing since joining the battalion. My feet were already very sore from Normandy and the running we had done before the invasion. At least now I felt they had a better chance of holding up during the hours of running I knew we would be doing in jump school.

First Sergeant Hazlett also told me that a reconnaissance sergeant position had been added to the battery's Table of Organization, and that I would be promoted to fill it if I completed jump school. He told me that I could take my leave in London, in one of several nearby towns, or at a place in the Scottish countryside. All army units are made up of individuals from diverse backgrounds—country and city boys of all variety. Being a city boy, I chose London even though I was told it was under sporadic attack by buzz bombs. Somehow, after Normandy, this did not bother me much, so I took my leave papers and boarded a train for Paddington Station on Monday morning.

My first problem was finding a hotel. One of my buddies who had returned from London recommended the Princess Royal and Mayflower hotels. The army service people were no help since they thought I was crazy for coming to London in the first place. I tried the Princess Royal but it had no rooms, so then I went to the Mayflower. It was also full, but after some begging I was told the top two floors were empty because a buzz-bomb strike would probably damage them. They offered me a room on one of those floors, and I gratefully accepted. (Oh, for the foolish joys of my youth!)

Everything was fine until nightfall. I was comfortably lying in warm water in a large, deep English bathtub when the first buzz bomb passed overhead. It shook the windows and even brought ripples to the surface of my bath water. That disturbance was caused by the reverberating, loud, putt-putt roaring sound of the bomb's ramjet engine as it flew over at an altitude of about five hundred feet. When the engine stopped, I almost dived underwater. I waited anxiously for the explosion and was happy to hear it explode some distance away. It took about five minutes before I thought about the people it may have fallen upon.

Although I had a normal desire for feminine companionship, I was afraid of contracting venereal diseases from prostitutes. Moreover, I was not at all skilled at picking up women. I wound up visiting museums, seeing the sights, going to plays and a classical music concert, buying books, drinking warm English mild-and-bitter beer, and eating good food. All this was interrupted frequently by buzz bombs. In all, about twenty-five of them fell within range of my hearing, and several were passing directly overhead when their engines stopped, as happened that first night. They were really scary things at night because the ten-yard-long exhaust flashes could be clearly seen from a great distance as they flew toward us. When the flashes and the noise stopped we knew they would come down within seconds. I dived into many curbside gutters around London. Most were clean but a few were dirty. After five days in London under such conditions, I took the train back a day early and rested in the quiet stable at Market Harborough.

Later, I learned that some of my more intelligent friends had taken London leaves but had stopped on the way in smaller English towns. There they found quiet atmospheres, English beer, good food, and plenty of nonprofessional feminine companionship. Apparently they found everything we had hoped London would offer but without the buzz bombs!

The comparison between our lives in England and in combat in Normandy was to compare order with chaos. The definition of chaos is "a lack of organization, active laws, government, or social order." Perhaps "the loss of civilization" is a suitable short definition. These definitions logically imply that chaos is the normal state of things, and it is in this chaotic state that mankind has overlaid some tenuous form of order with its ability to design organizations, laws, governments, religions, and social order.

A large percentage of mankind depends solely on a few organizers to determine the form of government and social order that prevails around them. In earlier times these followers—sheep, if you like—probably represented more than 95 percent of the total population. However, as the miserable Dark Ages gave way to the Renaissance, this percentage of sheep decreased until, by the twentieth century in some countries, it had fallen to about 75 percent. As more and more citizens participate in their government, the thin veneer of civilization becomes stronger against assault by tyrants, radicals, mob psychology, and demagogues.

In Germany in the 1930s, Hitler and his gang of thugs destroyed all semblance of civilization. This brought chaos first to their own country and then to their immediate neighbors. At first, the European Allies attempted to compromise with Hitler's aggression in order to gain peace at any cost. This was like negotiating with a lion not to eat any more antelope. After finally making the correct decision to destroy the colossus Hitler had designed, the Allies did not escape falling deeply into chaos themselves. Thousands of Allied servicemen and -women were thrown into the maw of war, often poorly equipped, poorly trained, and poorly or carelessly led. These people received a full dosage of chaos.

For the frontline soldier, battle was pure chaos. Everything was out of control. Anything could happen at any time. There was no personal security, and the system in which we lived was absolutely random. Stepping out of that chaos and into a civilized England—which, although not perfect, still had a substantial veneer of protections against chaos—offered a clear demonstration of what we were fighting for and what we hoped for, given the opportunity to return home.

Shortly before dawn on Monday, 31 July, they trucked those of us going to jump school to the Rutlandshire Royal Air Force (RAF) base near Leicester. Since there was less risk of broken bones and strains or sprains from parachute jumping if troopers were stronger than most soldiers, physical conditioning was emphasized during the first week. Those of us who thought we were in good shape soon learned what physical conditioning really was. Beginning that Monday we went on an eight-hour schedule of extreme exertion. We ran at double time for an hour, every other hour, four times a day. This amounted to more than twenty miles of running each day. If a soldier fell out of formation he had to do ten push-ups and then catch up with the formation. Nobody fell out after the first day, no matter how exhausted they might be, unless they required medical attention. The remainder of the daily schedule consisted of two hours of calisthenics, one hour of jumping from a seventeen-foot-high platform into a not-very-soft sandpit, and one hour of rope climbing. To my surprise, I found I was among the more poorly conditioned men in the group, and the rope climbing was almost my undoing. We had to climb thirty feet up a rope hanging from a beam at the top of a hangar, let go of the rope with one hand, and slap the beam. To qualify, this had to be done at least once during the week. I barely made it to the top a single time on the fifth and final day.

Exhaustion is not the right word to describe how we felt after each of those strenuous days. On the first day, we were so exhausted that some men had to be helped into upper bunks. The pain was all over our bodies. By the third day we began to feel human again, and by the fifth day we felt superhuman. By then we were convinced we could accomplish anything. In spite of a lack of interest in food because eating took away from our sleep time, we all forced ourselves to eat and drink since we knew we could not survive without sustenance.

Everyone became tense and grouchy, and on the second night I got into a fight. All I wanted was to rest, to be left alone, and read a book. However, three or four of my mates began to tease me about what today would be called my "nerdiness." As a result, I foolishly challenged one of them to a fight, although I was no fighter. I really began to question my decision when I saw that the one I had chosen to fight was an ex–Golden Gloves boxing champion from Massachusetts, Cpl. Albert S. "Nappy" Napolitano. We went into the shower, where I received a thorough beating. Fortunately, Nappy took some pity on me. He became one of my closest friends thereafter. No one else challenged my book reading again because they knew I would at least give it a try, even if I was a pitiful opponent.

Beginning on Tuesday of the second week the physical conditioning continued in the mornings, while in the afternoons we made parachute jumps. The greatest risk in a combat parachute jump is not the jump itself. The major risk a jumper faces is that he may be shot while he is descending, helpless and unable to defend himself as he dangles under his parachute. Combat jumps thus are made from a low altitude, minimizing a trooper's time in the air. The optimum altitude for a combat jump was supposed to be seven hundred to eight hundred feet.

When jumps are made at such a low altitude, there is little time for error. The mechanics that made a chute open included a strong, thirty-foot static line that each trooper clipped to a cable running the length of the plane. Slack in the static line was held together by rubber bands on the back of the parachute pack. As the trooper jumped, the static line fed out until all the slack was used up, at which point the static line pulled the back off the pack and the rushing wind pulled out a small pilot chute, which in turn pulled out the main chute. If the parachute was packed properly it opened easily. For the chute to deploy, open, and reduce the rate of descent to a safe rate from free fall requires about three hundred vertical feet, which takes about three seconds.

We carried reserve parachutes that had to be manually deployed by pulling a ripcord. These also took about three hundred vertical feet to open and slow the rate of descent sufficiently for a safe landing. This margin for error of only a hundred vertical feet meant the jumper had to count "One thousand one, one thousand two, one thousand three." If his main chute was not fully deployed by then, he had only another second to decide to deploy his reserve chute or it would do him little good since he would hit the ground with an impact that might kill or hurt him badly. To add to the stress, deploying both chutes at the same time was not wise because they were likely to become entangled and fail to slow a jumper's descent sufficiently enough for him to survive the landing.

Another problem a jumper faces, the opening shock, is usually not too serious, but it can become so if he makes a mistake or becomes careless. We usually jumped from an airplane flying at about 125 miles per hour. When the chute opened, it jerked us from 125 miles per hour to zero airspeed in just a few feet. Body position was very important in order to prevent damage to the spine. Fortunately, teaching troopers the proper position was fairly easy.

We made our practice jumps from a higher altitude than combat jumps, usually about a thousand to twelve hundred feet, thus making them safer. Death as a result of the jump itself was a rare occurrence in both practice and combat, but about 1 to 3 percent of troopers experienced injuries, most of which were sprains. Night jumps such as the one in Normandy posed other risks. Missing the intended drop zone, either because of bad weather or navigational error, was one. Another good example of pilot error was the improperly high altitude (about two thousand feet) from which the Normandy jump was made. This, along with cloud cover that obscured the drop zones, caused most of the more-than-expected jumping casualties the division experienced on D day. Even in practice jumps the pilots seemed unable to find the proper drop zones. It was widely rumored that the pilots were drunk on many combat jump missions.

On 7 August we made our first jump after completing our prejump training. Captain Alley, the rest of the battery officers, and some of our NCOs came along in support. All of us successfully completed the jump, and our officers congratulated everyone afterward.

Each of us had to make five jumps to qualify as paratroopers. My first jump was terrifying, but after surviving it a great feeling of accomplishment replaced my fear. My next two jumps went well, but I sprained an ankle quite severely while landing on my fourth jump. I was faced with the choice of making my fifth jump that night or repeating the entire course once my ankle healed. I feared that we might soon be ordered back into combat and that I would not have another chance to qualify as a paratrooper, which in turn might lead to my being ordered to a replacement camp.

The doctors thought my sprain was too severe to jump, and they advised me not to do so that night. Of course they were not the ones who would have to make the additional five jumps and go through another two weeks of jump school or perhaps be separated from valued comrades. They warned me that I might further damage my leg, but they said that if I was determined to proceed they would thoroughly tape both my ankles and wish me luck. Faced with choosing the lesser of two evils, I opted to have my ankles taped and make the jump.

A night jump is particularly frightening because you face the prospect of stepping out of a comfortable plane into black oblivion. After I made the jump, it seemed more like voluntarily deciding to step through a black portal into a coffin. Another problem is that the ground is darker than the sky, so it is difficult to distinguish details as you approach the ground. A road might look like a stream, and trees are hard to make out. These and other concerns added to the fear level in spite of the fact that the drop was to be into an open field lit by pathfinder lights that had been placed on the ground to guide the pilot to the proper area. Of course, by then we all knew that there were no guiding lights for most of the 82d's Normandy jumpers because the pilots dropped them from too high an altitude into clouds and because many of the pathfinders were dropped in the wrong positions. The bravery of those paratroopers who jumped into clouds and toward an unknown reception below them was far beyond the call of duty by any standard.

Although my ankle hurt so badly that I could only walk stiffly and with much difficulty, my last jump was successful. Actually, my concerns about my ankle were so great that all fears about the jump itself were completely blocked from my mind. The next day I hobbled up to receive my silver parachute wings from the recently promoted XVIII Airborne Corps commander, Maj. Gen. Matthew B. Ridgway, in a very impressive ceremony. I was far more proud of this accomplishment than either of my two college graduation ceremonies. I was glad to receive my wings but I silently hoped I would not have to make any more jumps. All of my friends successfully completed their jumps and qualified for their parachute wings.

Later, General Gavin, who had made three previous combat jumps and scores of practice jumps, suffered two compression fractures in his back on the daytime combat jump into Holland. This probably was the result of his plane being too low when he jumped, thus failing to slow his rate of descent sufficiently for an easy landing. Hitting the ground too hard sometimes caused such an injury. This goes to show that the air force pilots did not respect rank; they treated us all the same.

We were trucked back to Market Harborough on Saturday, 12 August. On the bulletin board was an item of personal interest: the promotion list that advanced me to sergeant. There were rumors that we would receive a full complement of new 105mm howitzers but instead we received two additional 75mm guns. Unfortunately, the powers that be failed to authorize the two additional trucks needed to tow them.

My promotion required that I be trained in two new skills. As the second in command of an observation team I would have to know a lot more about directing artillery fire since this would be my duty if the team's officer became incapacitated. He would also depend on my help in finding and directing fire on targets. Also, although it was unlikely, I might have to command a planeload of jumpers. Because of this I also had to be trained as a jumpmaster. The first part was easy since I'd had some experience in Normandy. A week of training was all it took to make me sufficiently proficient in fire direction to act as a standby and to provide the necessary assistance.

The next week they sent about a dozen of us (some men came from other outfits) back to our favorite airport for jumpmaster training. More—but much easier—physical training was required, then we practiced jumping out of a dummy airplane fuselage many times. After three days of this, we had to make two jumps, one during the day and one at night. The drill was that the jumpmaster would manage the jump of four or five other troopers and then follow the last one out. Fortunately my ankle had healed and all went well. Also, jumping proved to be much easier for me as a jumpmaster since I was so involved in getting my men properly set up and then safely out of the plane on time that my own jump turned out to be just a reflex action.

Shortly after I qualified as a jumpmaster we learned that we would be going into our next battle, wherever that would be, in gliders. It was reported that there were not enough parachutes available, but the fact that the operation was planned for daylight may also have influenced the decision. Those of us not immediately involved with the guns still hoped to land by parachute. We had all seen a lot of wrecked gliders in Normandy and we knew they flew only slightly better than bricks. Frankly, flying into combat in a glider terrified us much more than parachuting.

By then, the German front in Normandy had been broken, and throughout August, Allied armored and infantry divisions raced across France. The 82d and 101st Airborne Divisions were alerted to prepare for a drop near Lille in northern France to help the drive across the Low Countries to the port of Antwerp. It was hoped that this drive would not be stopped before the attacking force reached the good, flat tank country of northern Germany beyond the Rhine River, bypassing the Siegfried Line fortifications altogether. The Germans were expected to make a stand along the Belgian border, but when the British and Canadian forces passed through this area relatively easily, our alert was canceled.

On 13 September we were alerted for another mission and our training intensified. The British had reached the Meuse-Escaut Canal in northern Belgium and were preparing to cross it. Three airborne divisions were to be dropped in front of the British XXX Corps's armored and infantry divisions to allow them to move quickly north across the Meuse, various canals, and the Dutch estuaries of the Rhine: the Waal and the Neder Rijn. If all these waterways could be crossed over captured bridges, the Allied armies might be able to move around the Siegfried Line without heavy fighting and enter a part of northern Germany that could not be easily defended against our tanks. It seemed like a good idea, and the operation was given the code name Market-Garden.

5

Reflections on Elite Units

After a month of combat in Normandy, completing jump school, and being in the midst of preparing for another airborne assault, we began to wonder about the basic mission of airborne troops. The original plan for the airborne divisions was that they would make violent parachute assaults, fight for a week or two, and then be withdrawn from the fighting. They would join the reserves under the control of General Eisenhower, commander of the Supreme Headquarters, Allied Expeditionary Force (SHAEF), to prepare for another mission.

In Normandy, the 82d demonstrated its superior overall fighting qualities so army and corps commanders became reluctant to release it for return to SHAEF control. This tended to make the 82d the unit they would throw into action to accomplish an objective that other divisions had failed to achieve. This practice greatly increased our casualties and made it harder to prepare for the next assault. The officers with whom I made the recruiting trip after my return to England were concerned that staying in battle would be our undoing as assault troops. In fact, one of the problems was that although we had become "elite troops," this term did not always fit well with U.S. Army thinking.

Americans think of specially trained and selected elite units with mixed feelings. For generations, other countries, particularly the British, Germans, French, and Russians have used elite units effectively. The objections Americans have to elite units are based on the idea of democratic equality and that American boys can be made into soldiers of equal quality with equal ease. This idea harks back to the minutemen of the Revolutionary War. In World War II the U.S. Army found it needed elite units to compete effectively with enemies who showed this premise of "all men can fight equally well" to be false.

The airborne units and other elite American units called for volunteers only, then selected only those who passed much stricter physical and mental standards than were required of the rest of the army. The selected airborne volunteers next underwent a program of rigorous physical training that used many techniques designed to improve mental alertness. There followed the even more demanding parachute training school. A number of intermediate tasks had to be accomplished, including the satisfactory completion of five parachute jumps, before a trooper was awarded his silver parachute wings. Becoming used to meeting a long series of difficult objectives was just as important to the airborne volunteer's later combat capability and success as was the physical training.

Many men dropped out of this rigorous program and went back to regular army units without prejudice. This weeded out some of the volunteers who might have been weaker than those who succeeded and who might later have failed in their duties. I knew few men who completed the program who failed later. Those who succeeded developed a strong camaraderie with the men with whom they completed the strenuous training regimen. Whether these men succeeded because of what they individually brought to the program or because the program brought out the best in them, I do not know. I tend to believe it was a combination of these two factors, and perhaps others. I do know that I would rather have died than fail the men for whom I was responsible or my commanders and peers. I believe the majority of the men in the 82d shared that feeling, and it was a powerful contributor to the division's success in combat.

The mystique of being airborne attracted many of the highest quality leaders, both commissioned and noncommissioned officers, to the 82d. This was a great advantage we had over most of the infantry divisions. Included in the elite American divisions were the airborne, most armored, and a few infantry divisions (in the Pacific, marines would have to be added to the list). Those armored divisions that had been organized for several years and had seen some combat in Africa and Italy were excellent and could be depended upon to fight well if they were in the line next to us, responsible for our flank. The same could be said of the lst, 4th, and 8th Infantry Divisions and others that had previous combat experience. These divisions had gone through on-the-job training, a cruel culling-out process that reduced the portion of its men who were not capable of the rigors of combat for either physical or mental reasons.

All of these divisions had the advantage of having the best and most experienced commissioned and noncommissioned officers in their ranks. These factors meant that about twenty of the more than sixty American divisions in the ETO proved their ability to perform consistently, excellently, and dependably. These units and their men followed the doctrines that were developed in action and were aggressive in battle.

The other forty or so American divisions in the ETO did the best they could under the circumstances, but they were thrown into battle under the worst of conditions so they had little chance to succeed. They had no experience and they were made up mostly of draftees, many of whom were virtually untrainable. For the most part, they received the dregs of the American commissioned officer corps. Because of these problems, it should come as no surprise that these divisions were poorly suited for assaults or defending a key point against a battle-hardened elite German unit. After trying these poorer divisions in attacks against elite enemy units a few times, with regret and without publication, the high command turned to the better divisions for most major assaults and placed the poorer divisions in defensive situations. This decision was to bear bitter fruit in the opening moves of the Battle of the Bulge when elite German units assaulted a sector of the front defended, in part, by green, poorly trained American divisions. Most of these green divisions were broken up by the German attack, but many individuals and small units performed gallantly. They mustered enough strength to slow the German juggernaut and give veteran units time to come to their aid and defeat the Germans more easily.

Thus, despite its democratic tendencies, the U.S. Army informally set up two groups of divisions: those that did most of the hard fighting and a second, less skilled group that performed easier defensive tasks that were also necessary. The German army was similarly organized, and those of us who fought its elite units, as well as the poorer ones, could quickly detect which type we were up against. If our poorer divisions had performed at the same level our elite divisions did, the war would have been shortened by months. In deciding that these poorer divisions were unlikely to be able to improve enough to be effective assault forces, the U.S. Army faced the same facts and made the same decisions as did the Germans, British, and Russians.

As stated previously, the key to the 82d's success was its excellent leadership. My experience was that the leaders who were really effective shared everything with the troops they were responsible to lead. These men subjected themselves to the same rigorous training their men went through. To some extent, officers were forced to adopt this mentality by the vigorous training and the likelihood that an airborne division would be isolated from other support for extended periods of time. The idea that leadership results from an officer rising up, running toward the enemy, and shouting "Follow me!" is fundamentally faulty because it leads to an inordinate loss of leaders. Simply stated, such action results in an unorganized attack that will prove ineffective. A good leader describes the intended attack so everyone knows what the objective is, his part in it, and when it is to occur. Then the leader goes with his men, exposing himself to the same—but not greater—dangers than his men face.

Until World War II and for part of it, officers in the British and American armies wore distinctive uniforms in battle that led to inordinate and foolish losses. Ending this nonsensical practice made it easier for officers to survive so they could do their duty and lead. Battalion, regimental, and division commanders led assaults less often. Nevertheless, in the 82d these higher commanders were always visible and frequently participated in action where it was hottest and most critical.

During combat maneuvers our high commanders were always near the front. All officers in the division parachuted with their units whether a jump was for combat or practice. No officer in the 82d would stay back in safety while his unit was in jeopardy; if he did, he would have been relieved. This strong leadership was the basis of the division's great success in combat in the ETO.

From a personal standpoint, I know I was on the physical borderline for meeting the requirements of the 82d. The attributes that led to my acceptance as a leader were willpower, a fair level of intelligence, and better than average judgment in tight places. There were many with similar detriments and attributes, but some had great physical skills along with mental strengths.

The diversity in the 82d taught me a great lesson in tolerance. Although there were no blacks in the division (the armed forces were segregated in World War II), its members were an otherwise excellent sampling of the entire U.S. population. The 456th PFAB, of which I was a part, had members from all of the states and from a variety of religious persuasions, cultural and social backgrounds, and intelligence levels. Our ranks included southern hillbillies, two Mafioso, a college professor, a number of college students and graduates, derelicts, Old Army soldiers, and about everything else imaginable.

Few men in this diverse group had much in common. It might have been expected that this diversity would have resulted in the formation of cliques, which in turn would have led to intolerance. It soon became apparent to all that a group composed solely of intellectuals or hillbillies could not perform its assigned task by itself. Because of the overwhelming requirement for teamwork and mutual support, the human tendency to form adversarial cliques was minimal. In fact, a general tolerance developed between all members of the division.

This lesson in tolerance was a lifelong lesson to our members. I regret that blacks were excluded because I believe the country would be better today if they had been members of all the World War II fighting divisions. Today's army is proof of that.

6

Into Holland by Glider

It took some time for the high command to decide whether we would move to our next battle by parachute, glider, or truck, so we trained for each of these possibilities in a somewhat confused manner. Finally it was decided that the 456th PFAB would go into battle by glider. For 95 percent of us this would be our first glider ride, and we would have no practice, so our first ride would be to a point unknown to us where Germans would probably meet us with guns firing. The battalion would go in three parts. The first, an advance party of about twenty officers and men, would go in by parachute and glider on D day. The second group of about 350 officers and men and the artillery pieces would go in by glider on D-plus-1. The third group, consisting of about a hundred men, would arrive about a week later with the rest of our vehicles and heavy equipment. I was assigned to the second group.

There was a shortage of glider pilots, so only one could be assigned to each glider instead of the usual two, and the highest-ranking occupant was called upon to serve as copilot. A few days before we were scheduled to move to the airport, I was assigned to be the copilot of a glider that would carry a jeep and the three enlisted men of our observation team. Our lieutenant would parachute in with the 505th PIR headquarters. This assignment brought me into the small group of noncoms who joined the officers of the battalion three days before D day at a presentation of the confidential details of the planned assault. For security reasons, every major operation had its own designated D day and H hour. That way, people could talk about D day without disclosing the actual date of the operation, in this case Market-Garden, until all dates were set and arrangements made. Market-Garden was a bold and ambitious strategic stroke that had the potential to shorten the war. Market was the code name assigned to the airborne portion of the operation. Its goal was to secure a series of bridges over rivers and canals between the British front line near the Belgian-Dutch border and Arnhem on the Neder Rijn and open a corridor through which armor could move with little opposition. Garden was the movement of British armor through the corridor to "reap the harvest of Market."

As the British XXX Corps crossed the Meuse-Escaut Canal, the 101st would drop in the vicinity of Eindhoven and secure bridges over the Wilhelmina and Willems Canals and the Dommel River; the 82d would capture bridges across the Maas (Meuse) River near Grave, the Maas-Waal Canal, and the Waal River near Nijmegen; and the British 1st Airborne Division would seize the highway bridge over the Neder Rijn at Arnhem. The corridor thus formed would be more than seventy-five miles long. If successful, it would open an easy route into the northern German plain, territory that the Germans would find difficult to defend against the superior numbers of Allied armor. The best aspect of the move was the fact that the strong defenses of the Siegfried Line would be completely flanked, thus avoiding what all knew might be a bloody battle to breach those formidable fortifications.

One important negative factor was that once the airborne divisions were dropped along the seventy-five-mile corridor, the Allied strategy would be fully disclosed since the armor had had no choice but to move through it as quickly as possible. For the operation to achieve its full strategic potential, XXX Corps's divisions would have to move swiftly through the corridor and into Germany before the Germans could muster enough forces to stop them.

In hindsight, it is apparent that the operation was planned too quickly and the need for speed was not sufficiently emphasized. There was also a great intelligence failure because the German 9th and 10th SS Panzer Divisions were refitting in the Arnhem area. The divisions were identified as being on the scene but were incorrectly

considered to be ineffective because of recent fighting. We did not
know any of this when we landed, so all were optimistic about our
prospects of ending the war by Christmas.

To ensure success, the British had to cross the Meuse-Escaut
Canal and reach Arnhem in just two days. This was a tall order, much
harder to do on the ground than on a general's sand table. Equally
critical was that all of the bridges along the route be secured. The
82d's mission was to take the large road bridge over the Maas River
at Grave, at least two of the five smaller bridges over the Maas-Waal
Canal, and the huge two-thousand-foot, four-lane road bridge over
the Waal at Nijmegen. We expected all of them to be wired with explosives and ready for destruction. If the Germans succeeded in blowing just one of the key bridges this could defeat the entire plan, so
it was essential that they be seized quickly. The planners also assumed
any German counterattacks along the corridor would be weak, and
they thought the Luftwaffe was beaten and would not be an important factor.

We knew something was really up when our battalion headquarters and Battery A were moved to the airfield at Langar on 16 September. There were more transports and gliders lined up there than
we imagined existed, and we knew this was only one of many airfields
that were to be used. Sure enough, on Sunday the seventeenth we
loaded our glider with our jeep and some supplies. Then we watched
as planes loaded with the 505th PIR's paratroopers took off. They
would precede us by a day. Soon the clear, blue sky above was full of
planes that were forming an air train of about seven hundred aircraft, of which about a hundred left from Langar. They moved to the
east after completing their formation at about 1030. Included in that
first serial were two planes carrying our battalion commander, Lt.
Col. Wagner J. D'Alessio, and ten men who would parachute in with
him, along with two planes towing gliders carrying other troopers
from battalion headquarters and their equipment.

Late that afternoon, the troop-carrier planes came back. Ninety-
six of the aircraft that left Langar returned; about ten were damaged.
The pilots reported that they had dropped their loads right on target. They said they encountered heavy flak along the Dutch coast and

that they had observed some German resistance around the drop zones. All in all, the first day's drop was considered a success.

The eighteenth was clear, sunny, and beautiful. Battery A required twenty-three gliders to carry its three officers, 105 men, and their guns and light equipment into Holland. Our lieutenant had gone in with the advance party, and I had orders to meet him with the rest of our observation team at the 505th's headquarters, wherever that proved to be. I rode in the copilot's seat of our glider and had a great view of everything. As we sat on the runway before takeoff, the pilot gave me a quick lesson on how to land a glider in case he was killed or wounded. The lesson continued for a half-hour once we were in stable flight headed east toward Holland. Since we were expecting to fly through some antiaircraft fire, the pilot's loss was a reasonable possibility, and the thought of landing that thing terrified me more than being hit myself. It at least kept my mind off other possible disasters we might face.

Shortly after takeoff, at about 1300, we noticed that one of the gliders ahead of us seemed to be out of control. It just could not fly straight behind its tow plane, and soon the pilot cut it loose. Both the tow plane and the glider landed on the runway below. I found out later that it was our battery commander Captain Alley's, glider. Its rudder had jammed, and the pilot barely managed to land it safely. After they fixed the rudder, the tow plane lifted the glider a second time and they followed us and landed in the drop zone just a few minutes after we did.

We crossed the North Sea and then the Dutch coast between the Waal outlet and the Schelde estuary, where the Canadians and British were fighting to clear the sea entrance to Antwerp. As far as we could see there was a continuous stream of planes and gliders. Occasionally a German antiaircraft gun would open fire and threatening puffs of exploding shells appeared around us. When this happened, the P-51 and P-47 fighters that accompanied us dove on the guns and strafed them. They were very effective, for soon the ground fire directed against us ceased.

My luck held. Our pilot made it to the drop zone unhurt, so I did not have to land the glider. Our tow plane cut us loose over the drop zone, located between Groesbeek and Mook, at about 1450. Our landing was rough, and we skidded into another glider; fortunately no one in either one was hurt. The body of our glider was bent, so we could not get the jeep out. We were in a field of sugar beets that stood almost a foot tall. We had been told that German panzers were likely to be in the Reichswald, the dense woods located to the east across the nearby German border. Enemy troops along the edge of the Reichswald were firing small arms and mortars into the drop zone from about three hundred yards away, which meant we had landed in Germany. Fortunately they were short of machine guns and were poor marksmen, so only two Battery A troopers were hit. We wanted to get away from the glider as fast as possible but we needed our jeep and equipment, and that meant getting help. We were so hyped as we ran to a nearby road in search of assistance that each of us must have fallen over the beet plants ten times.

We encountered an infantry heavy weapons company moving south on the road. I asked their officer if he could help us remove our jeep and equipment from the glider. He sent about twenty men back with us, and we trotted to the glider through enemy fire. It took us about ten minutes to tear the pipe-and-canvas glider apart sufficiently enough to recover the jeep. It was hard driving through the beet field because the Germans were firing mortars at us, but we survived. Since our helpers were also headed to the 505th's headquarters we loaded some of their mortar ammunition and other heavy equipment into our jeep and trotted along on foot with them.

Second Lieutenant Harvey Bascomb, our team leader, was waiting for us when we arrived. He had injured an ankle when he landed and was painfully hobbling around. Without a doctor to examine him it was impossible to tell whether it was broken or just badly sprained. He was very glad to see the jeep. Lieutenant Bascomb was a replacement officer who joined our battery after our return from Normandy. This was his first action, and he was more nervous than the rest of us. That Monday afternoon, after our arrival fifty-five miles behind German lines, action became light as soon as the local defenders realized they could do nothing to evict us. We had taken the enemy by surprise and were successfully building our strength, but we knew they would react soon and violently.

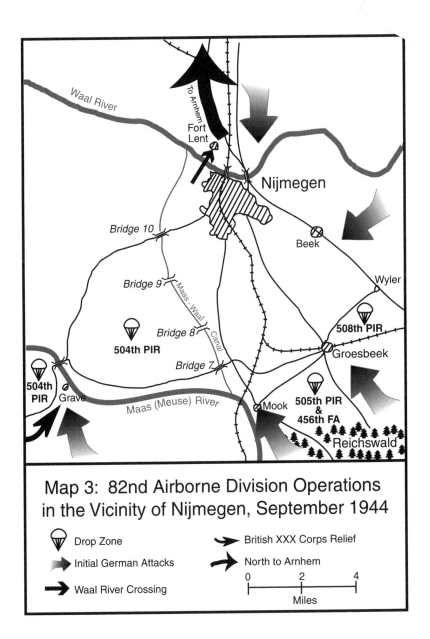

Map 3: 82nd Airborne Division Operations in the Vicinity of Nijmegen, September 1944

Battery A was complete with all its guns and observers and was laid and ready to fire near a 505th PIR outpost by 1700. Batteries C and D were not as lucky as we were. Battery B had taken off from the RAF field at Cottesmore, and Battery C flew from the RAF base at Fulbeck. Both batteries were to land in a different drop zone from ours. It was under heavier attack and only about half of their gliders landed in the intended drop zone. The remainder were scattered in nearby fields.

In separate incidents two pilots towing gliders from Batteries B and C lost their way and dropped them between the areas controlled by the 82d and 101st Divisions. In each case the Dutch underground came to their aid and smuggled the troopers and all of their equipment to a 101st Division outpost. They later rejoined us when the corridor was opened by the British armor.

Battery B lost six men, including its first sergeant, when their glider and its tow plane were shot down in flames by enemy antiaircraft fire over the Dutch town of Molenhoek. Among those lost were Pvts. Harry C. Guiltner and Donald E. King, both of whom had been my friends in Wales and joined the 456th with me.

We had landed in a picturesque, pastoral area with windmills, beautiful woods, quaint cottages, and rich green meadows. As yet it was unspoiled by war. So far, only light weapons were being used in the fighting, and damage to civilian property was negligible. However, when the Germans brought heavy artillery and bombers against us, we all knew the damage would be extensive. The Dutch also understood this and almost welcomed it because they hated the German occupiers so much. Dutch civilians, including beautiful girls in wooden shoes, brought us food and drink. I particularly remember the dense, dark bread with fresh country butter they gave us. It was delicious. We were all impressed by the fact that these people had been almost starved during the German occupation, but they freely shared what they had with us in spite of the fact that they knew we had brought violent war to their neighborhood.

Soon after the landing an enemy train moved into and then out of our defensive perimeter on its way to Germany. It caught us by surprise. We had not expected to encounter enemy trains in our drop zones. General Gavin was furious and chewed out two regimental commanders and anyone else in sight. A half-hour later another train, this time from Germany, tried to move through our positions. This time we were ready, and someone fired a bazooka rocket into the steam locomotive. Steam spurted from the boiler as the train slowed to a stop. The bazooka gunner fired another rocket into a tank car containing oxygen. It was attached to a tank car carrying hydrogen for V-2 rockets. There was a huge explosion and we saw no more enemy trains after that. Fortunately none of us was hurt.

Initially, the 456th was in support of the 376th PFAB, which had parachuted in on the seventeenth. Our battery and most infantry positions south of Groesbeek were on the highest ground in Holland. This was good because the Germans would have to attack us by moving up hill, which is never an easy task. On the bad side was the lack of protective cover such as woods, walls, and buildings. The Germans could see our positions and everything we did there on the open ground. Our ability to move was limited because the Germans tended to fire at anything that moved. No one had to order a soldier to dig in. On D-plus-2 and D-plus-3 the battery was used to help man the 505th's perimeter because infantry troops were scarce.

By nightfall on D-plus-2 our situation had improved and it was likely the 505th could hold its perimeter and make ready for the next day's landings. The main force of the British XXX Corps did not make it to our area that day; they were at least a day behind schedule. A strong force of SS *panzergrenadiers* supported by tanks defended the city of Nijmegen and its critical Waal River bridge. Although the bridge remained intact, if the Garden part of the operation did not get back on schedule the next day, failure was likely. But that was of little concern to us ordinary soldiers at the time; we were simply fighting to stay alive.

Colonel William B. Ekman, the 505th PIR commander, was concerned by the possibility of a German attack coming out of the Reichswald to the east. The regiment and its supporting units manned a seven-mile-long defensive line facing east and south. This was a long front for a single regiment, and it meant our position was weak, consisting of a series of strong points with undefended spaces between them covered only by patrols. There was no way we could hold off a determined attack by a sizable force of high-quality German troops supported by tanks.

On D-plus-3 the 456th was assigned as Colonel Ekman's only artillery support. More artillery and another regiment of infantry were due the next day by glider. He ordered most of our battalion to prepare to fire to the east. Our observation team remained at the 505th's headquarters, another was put in one of the eastern strong points, and a third moved to a position facing south. Our main hope was that we could hold out long enough for reinforcements to arrive. Hopefully that would happen before the Germans mounted a serious attack against us. All were buoyed by reports that elements of the British Guards Armoured Division's reconnaissance party had entered the 82d perimeter at Grave on the morning of D-plus-2. The reality was that this advance party consisted of only a few jeeps and armored cars and was in no position to give us much help. We could only hope their main body followed closely behind them.

At dawn on the twentieth a strong German attack drove elements of the 82d out of Wyler, Germany, and recaptured about half of the drop zones near Groesbeek. Infantry supported by artillery fire stopped the attack, but the troopers were not able to recover the town or all of the drop zones. This was critical, not only because of the danger to the men in the gliders that were expected later that day, but because the troops already on the ground were rapidly running out of ammunition. Fog in England in the takeoff area delayed the incoming flights, but at about 1500 on D-plus-3 hundreds of gliders carrying infantry, artillery, and some ammunition arrived.

The Germans opened fire on the incoming gliders as we watched helplessly. Enemy fire and our smoke shells exposed the fact that German troops were waiting for them, so most of the glider pilots tried to land close to friendly positions. Troopers whose gliders landed among the enemy were forced to fight their way out. Although both sides suffered heavy casualties, only about 10 percent of our incoming artillerymen and guns were lost. Some of these casualties were wounded and were recovered during the night. The planes carrying supplies to be dropped by parachute were warned of the situation on the ground, so almost all of the much-needed ammunition fell in friendly territory and was quickly recovered. These successful landings greatly increased our strength. At the same time, the Germans proved to be of low quality, made up mostly of convalescents, newly recruited boys, and rear-echelon soldiers.

A battalion of parachute infantry supported by a battalion from the British Guards Armoured Division, the spearhead of XXX Corps, attempted to seize the Waal bridge on D-plus-3 by working its way along the river beyond Nijmegen to an area east of the bridge. They made it to within four hundred yards of the bridge, but they were unable to get any closer because of the determined German opposition. The paratroopers held their position until after dark. About midnight, a patrol that included some airborne engineers was sent to the bridge. The engineers climbed all over the lower bridge structure, defusing demolition charges and cutting wires. Because the Germans would no doubt inspect the wiring using binoculars in the morning, the engineers would cut a wire and then carefully tape it back together, leaving a gap in the copper wire beneath the insulation. If the Germans discovered one of these breaks the only practical thing for them to do would be to rewire the whole demolition system. The process of recovering the demolition system might take them a day to complete, and it would have to be done under our sniper fire. After the patrol returned, the battalion retreated.

The arrival of XXX Corps's main force at the Grave bridge in the 82d Division's perimeter late on D-plus-2 was another morale booster, especially after the 325th GIR's scheduled arrival on D-plus-3 was delayed for another day by bad weather in England. This reinforcement by British armor would help us gain the Waal bridge. No one had word about the British paratroopers fighting in Arnhem but we knew their situation had to be precarious considering all of the delays and the strength of the German opposition.

From a personal standpoint, my first three days in Holland were a blur. The 456th PFAB, including Battery A, fired on targets at all points of the compass. This meant the observation parties went from place to place to try to detect the enemy threats and engage them with artillery fire. A shortage of ammunition made observed firing essential. Running around that open terrain was very dangerous, so an attempt was made to minimize movement by sending the nearest party to a new target area. Despite those precautions I had to move around a lot, and I was fired at more in those two days than during any week of the war.

One such incident I recall was when scouts brought in a report on D-plus-2 that Germans were attempting to bridge the Maas to our west. Lieutenant Osmussen and his party were with the battery "resting." His noncom had been hurt, so I was ordered to replace the man temporarily. This worked out well since it helped ease Lieutenant Osmussen's movements around the area. His plan called for one of the infantry scouts to lead an infantry company and me to the threatened point. He would then go there and meet us. This worked out well. Because the Germans had trouble observing the land west of our airhead, we were only fired on twice.

When we arrived, we saw a battalion-sized German force waiting for some engineers to build a bridge across the Maas. They were about halfway across and had a few men on our side stringing cable to hold the bridge in place. Our infantrymen quickly killed or captured those on our side of the river and cut the cables. We directed artillery fire on the enemy on the other side and on the bridge itself. Soon the beginnings of their bridge floated away and the remaining Germans left the area. We noted a dozen or more dead on each side of the river. The company left a platoon behind and the rest of us returned.

Sleep was at a premium. I do not think I had more than six hours during those three days. In spite of the lack of sleep, most of us were still hyper. This action against the enemy on the Maas River was typical of four others I participated in during that period.

The German defenders at the Waal bridge had thwarted all efforts to take it from the south end. General Gavin had earlier suggested that assault boats be brought up and paratroopers from the 504th PIR cross the Waal and attack the north end of the bridge simultaneously with attacks by the 505th and the British armor from the south. Although the paratroopers had undergone no training with assault boats, the skeptical British, having no better alternative to offer, approved the plan.

Although our battalion seldom supported the 504th, since maximum artillery fire was needed to support the crossing, my observation team was sent to the south bank of the Waal near a railroad bridge that was also to be captured. Dutch homes were built close to the edge of the river and they would provide good cover for the infantrymen and boats as they prepared for the river crossing. The Germans had concentrated their forces at the north ends of the two bridges and on the ground between them. A large power station was situated about a mile west of the Waal road bridge. Because the north bank seemed weakly defended there, it was selected as the crossing site. We set up our observation post on the roof of the power station, from which we had a clear view of the opposite bank, the defenders, and the full length of the railroad span. In the distance we could see the road bridge through the railroad bridge.

There was a delay getting the boats up, and they finally arrived about 1400 on 20 September. While they were being hastily assembled we fired a strong artillery bombardment on the German positions on the opposite bank. The crossing finally got underway at 1430 just after British fighter-bombers pounded the enemy and artillery smoke shells were fired into the landing area. About two dozen boats were available, each carrying about twenty men.

The current in the main river channel was very fast, and when the boats reached it many of the inexperienced crews lost control. Those boats became easy targets for the few defenders on the north riverbank, and some men were lost as six boats were destroyed in the first crossing. Most of their occupants swam safely to the south bank, however. The bulk of the remaining troopers reached the far shore and charged the defenders as soon as they touched ground. Soon all of the enemy were wiped out with the exception of a few who were captured. About half of the boats survived to cross again, taking a second wave that made the trip with little opposition. They captured the north end of the railroad bridge quickly. A battalion attacking from the south linked up with them not long after that. The unexpected river crossing and the speed with which the railroad bridge was taken completely surprised the Germans. It was such a glorious and fascinating panorama that we lost track of the fact that men on both sides were dying before our eyes. Once the two battalions joined, they were strong enough to make good progress against the north end of the road bridge.

A well-coordinated attack by the 505th and the British Guards Armoured Division had begun earlier in a drive through Nijmegen to reach the south end of the road bridge. This combined attack from north and south was too much for the German defenders, who broke and retreated to the north. The paratroopers on the north bank killed many Germans as they fled from the area. When German engineers attempted to blow the bridge, the demolition charges failed. The Dutch underground, airborne engineers, artillery fire, or the efforts of all had cut enough wires to prevent the charges from exploding. British tanks streamed across the bridge and a firm bridgehead was soon established. General Gavin was in a state of near panic as he sought to get relief to the British paratroopers in Arnhem, and everyone was furious when Field Marshal Bernard Law Montgomery ordered the British to halt and wait for their infantry to come up from Grave.

That night the last of the British and Polish paratroopers in and around Arnhem either surrendered or attempted to escape to the south side of the Neder Rijn. The overly ambitious Operation Market-Garden had ended in abject failure. Designed to shorten the war, because it had drawn all available reserves of men, ammunition, fuel, and supplies from our other offensive efforts, it actually prolonged the war by allowing the Germans to organize their Siegfried Line defenses. Montgomery had always fought ponderous, meticulously planned battles. Allowing him to command a lightning strike of the boldness of Market-Garden was just too much to expect. The lion's share of the blame for the operation's failure should probably go to General Eisenhower, who approved the plan.

Lieutenant Generals Brian Horrocks, the XXX Corps commander, and Frederick Browning, deputy commander of the First Allied Airborne Army, performed very well in spite of Field Marshal Montgomery's almost continuous distant micromanagement, which only tended to slow things down. We were proud to fight beside XXX Corps' British and Scots divisions, which were made up of excellent soldiers. Browning and Horrocks called our crossing of the Waal one of the most gallant operations of the war. The Guards Armoured Division commander said the 82d gave them better infantry support than they expected or were used to, and we in turn believed that their armor gave us unusually fine cooperation.

Although I may criticize chairborne generals from time to time, no one could criticize our airborne generals. Ten days after the event, General Gavin was found to have fractured two vertebrae. In spite of extreme discomfort and being unable to walk without help, he stayed with his troops and performed his command responsibilities. He went to every threatened point or wherever an attack was to be made. Gavin and his subordinate officers took the same hard training we all did and they never asked anyone to do something they were unwilling to do themselves.

The Germans believed that the intact Waal Bridge represented a serious threat to their overall defense, and on the twenty-first they began determined efforts to destroy it. The first of their jet airplanes was committed that day. These efforts were really rather comical. Their Messerschmitt Me-262s would swoop in at over five hundred miles per hour, too fast for them to drop their bombs accurately. Our antiaircraft guns, designed to engage planes capable of much less speed, were ineffective against them because they could not traverse quickly enough to hit the jets. A jet would go by followed by its engine noise and then by a series of smoke puffs from our antiaircraft shells following the jet like a string of black pearls.

At this time the great assault ended and we began a process of consolidating our positions, expanding them where reasonable, and holding on to what we had.

7

The 82d Airborne Fights as Infantry

After a week of intense action trying to make the overly ambitious Market-Garden assault successful, we were spontaneously transformed from an airborne assault division into a truck-borne infantry division by the stroke of some general's uncaring pen. During that week we had been under maximum stress and almost continuously in some kind of action, firing on enemies at all points of the compass. These efforts resulted in heavy casualties. German aircraft, mortars, and artillery fired on the battery several times every day, and our forward observation parties were also frequently attacked. During that week Battery A suffered nine casualties of all types out of about seventy-five men engaged.

The battery was involved in some heavy action while I was away from it. On 19 September, while scouting for a new position, Captain Alley and First Sergeant Hazlett were strafed by an Me-109 firing explosive 20mm cannon shells. They dove into a haystack and somehow escaped injury. In another incident that day, Lieutenant Osmussen and his observation party came under heavy mortar fire and two of his men were wounded. On the twentieth and twenty-first, enemy patrols almost entered the battery area and two German soldiers were captured.

While I was with Lieutenant Ross's forward observation team in the vicinity of Mook on the twenty-first, Lieutenant Osmussen and his team again received heavy mortar fire. Corporal Fitch H. Rowley was killed, and Osmussen and Pfc. George A. Black were seriously wounded. Several of the 505th troopers who were with them were also killed or wounded. Lieutenant Osmussen was a big, happy, and enthusiastic man who had played football for the University of Minnesota and had hopes of a career in professional football. His wound, which resulted in the loss of the use of one of his arms, ended that ambition. The wounded were evacuated, but Rowley's body had to be left behind by the retreating troopers. A year later, on the anniversary of Market-Garden, Captain Alley sent a party to the area with a sketch map showing where he thought the man was lost. The party found two skeletons in the area. They identified one of them as our comrade's by the dog tags around its neck. The other skeleton was that of the 505th trooper who was guarding the party. Both sets of remains were given a proper military burial.

On 21 October we expected that enemy planes would again be flying, looking for targets of opportunity: us. This had been going on for several days, with most of their activity occurring within the first three hours after dawn. That day proved to be different. When about ten Focke Wulf Fw-190s and Me-109s came at us from the east, over the Reichswald, about twenty P-51s and P-47s pounced on them. The enemy planes were flying at about a thousand feet, preparing to bomb and strafe our positions. The ensuing dogfight occurred at this low altitude, some of it directly overhead. It lasted only a few minutes, during which the sound of thirty airplane engines roaring at full throttle and the firing of more than a hundred .50-caliber machine guns and 20mm cannon was overwhelming. Four German planes and one American plane were shot down within our view. All of the pilots perished. The engagement ended when the remaining enemy aircraft fled over the German border with the American fighters on their tails.

We found ourselves captive in a defensive line for more than six weeks after we had successfully completed our part of the Holland airborne assault. Unfortunately for us, the Germans thought the presence of elite units in Holland, such as the U.S. airborne divisions and the British XXX Corps, indicated that another assault would soon take place in the area. This attracted some of the higher-quality enemy units to fight against us. Their presence caused us more casualties.

A learned sage of some war once said: "A soldier's war is the combination of very short periods of lively action with accompanying absolute terror, interspersed with much longer periods of absolute boredom." This quotation aptly describes my experience in Holland during those six weeks. I remember incidents and have visions of the scenes I saw during that period, but there is no continuity to them. I have used a combination of my memory and documents I recently obtained to produce a description of those events. When the two sources conflict, I have relied on my memory of them.

On 25 September our rear party of about sixty men arrived after their long and hard sea and land movement. We would now be able to move the guns with trucks rather than having to manhandle them from position to position. The battery had been firing about five hundred rounds per day, so we really needed the ammunition and supplies they brought.

In late September, the 505th, supported by our artillery battalion, was assigned to defend the eastern portion of the island we held between the Waal and the Neder Rijn. Part of the island was below the level of the rivers and was protected by dikes. Dairy farms dotted the flat, rich meadows on which many milk cows were grazing, ignorant of the war going on around them. Ground water just below the surface made digging in impossible. The Germans looked down on the meadows from their positions twenty feet above along the dike. Our only alternative was to occupy a series of strong defensive positions in farm complexes or in the many small copses of trees or rock piles that were scattered about. From the German standpoint, attacking across those flat, open meadows would have been suicidal. A stalemate therefore existed along that part of the front.

Our four-man observation team led by Lieutenant Bascomb shared a dairy farm with an infantry platoon. The farm consisted of a house, a barn, and other buildings, all surrounded by a stout stone wall. The Germans were positioned along the dike about three hundred yards to the east. From there they dominated our position. Because of the flat, open land between the opposing positions, a "live and let live" situation quickly developed. The Germans seldom wasted ammunition on one or two GIs out in the open, but they would fire on three or more. The only time it was safe to move outside the complex was at night. Only then could we receive ammunition and food or be relieved by other troops.

Since we were just east of the road bridge over the Waal, we almost daily saw Me-262 jets pulling out after attempting to bomb the bridge. The noise of the bombs, our massed antiaircraft guns, and the jet engines was deafening. In addition to committing much of their waning airpower, the Germans used bombs on floats and frogmen in their attempts to destroy the bridge. Nothing worked until 28 September, when they finally succeeded in heavily damaging it. Later that night the bridge was made completely unusable, but by then our engineers had built several pontoon bridges over the Waal, so the German success affected us little. On the night the road bridge was damaged, two of our observation parties—including the one I was part of—were trapped for a short time north of it. After receiving orders to return to the battery, we found a pontoon bridge and made our way back.

On clear days we could see streams of hundreds of American bombers flying east to bomb German cities. These planes were flying the same route we had used to fly to Groesbeek on 18 September. The Germans met the bomber streams at their border with massed antiaircraft fire and fighters, and we saw many bombers fall out of the sky.

One day, a twin-engine B-26 medium bomber was hit just to the east of our position. The pilot attempted to return the burning plane to friendly territory, but something made it unflyable as it passed overhead. Four men jumped from the plane. Two parachutes snagged on the plane and both men fell to their deaths. A third man landed safely about a hundred yards from our position, and the fourth man's parachute was damaged and partially collapsed. He made a hard landing nearby. We yelled to both of them to lay flat and wait for someone to come out for them. One of the airmen yelled back that his legs felt broken and that he was really hurting. Several infantrymen crawled out to guide the uninjured man back to the complex. He turned out to be the pilot, and he was very happy to reach the relative safety of our position.

We had one medic in the complex, and he had a stretcher. I organized a group of six volunteers to crawl out to bring back the injured man. There was a partially water-filled ditch near the man that also passed close to the complex. We crawled along the ditch to a point about twenty yards from where he lay, then slithered out to him on our bellies using our elbows and knees to propel us through the high grass. We could not tell the extent of his injuries, but a jagged end of broken bone protruded from one leg. Regardless of how seriously he was injured, we could not leave him where he was, nor could we wait for dark and a doctor to come out to treat him on the spot. The medic had brought some splints, which he placed on both legs since we wanted to protect him against further injury. We then bandaged him as best we could and gave him a morphine injection. Once we got him on the stretcher, it took all of our effort and about fifteen minutes to drag him the twenty yards to the ditch. By the time we reached the ditch we were all exhausted, and the injured aviator was in severe pain exacerbated by our unavoidably rough handling. Once we were in the ditch, it was easier to move and we made it back to our position in about ten minutes. Despite the morphine, he said his pain was almost unbearable. Although he was badly hurt, we believed he would survive. The problem was that he could not be evacuated until after dark, which meant waiting another eight hours. All we could do was give him more morphine and try to console him. After dark, the pilot and the injured airman were evacuated. We heard no more of the fate of either man.

We learned that the division was now part of the British Second Army and totally under British command. This wouldn't have been so bad except that by D-plus-10 our rations had run out. Now the British were responsible for feeding us. Although army chow was never of gourmet quality, it was far superior to British rations. There were four variations of American rations. A "ten-in-one" ration was a single carton of food containing one day's rations (three meals a day) for ten men. It consisted of cans of eggs, wieners, stew, hash, chocolate, and powders from which to make coffee, soup, and lemonade. Most of the time the cooks were issued the ten-in-ones and prepared our meals in field kitchens, but sometimes we received the cartons directly. C rations were designed to feed one man for three days. Each man prepared his own meals, and these consisted of stew, Spam, puddings, and the like. They were also bearable. One K ration fed one man for one day, and these were the worst. They came in a box containing canned eggs and deviled ham, crackers and cookies, cheese, a chocolate bar, and powdered coffee and lemonade. We usually ate them cold. K rations would keep a man alive for days, although no one could stand them for very long. The D ration was designed for sustenance only and consisted of a single large chocolate bar enriched with vitamins. On rare occasions the cooks were issued bulk raw ingredients such as meat, potatoes, flour, vegetables, and other staples. Unfortunately, many cooks were excellent at ruining good ingredients. Reflecting on army cooking after many years, soldiers looked on cooks as "the lowest of the low." Most of them received little training and they usually did not have much to work with. They were just kids like the rest of us and did the best they could under terrible circumstances. All these U.S. Army rations were well designed from a nutritional standpoint. No one would starve, and they supplied adequate energy for fighting.

British rations were designed to feed one man for fourteen days or fourteen men for one day, so they were known as fourteen-in-one rations. I have tried to forget the items included, but all were canned and among them were steak and kidney pie, mutton stew, scrambled eggs, kippered herring, plum pudding, and something called treacle pudding. Besides our unfamiliarity with these dishes, the main differences between British and American rations were the quality of the ingredients and the seasoning. Many British meat-based items had a rank taste and smell and seemed spoiled, whereas American rations seemed fresher and were of much higher quality. We ate British rations for six weeks, and this brought many American soldiers very close to mutiny. The British soldiers shared our feelings about their food and said they thought our rations were a real treat.

One advantage to being attached to the British army was the rum ration. Every British soldier received two ounces of Jamaican rum each day. As a part of the British forces we also were entitled to this ration. When the British delivered the rum directly to our unit we usually received it. However, since it is against regulations to give liquor to American soldiers on duty, most of the time our higher headquarters confiscated it.

Our observation team was in the rear area resting and eating British rations for a day before we went back to our complex. It had two attractions: cows we could milk and some healthy yearlings. We had not had fresh meat since leaving England, and one of the men in the compound had been a butcher in civilian life. After our return we spotted an attractive young heifer about a hundred yards away, close to the ditch we had used to rescue the airman. We could not just walk out and shoot the animal and drag it back because the Germans might shoot us. So, we worked out a plan. We had one thing going for us: the Germans were not likely to shoot at one or two soldiers.

Nevertheless, it was a stupid plan that could easily have drawn fire from the enemy dug in just three hundred yards away. Since I had a .45-caliber pistol, I was to crawl out and shoot the beast. Four other men would then join me and we would drag it back to the compound for the butcher. When I was about six feet from the bovine, it looked down at me and I fired at its head. It just shook its head like it was shaking away a fly! Only after I fired five more shots did it fall dead. I never had much faith in my pistol after that. I had hit exactly where I was aiming with each shot fired at short range. The animal probably weighed close to three hundred pounds, and the five us could not handle it without standing up. We wound up waiting for four more men to come out with ropes. We tied several lines to the animal and then dragged it in. The meat was a little tough but the steaks were better than anything we had had in a year.

Two weeks later we were moved south away from our pleasant farmhouse to the woods near Mook. Thick woods are a terrible place in which to fight. Although trees may offer some protection from small-arms fire, shells that burst high up in them scatter a shower of deadly wood fragments and steel splinters on soldiers on the ground below. The best protection is a deep foxhole with sturdy overhead cover. Sometimes the trees mute the effect of shellfire compared to a shell exploding on the ground. Sometimes tree bursts are far more deadly than ground bursts. An attacking enemy may come upon a

[handwritten in left margin: Dutch cow is butchered.]

soldier more suddenly in woods than in the open, so personal security is harder to maintain in woods.

Soon we found that the Germans opposite the 505th were from the 1st SS Parachute Division, one of the most elite units in the entire German army, although it was technically a Luftwaffe division. Fighting between the two opposing parachute divisions soon became vicious in spite of the fact that no major offensive operations were ordered by the commanders on either side. Bloody fighting for a few useless acres that brought negligible advantage took place every day.

At the 505th's headquarters I observed a tragic example of just how senseless this fighting could be. An SS parachute major had been knocked out and slightly wounded by a shell burst. He was brought to headquarters for interrogation but he refused to answer any questions. One of our doctors was in the area examining men who had been slightly wounded but were still fit for duty. He was asked to examine and treat the German major's wounds. The doctor pulled up the German's tunic so he could bandage a graze and several superficial puncture wounds on the man's side. As the doctor was treating him, the major pulled a knife from his sleeve and killed the doctor. Four nearby troopers emptied their guns into the German, killing him instantly. We surmised that this Nazi fanatic could not accept defeat, surrender, or captivity. We figured he resented the fact that he had been rendered unconscious, allowing him to be captured—a fate worse to him than death. He knew his action would result in his death but he both wanted to die and to take with him the most valuable American he could find. Apparently in his mind, killing a doctor would cause many other troopers to die from lack of care. This was a clear illustration of how devoted and fanatical these SS soldiers were to Hitler and their Nazi cause. They would never give up until they were dead, wounded, or hopelessly defeated. This and similar incidents made the fighting between the 82d and the SS paratroopers a no-holds-barred, to-the-death struggle. Shooting helpless prisoners was against the rules of war and most soldiers considered it reprehensible. Nevertheless, after the doctor died, both sides began to kill prisoners without mercy. After two weeks of this pointless killing, both sides informally stopped it.

During the period 1–7 October the Germans launched numerous counterattacks. It was a continuous series of actions during which the enemy gained a few yards of the territory we held. We would then regain it and capture some of theirs. All of this time we directed fire against any enemy forces we could see. Groesbeek was bombed daily, and our positions were shelled each day. The 456th PFAB was close enough to the line to be probed by enemy infiltrators. We killed three and captured three during this period and drove many more away before they reached our outer perimeter.

The best estimate I can make of the timing of the strange, dangerous but adventurous incident I am about to describe is that it happened on the night of 12 October, plus or minus a day. This estimate is based on my memory of a complex series of events and a recent reading of Captain Alley's combat log.

We held a small portion of the woods east of Mook, the Dutch extension of the Reichswald, which is a German state forest. Across the border, which was not well defined on the ground, was a series of forts that made up part of the northern end of the Siegfried Line. Patrols the infantry sent out discovered that German soldiers spent most of their time holed up in the relative safety of their houselike bunkers, leaving the spaces between them lightly occupied. The patrols also found that high ground on the eastern end of the woods overlooked the German rear areas, including their major supply and ammunition depots.

Since one patrol of three infantrymen had made it to this high ground and back safely, someone got the bright idea of sending a stronger force there escorting an artillery observation team. Our team was in the CP of one of the 505th's battalions, so we were given the duty. I saw Lieutenant Bascomb, our team leader, in animated conversation with the battalion commander that afternoon, and it seems likely we were given this assignment without our battery commander knowing all the details.

That night, a platoon of infantry led us to our destination—an old, broken down, vacant, stone building overlooking the target area. It was almost three miles from our starting point, well beyond enemy lines, the Siegfreid Line defenses, and onto German soil. We were not trained for patrolling, but we were with experts. They told us to move slowly and silently. We left at about 0200 and reached our destination at about 0330. The patrol left us there alone. Even before the sun came up, we recognized that our position was relatively secure as long as we did not give ourselves away inadvertently. We thus had to be very careful about any movements we made. We were very quiet and cupped our hands around the ends of our binoculars so that no sunlight would reflect from them.

We had good maps of the target area and after studying it for over an hour we were able to plot several likely targets on the map. When we had completed this process, we radioed the locations to the battalion fire control center. Using the radio was risky because the Germans were experts at locating radio transmitters. It was too dangerous to fire single rounds to correct the aim of the guns because some German officer would almost certainly conclude they were being directed by observers and send out patrols to look for us. If fire suddenly fell on their positions, we hoped the enemy would conclude it was being directed against map coordinates based on information from Dutch spies or from one of the several spotter planes we had in the area.

A British battalion of twelve heavy 155mm howitzers had been brought up to add to the weight of fire. They and two of 82d's battalions, thirty-six artillery pieces in all, fired a "time-on-target" mission—meaning that all thirty-six shells fired would explode without warning in a grid on or over the target at the same instant—on our first target, a suspected ammunition dump. They included a mix of airbursts that spread shell fragments over the area and some high-explosive shells that detonated on contact. We observed several large secondary explosions indicating that we had indeed hit an ammunition dump.

Based on where the first shells actually fell compared to where they were directed by map coordinates, we made a slight correction which made later fire against other map coordinates even more accurate. An hour later we called for fire on a busy major road crossing with an apparent motor pool adjacent to it. An hour after that we hit a third target that looked like some kind of headquarters. The battalion commander said we had done enough and should not endanger ourselves anymore. We were ordered to study the area until dark and mark the map with more targets so they could be fired on during the night or the next day after we pulled out.

Although we were all fearful, the stress of the situation was really beginning to affect Lieutenant Bascomb. He was unable to sleep, had the shakes, and was having trouble making decisions. Our mission behind enemy lines was unusual for all of us and had a much higher element of risk than anything we had ever faced.

The rest of the team had been in jeopardy before in Normandy, but the three weeks in Holland were Bascomb's first action, and that action had been fierce with no rest. Things were turning out to be far different from anything he had expected based on his previous training or experience, or even compared to the tales he had heard from Normandy veterans. We were all scared, but he was beyond scared, close to being paralyzed. We had all been close to paralyzing fear before, so we were sympathetic and tried to help him out as best we could.

The infantry platoon was due to pick us up about 0300 because it was the time most soldiers, including the Germans, were least alert. When the platoon was a half-hour late, we really began to worry and think about what we would do without their help. We did not think we could spend another day where we were without being caught. We were not trained or competent to get back to our lines through the German positions without expert help but we decided we would try if the infantry did not show up by 0400. They arrived in the nick of time, almost an hour late. They had sighted a German patrol but said they did not think they had been seen. As we headed back to our lines we were slowed when we ran into a small enemy patrol and got into a firefight. The sky turned gray with predawn light and we spotted a stronger German force chasing us. Another firefight ensued, and Lieutenant Bascomb, who was becoming more and more frantic as time passed, dove into a foxhole filled with dead soldiers who had been killed in fighting there two weeks earlier. Why anyone would choose to dive into a hole occupied by putrid, two-week-old corpses was beyond us, but this was a measure of his desperation. We could not persuade him to come out. There was just no time to talk or for persuasion or discussion, so our training kicked in. We had only a few seconds to move on or we would be left behind. Our radio operator, Cpl. Jim Hancock, and I jumped into the hole and dragged the lieutenant out. When he did not instantly move out with us on his own I hit him in the jaw with the butt of my M1 rifle and knocked him out cold. I gave my rifle and pack to Jim and slung Bascomb over my shoulders in a fireman's carry. I ran several hundred yards to safety. When he regained consciousness and I finally recovered my breath, we found ourselves in a mutually embarrassing situation: I had struck an officer, and he had shown what might have been considered to be cowardice in action. Both were court-martial offenses, but he appreciated what I had done. In the end we all agreed to forget about the incident.

Thinking back to our feelings about Lieutenant Bascomb, we really did not think of him as a coward. All of us were dealing with a very high level of fear. Although the rest of us were still able to fight our fear and continue to function, he had reached the point where that last bit of stress had pushed him over the edge to mental paralysis. Everyone has a different threshold at which this happens, and all of us came very close to it at one time or another, particularly on that night. No one is immune to fear. We knew from experience that a man could become limp and numb with fear and then suddenly recover from it, so we hoped that with reflection and more experience he would overcome his problem. In the meantime, we could not depend on him in his present condition because he might endanger our lives. Until he conquered his fear, we were all prepared for me to take the leadership role. We realized this was exactly what I had been doing for the past several days, and this incident simply brought it to our attention.

Two days later, First Sergeant Hazlett called me in to talk about the incident. He told me that an infantry officer had seen most of the events and reported the incident. He asked me to tell him what had happened. I told him everything that had occurred, emphasizing the fact that none of us had been trained for night patrols and that we should never have been sent on such a mission in the first place. He asked me why I had not filed a complaint against Lieutenant Bascomb. I told him we had been behind enemy lines and had to handle matters as best we could. We had performed our assignment well whether he was in the lead or not. I also told him we hoped things would iron themselves out when we returned, and I feared making a court-martial case out of it since the outcome of such a case was so unpredictable. He said I had done okay but that I should have "turned in the bastard."

Nothing further came of the incident. In a recent reading of Captain Alley's log I learned the following details, which partially explain why. On the night of my conversation with Hazlett, 14 October I think, about twenty-five 170mm rounds landed in the battery area, wounding four men and damaging most of our vehicles. Hazlett spent the next several days concentrating on restoring the command to order. The next two days were quiet, and we received our first mail since leaving England.

On the night of the sixteenth, things really blew up. Lieutenant Ross had just come in from a forward observation position for a rest and was sharing Captain Alley's dugout. At 0140, shells began to fall throughout the battery area, and four large rockets, "screaming meemies," hit just outside their dugout. After checking himself out and finding he was slightly wounded, Captain Alley found that Ross had been severely wounded. Unable to find his flashlight, he gave Ross a morphine Syrette, which he administered to himself. Alley called for a medic and went to see if Hazlett, who was in a foxhole nearby, was okay. The first sergeant was also seriously wounded, and both Ross and Hazlett were evacuated in the same ambulance. Ross died in the hospital ten days later, and Hazlett lost his left leg above the knee. One of the finest regular army soldiers I ever met, Hazlett was allowed to complete his thirty years of service with the aid of a prosthesis.

With all this confusion, it is not surprising that nothing further happened with regard to Lieutenant Bascomb or me. We later served together on several observation missions but we both thought it best to forget about the night of 12 October.

Living in the field with an army in combat has probably not changed very much since Roman times. After living in houses, apartments, and dormitories with mother's well-cooked food, baths, real toilets, and comfortable beds, the difference for most of us was like

1st Sgt. Hazlett looses a leg.

going from home to prison, or perhaps going back to the Dark Ages. We lived underground most of the time, and when we came out for any purpose we were always alert for the sound of an incoming shell, careful always to keep track of the location of a nearby hole into which to dive.

The closest thing to a foxhole is a grave. The purpose of a foxhole was to protect its occupant from shell fragments if artillery or mortar shells fell nearby. No hole was effective against a direct hit. We dug ours about seven feet long, two feet wide, and four to six feet deep. If we had the time, we added a foot-deep sump at one end of the hole in which water could collect to keep the sleeping area dry. We also placed logs crosswise over the hole, when time permitted and they were available, to protect against tree bursts. Living in a hole like a rabbit, no matter how well it was improved, was damp, confining, and extremely claustrophobic.

Sanitary matters were another consideration in the field. We took very infrequent sponge baths using water warmed in our steel helmets. I had two basic conditions under which I lived while in combat: usually I was part of a four-man group, but the rest of the time I was part of a larger group of close to a hundred men. When I was with a large group there was nothing grosser than squatting over a slit-trench latrine with my pants down doing my morning duty alongside a dozen other men. Since I was shy about my personal habits, I much preferred the privacy that came with being in a small group.

Four of us who had been buddies since before Normandy often dug our foxholes close together near our battery headquarters. We cooked our British rations together and washed clothes for one another when one or more of us went out on other duty.

The same night Lieutenant Ross and First Sergeant Hazlett were wounded I was out on an all-night observation mission. Early the next morning I returned and saw a lot of activity as I approached the vicinity of the battery's outer line of guard posts. When I realized what had happened, I was sick to my stomach. One of the shells we had heard during the night had struck a tree, spraying one of the outpost dugouts with fragments, killing two of my friends, Cpl. Manuel R. "Manny" Grasso and Pvt. Gillis R. "Gil" Harris. What I walked into was the graves registration people bagging and removing their bodies. After seeing that, sleep was impossible. It was only by chance that I had escaped the same fate.

When I reached my hole near First Sergeant Hazlett's, I learned about him and Ross and discovered that the same rocket that wounded them had shredded all the equipment I had left there. I was also affected by the fact that the number of my close friends who had been killed or wounded had risen to twelve. That number did not include the many other men in the battery with whom I was less well acquainted who became casualties. My subconscious was telling me that being my friend might have been the cause of their deaths or maiming, and this feeling became the basis of a self-consuming guilt trip. Such thoughts are nonsense but, as was the case with many soldiers, my subliminal emotional mind did not respond to rational thought. Many of those still alive had a similar guilt response to the deaths or serious wounding of their friends. The deaths of my two close friends, Gil and Manny, along with the maiming of Hazlett and Ross, would continue to have a powerful effect on me long after the war ended.

Although I did not experience it, another common reaction to the death of a buddy was to act as if he had never been there at all. Although some criticized this reaction, it was merely a way of coping with an unbelievable event. It must be remembered that only a few months earlier, these men had been carefree kids, threatened by nothing and with all the comforts of home.

Before we left Holland, one of our men was involved in a strange incident. Most of us had noticed that he had secreted an old leather briefcase in his hole. Someone reported this to an officer, and the briefcase was found to contain several hundred thousand deutsche marks. He said he found the briefcase in a building the Germans had previously occupied as a headquarters. Plans were made to court-martial the man but the charges were dropped when it was discovered the money was worthless.

Holland, a pleasant land of windmills, wooden shoes, and dikes, had not been kind to Battery A. A total of 170 of us parachuted in, landed by glider, or came by ship and truck. When we left, Battery

A had six commissioned officers, forty-five noncommissioned officers, three medics, and eighty privates. In the fifty-four days we were there 15 percent of our men became casualties, including four who were killed or died of wounds.

On 11 November the division was finally ordered back to France to refit and prepare for the next operation. It was about time for all of us. If we had stayed much longer, many men would have become candidates for a funny farm.

15 % casualties in Btry A

8

On to France for Rest and Refitting

A Canadian division had been fighting hard for three months to clear German defenders from around the Schelde estuary in order to open the port of Antwerp so it could begin supplying the Allied armies in the north. Once these actions were completed, the Canadian division replaced the 82d Airborne in the line east of Mook. At about 1800 on 11 November 1944 we fired all our guns in a traditional salute to fallen comrades and moved out through our old drop zone between Mook and Groesbeek to an assembly area at Hesch, Holland. It took a day to organize the division's move. On the thirteenth we were loaded into vehicles for the trip to France. I rode in a chilly open jeep.

We left Hesch at about 0600 and headed south on the same road the British XXX Corps had used to come to our relief in September. The burned hulks of vehicles that had been pushed out of the way still lined the road. Many other signs of the fighting the British XXX Corps and the 101st Airborne had done to secure the corridor were still apparent. We passed through the city of Eindhoven, which had been bombed and shelled during the fighting, and then crossed the bridges the British had built over the Meuse-Escaut Canal just south of the border between Holland and Belgium. After crossing the canal we moved into territory that had seen little fighting and continued south to Leopoldsburg, where we were billeted for the night in tents at a British camp. We left on the last leg of our trip at 0600 on the fourteenth and arrived at Camp Suippes, near Épernay, at 1000. This was a very large French army camp and barracks complex near the medieval city of Reims. There we were housed in old but well-built

84

French army barracks situated in the midst of the battlefields of World War I. Three other sergeants and I shared a comfortable, well-heated room. After two months of living in cramped, damp foxholes in the cold of the oncoming winter, with slit-trench latrines, no baths, and frequent death, this was a wonderful billet.

The 82d and 101st Airborne Divisions again had been assigned to SHAEF headquarters to serve as the main theater reserve. Both divisions were to be given time to refit, rest, and integrate replacements for the many casualties they had suffered during the heavy fighting in Holland in preparation for responding to any unforeseen event.

I had no important responsibilities involving subordinates while not in action, so I was part of battery headquarters in barracks situations. Because I spoke some French, I was assigned the mission of coordinating with the locals to provide wholesome entertainment that would help get men's minds off the war, at least for a few hours. Everyone had a need to blow off steam after the tension and stress of two months in action in Holland. Many men stood in line for hours at whorehouses. Others drank themselves into a comfortable oblivion, where they remained for hours and sometime days. Such actions were reasonable responses to the need to cope with the horrors of war.

As if we did not need more pressure and stress, a week after we arrived in Camp Suippes four or five weeks of our mail caught up with us. We all were still thanking our lucky stars for being alive when many men received bad news from home in the form of the dreaded "Dear John" letter. By then, most of us had been overseas for close to a year, and even longer in the case of some of the old-timers who had been with the outfit since North Africa and Sicily. This elapsed time allowed many sweethearts and wives to find other interests and other men. Although one or two of these letters arrived with every mail delivery, a much larger number seemed to arrive that day at Camp Suippes. The news that a wife or sweetheart had decided to join another man was devastating. Many men wondered what they had done wrong. In fact, the only thing they had done was to be drafted or enlist to serve their country in war. Many victims believed this was the end of their lives. I hope they all recovered and found more loyal spouses later. However, I am sure some just gave up and took the next opportunity to die.

I had dated a girl named Sylvia in Wyoming, Ohio, six or eight times during my senior year of high school and my freshman year at Purdue. Although we had no serious arrangement, we corresponded throughout my service. As the war went on, she became "the girl back home" to whom I wished to return. After the war I learned that Sylvia had corresponded with four other servicemen on the same basis as she had with me. Although I was devastated at the time, I now appreciate that this was her contribution to the war effort. While nothing serious ever came of our relationship, I have always been grateful that Sylvia never wrote a "Dear John" letter to me.

On our second weekend in Épernay the whole division was restricted to post because there had been too much hell raising in the nearby French towns the previous weekend. A fair number of troopers had been arrested and were in the guardhouse, charged with various offenses ranging from rape to public drunkenness. That was when I was assigned to find a French entertainment troupe of some kind to give us a high-quality Saturday night show. I talked to a special services officer in SHAEF's forward headquarters who suggested I contact a good troupe he knew about near Saint-Denis, a nearby northern suburb of Paris that had been liberated four months before. I collected some money from funds contributed by the troops for such purposes, as well as some other valuables like coffee and cigarettes. I obtained orders authorizing a driver and me to go to Saint-Denis and suburban Paris, but we were not allowed to go into the city center. Thus prepared, we set out in a six-by-six truck early on a Thursday morning.

My French was improving but it was still poor. Luckily, we found the troupe where the officer told us it would be. The troupe consisted of a magician (the leader) and a female helper, two jugglers, two mimes, and two statuesque dancers. We did not know what statuesque dancers were, and my French was not good enough to determine exactly what they did. Finally, I asked the magician if they were strippers.

"*Oh, la, la, Strippeurs? Non! Non!*" he replied emphatically.

Although this made it clear to me what they were not, I still had no idea what their part of the act involved. However, the troupe sounded good since language was not an essential part of the show. I negotiated a price for a Saturday show, the equivalent of $100 in invasion money, eight cartons of American cigarettes, and ten pounds of coffee. I later discovered I had paid too much since the cigarettes and coffee had a very high value on the French black market.

I also had to promise, on my honor, to provide them with good living quarters for two nights and provide an armed guard on the ladies' quarters to keep them from being raped by American soldiers. This latter requirement indicated how much many French women feared soldiers in general. Although we were their friends and the Germans had been there as enemies, the French saw both groups as simply large armies occupying their country.

The troupe invited us to stay as their houseguests for the night, and on Friday morning we put them in the back of the truck with their equipment and drove back to Épernay. When I told our new first sergeant, Evan W. Prosser, about my promise, he thought I was crazy. Still, he arranged for the quarters and the armed guard. Several of us spent all day Saturday helping the magician set up the stage. Since he also acted as master of ceremonies and knew only about twenty words of English, he insisted that I translate for him during the show. Because of the inadequacy of my high school French, we practiced this together for three hours.

I had the idea that if I could find another unit interested in the show, they might cover the costs, and we would get our show for nothing or even make a profit. In the afternoon, I visited the special services NCOs of two of our infantry regiments, told them about the show I had arranged, and invited them to send a few representatives to see it.

The show went well. The statuesque dancers turned out to be two very well built young ladies who appeared completely nude. They struck numerous still poses and moved only when the lights were turned off. We judged every part of the show to be great, but the statuesque dancers were a real hit. The guard detail on their rooms had to be doubled that night. I succeeded in arranging two more shows for the troupe on Sunday with the two infantry regiments. I negotiated their fee for each show at one-and-a-half times what we had paid, and each regiment gave us ten pounds of coffee. The coffee and a small commission went into our treasury for future recreation costs. One regiment also agreed to take them back to Saint-Denis. All in all, the whole effort proved to be a great success.

The next week, I arranged to have three chefs from Reims come to our kitchen on Saturday and cook a great French meal. The U.S. Army supplied most of the raw materials, and it was amazing to see what really good cooks could do with the same stuff our cooks ruined every day. Although this exercise was a success, it was not as well received as the stage troupe had been. Additionally, our cooks hated me for some time afterward because they were convinced I had brought in the French chefs for the sole purpose of showing them up. I guess I did.

After three weeks, we were all rested. Barracks life had become boring because we had nothing useful to do besides training and physical conditioning. We spent a lot of time marching and practicing various maneuvers in the old World War I battle area. Although no one wanted to go back into combat, most of us were developing a fatalistic attitude about war since we all knew we would be returning to the fight sooner or later. Some men in the outfit had fought in Africa, Sicily, Salerno, Anzio, Normandy, and Holland, and many felt they had used up all of their good luck. They saw more combat as an unreasonable demand upon them.

There are three times most soldiers worry about combat. The first is well in advance of a fearsome event in which they might personally become involved. The second is while they are in action. Finally, after an action is over, they brood over how bad it was and what terrible things might have happened to them. Those who took this three-worry attitude were more likely to go crazy than those who tried to live solely in the present and limited their emotional expenditure to concentrating on their individual part at the time of the action. This is not to say that careful preparation is not needed. In fact, such preparation helped reduce later worrying. The old saying "Don't cry over spilled milk" says a lot about the futility of worrying about something that is over. It was not easy to develop a one-worry attitude, but those who were able to do so reacted better to unexpected threats and were better able to maintain their sanity.

On the fourth weekend the whole division was again confined to post because there had been a lot more hell raising the previous weekend. On 15 December First Sergeant Prosser suggested that, since we were in the midst of the French champagne country, we hold a controlled champagne party that Saturday night. I was assigned to go into Reims with a truck and driver to buy some champagne. The third winery we visited was that of Veuve Cliquot. There I negotiated the purchase of fifty cases of champagne for a dollar a bottle plus fifty pounds of coffee. The six hundred bottles amounted to about one-and-a-half bottles for each soldier (including all officers and enlisted men) in the battalion who were present and not on leave. This was a bit more than the first sergeant had bargained for. Moreover, since some of our men were nondrinkers, each drinking man would have two bottles or more.

The day I bought the champagne, the first signs of a German offensive became apparent to some of our high-ranking officers but not to us. No one apparently thought it was too serious a threat because the high command intelligence officers thought the Germans had already been beaten. That night, 16 December, many heard a faraway rumbling noise that sounded like distant, heavy thunder. After darkness, some thought they saw lightning in the distant sky to the northeast. Everyone knew that lightning was unlikely in December, and no one wanted to consider the other alternatives.

That same night I made the serious mistake of keeping two full cases of champagne for the sergeants' rooms. We invited the first sergeant and two platoon sergeants to join the four of us for a private party. They did, and by midnight the seven of us had finished all twenty-four bottles. Somehow we managed to make our way back to our bunks, where we each passed out.

In the 1970s the Ultra secret was disclosed to the public. Ultra was the Allied code name for intelligence obtained from encrypted German radio transmissions. Although we did not know it at the time, Ultra had greatly influenced the 82d's actions in Europe up to December 1944, and after that it was to influence our lives in a negative manner. How Ultra came about is a fascinating story. In 1939 the British had developed a very primitive computer. That same year, Polish spies stole a German Enigma encrypting device in such a way that

Prelude to Bulge

the Germans never became aware they had lost it. After a great deal of clever and hard work, the British were able to use these two devices to read almost all orders issued to and by major German commands on a timely basis. This was close to being able to read all the enemy's mail. When the United States entered the war, the British made this information available to the Americans and allowed them to participate in the work supporting the effort.

Allied intelligence officers were faced with two main problems regarding their use of Ultra. First, they were concerned that the Germans might pass along misinformation at some critical time in order to lure Allied forces into a trap. Second, if the Allies used Ultra too consistently and always made exactly the proper response to every German move, the Germans might figure out that the Allies had the ability to read their most secret correspondence and cause them to stop using the Enigma device. It was a fine line, and the Allies adhered to it well. Some lives were lost as a result, but Ultra remained the best kept secret of the war and many more were saved because of it.

Another problem with Ultra was that many important Allied commanders, particularly Americans, did not trust it. Some high commanders were able to overcome most of their skepticism, but apparently no one ever completely trusted the Enigma information.

Even though these considerations were valid concerns, American intelligence staffs generally passed along weak information in general from sources other than Ultra. That high-level American intelligence officers had Ultra available to them and still performed so poorly shows just how pitiful their skill level was in World War II.

In December 1944 the Germans suddenly ceased using their Enigma encrypting devices all along the western front. Apparently, just as American intelligence staffs had become accustomed to using Ultra and began to depend on it, the source completely disappeared. This left the Allies with aerial reconnaissance as their only reliable source of intelligence information. The interrogation of captured enemy soldiers was another source, although this was not considered fully reliable since both sides planted false information by allowing loyal soldiers to be captured so that they could feed misleading information to the enemy. Moreover, with little fighting going on, few prisoners were being taken.

The weather in Belgium was too bad for aerial reconnaissance, and the Germans were able to concentrate two panzer armies and other supporting infantry forces along a narrow front in the German forests extending from the Ardennes without the Allies recognizing that any threat existed. The flashes we had seen and the sounds heard on 16 December were the opening assault by this twenty-six division German force. To make matters worse, SHAEF was certain that the Germans did not have the men, equipment, and supplies to even attempt such a large offensive venture this late in the war. It was many costly hours after the German offensive began before the high command woke up to reality.

That was the sorry situation in which the only divisions in SHAEF reserve, the 82d and 101st Airborne, found themselves in that terrible winter of 1944.

9

Into the Bulge

When it came at last, morning seemed most unusual to me. In a personal fog, I barely recognized three things. My bunk had become hard and rough. I had a terrible headache, was fully dressed, had a pack strapped on my back, and was wearing a steel helmet. Realizing I was in the back of a moving weapons carrier, I struggled onto one of the benches on the side of the back compartment.

My friend Cpl. Jim Hancock explained the situation to me, as he understood it: German armor had broken through our lines in Belgium on 16 December and had begun making a deep penetration. The action toward which we were rushing later became known as the Battle of the Bulge. Shortly after midnight on the seventeenth the 82d was alerted for the move to Belgium to shore up the defenses, and it began the move at about 0700 on the eighteenth. Later, we learned that as acting XXXVIII Airborne Corps commander, General Gavin had decided that the 82d was in an adequate state of preparedness to move out within six hours of the original alert. That was a day earlier than his SHAEF orders required. Jim Hancock told me that the other five drunken sergeants and I had been dressed and thrown with our equipment into the back of the truck we were now riding in.

When I told him there had been seven of us at the party, including the first sergeant, Jim said First Sergeant Prosser had seemed normal and that he had helped manage the battery's efforts to prepare for the move. His help proved to be critical because two of our officers were on leave in England. I was amazed. Prosser had either drunk less than the rest of us, had a hollow leg, or had the willpower to overcome his condition and act normally, fully performing his duties. I knew he was a tough man with great determination, so I figured the latter was the most likely alternative.

The 456th received orders at 0100 on the eighteenth to be ready to move within eight hours. Shortages of ammunition and other necessities had to be made up and preparation for the move began at 0130. Jim also told me that at the time we received the orders to move the division had only about 20 percent of the trucks and vehicles needed to make such a move quickly. Sending a group of noncoms from each battalion in the division to pick up the needed trucks from the huge SHAEF motor pool nearby solved this problem. Because they lacked written orders authorizing them to pick up the trucks, the few officers present at the motor pool during the early morning hours ignored their requests. However, since the 82d men were all armed, they simply arrested the motor pool officers, their men, and the military police guarding the motor pool. They were not about to let a few rear-echelon troops, particularly military policemen, stop them from following their orders to "go and fight the Germans." I'm sure they must have had fun arresting and detaining the military policemen since the shoe was usually on the other foot. The 82d men commandeered some five hundred trucks and kidnapped about three hundred drivers. They also took extra cans of gas for each truck and several truckloads of gas in cans since there might be none available along our planned route. The 101st Division's noncoms arrived just after ours left and took another five hundred trucks. Because they arrived second, the 101st had to use cattle-hauling trucks. This operation may sound unorthodox, but getting all the required paperwork together would have taken a day or more—and we still would have been given the same trucks. The noncoms just eliminated a lot of unnecessary army paperwork, allowing the division to move a day early. It's a good thing we did. If the Germans had been allowed another day to drive west before we arrived, breaking their offensive would have been much more difficult. As it was, we barely made it to our positions on the northern shoulder of the bulge.

We later learned that our mission had been to move to and occupy Bastogne. However, our orders were changed en route. The 82d wound up going to the north side of the German penetration, where it was thought the greatest crisis existed. Our destination was the vicinity of Spa, Belgium, where the U.S. First Army headquarters was located. The same orders directed the 101st to follow us but to stop at Bastogne to defend that important road intersection. As we headed north we passed a number of disorganized units and groups of trucks streaming south to get away from marauding German panzers. A battalion of antiaircraft guns that had been moving south was stalled alongside the road. Its vehicles had run out of gas. The men in that battalion told us they had been driven out of their position by German tanks and that the Germans were already more than fifty miles to the west of us. Some of the antiaircraft artillerymen said their battalion had been ordered back to help defend Paris. This was typical of the panic and wild rumors that were flying everywhere around us. However, being combat veterans, we believed little we heard from the rumor mills. All of the fleeing troops we encountered told us the Germans would surely kill us if we kept heading toward them.

Whether the following was really true or not, and I think it was, we were later told that German spearheads were moving westward through Houffalize at the same time American convoys were moving north through the same intersection there. American and German military policemen reportedly directed traffic through this intersection at the same time for several hours. This was logically possible because neither army's military policemen were qualified to fight enemy troops since they were lightly armed and untrained for such fighting. One need only think of the position of a military policeman, directing traffic at an intersection, if he decided to challenge a column of tanks. Moreover, the German panzer spearheads were under orders to move west as fast as they could. It is likely their commanders would have preferred to keep moving rather than halt and engage in small, unnecessary fights that would prevent them from reaching their objectives in accordance with their tight schedule.

Regardless of the truth of whether both American and German military policemen directed traffic at the Houffalize road junction, this intersection posed a major threat to us. The whole division was riding north in thin-skinned trucks and other vehicles, and large German panzer formations had already passed through the same intersection moving westward. A collision between our column and German panzers would have led to a one-sided and hopeless battle for us, and much of the division would have become dead meat. The 456th PFAB was particularly exposed in this situation. We were three hours behind the head of the 505th RCT's column, bringing up its rear. Battery C, the last unit in a trailing serial, was fired on by German guns at the Houffalize intersection. They were not stopped and suffered no casualties. It was only through the greatest of good luck that the entire 82d Airborne Division passed the intersection without any serious interference.

Spa is about 130 miles north of Reims on a straight line. After 157 miles of travel by road, the vanguard of the division reached the small town of Werbomont, about fifteen miles southwest of Spa, at 1930 on the eighteenth. An advance party had set up the division headquarters there earlier that day. The two opposing armies were intermixed over hundreds of square miles, so a clear description of the battlefield situation was not possible. Still, several fragments of information were known. To say that confusion and chaos ruled everything would be a great understatement. A powerful German panzer spearhead was known to be north of us between Werbomont and Spa, and a large American force of mixed armor and infantry from various defeated divisions was partially surrounded at Saint-Vith, about twenty miles to the southeast. Another even more powerful German panzer force had passed through Houffalize and cut off our communications to the south.

As we arrived on the eighteenth—and for several days thereafter— we saw or heard buzz bombs flying westward every five minutes or so. Several were seen to cut off to our north in the vicinity of where we thought Liège was located. These flying bombs made a really disturbing racket.

The division had been ordered to help neutralize the panzer force to the north and rescue the Americans in Saint-Vith, as well as to set up a defensive line to prevent any German movement toward Liège, one of the larger cities in Belgium, on the Meuse River. Although we all knew it would not be a picnic, we were glad to be out of the thin-skinned trucks.

The 505th had been ordered to march eastward about ten miles over the high ground to the Salm River and set up a defensive line along it. The Salm flows north and joins the Amblève River a mile north of the small hamlet of Trois Ponts. The 456th arrived at Werbomont a few hours later than the 505th and was ordered to move east and find a suitable position from which to give supporting artillery fire from about two miles west of the Salm.

Our observation team, led by 1st Lt. William Cameron, was ordered to proceed east to find a suitable observation post above the town of Trois Ponts. Lieutenant Cameron had been on detached service but rejoined the battery as a replacement for Lieutenant Ross. I was assigned to be his reconnaissance sergeant. There was a shortage of good maps, so Lieutenant Cameron and I were told to inspect the situation maps at division headquarters, make our own sketch map, and work out a route to our destination. The situation maps indicated that elements of the German 1st SS Panzer Division were probably in a valley near the small town of La Gleize on the far side of the Amblève River to our north. Strong German panzer and infantry units had recently passed westward through Houffalize to our south. It was thought the route to the south would be cut the next day—if it had not been already. The map depicted other panzer units east of the Salm River moving westward, but they had not yet crossed. Indications were that they were bypassing a substantial pocket of American forces at Saint-Vith. The 82d was ordered to defend a linc along the Amblève to the north and the Salm to the east. From what we saw, the division needed to keep the German panzers from crossing these two rivers in force or we would be in big trouble ourselves if the Germans continued their drive to the west unchecked.

Our further examination of the division situation map showed that our position had great similarities to the one we had held in Holland at the beginning of Market-Garden. Powerful panzer units had been identified to our north, south, and east, and there were no sizable, effective friendly units in place to help us if the Germans worked their way around to attack us from the west. Our position was as close to being surrounded as it could be. Yet in the face of all this chaos and confusion, rather than being fearful, the division's confidence was high. Everyone at headquarters thought the Germans in our vicinity were in far greater trouble than we were.

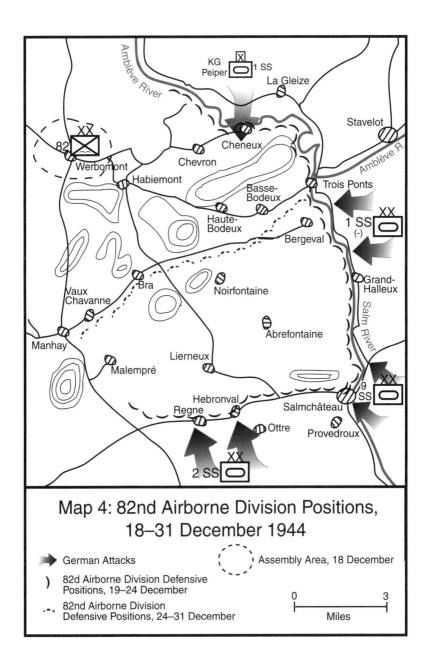

Map 4: 82nd Airborne Division Positions, 18–31 December 1944

German Attacks

Assembly Area, 18 December

82d Airborne Division Defensive Positions, 19–24 December

82nd Airborne Division Defensive Positions, 24–31 December

0   3

Miles

The maps showed the Ardennes region to be rough country full of rivers and streams that had carved deep valleys. The main paved roads followed the valley floors, and the high ground between the valleys consisted mostly of flat, heavily wooded plateaus. Almost all of the roads over the high ground were rough, unpaved timber tracks. About twelve inches of snow covered the wooded high ground. When the sun occasionally reached the roads it made the snow shallower but caused the surface of the dirt roads to become frozen and icy. Sometimes, in the afternoon, the roads were covered with a mush of ice fragments and dirt that was not quite mud.

We started east in our jeep over an icy, snow-covered logging road. Lieutenant Cameron and I were walking about ten yards ahead of the jeep with about a five-yard space between us. After going about three miles, Cameron needed to answer a call of nature, so we stopped while he did so. A jeep moving in the opposite direction appeared a few minutes later. Rumors were rampant that Germans in American uniforms, riding in captured jeeps, were moving through the area spying for their advancing troops. To further complicate matters, we had not been told the First Army password, and the division had not yet issued one of its own. The two jeep loads of soldiers pointed their weapons at each other and stared each other down. Finally, a man got out of the jeep and slowly approached us while his companions covered him.

He stopped a few feet away and asked, "Who pitched two consecutive no-hitters a few years ago?"

"Johnny Van der Meer," I replied. Instantly, the tension faded away.

The man then identified himself simply as "Jim Gavin." He asked if we were lost and where we were going. I explained that we were moving east to find the 505th's headquarters, and he asked if we had an officer with us. About this time, Lieutenant Cameron walked out of the woods and joined us. General Gavin said he had just come back from the Salm. He said there were indications that small German patrols might be in the area around us and cautioned us to be alert for them. He suggested that we follow his jeep tracks through the snow back to 505th's headquarters near the Salm, adding that it would probably be best if a couple of us walked ahead of the jeep so we could see them better. He gave us more information about the general situation along the Salm. Everything was still quiet there, and he said the 505th was confident it could keep the Germans from crossing the Salm. He added that they would be happy to have our artillery to support them.

We followed General Gavin's jeep's tracks easily. We were lucky that we were not advancing through land the Germans had recently occupied. They surely would have planted many antipersonnel and antitank mines along roads like the one we were following. Our previous fighting experience convinced us that German mines were among the most effective of their minor weapons, and they were terribly frightening to all of us.

Just before dawn we found a two-story farmhouse on the hill overlooking Trois Ponts and hid our jeep in the woods behind it. While Lieutenant Cameron and the radio/telephone operator set up our position, the driver and I walked down the hill to the 505th's headquarters. The bridge at Trois Ponts had been blown. About two miles to the north, a German self-propelled antitank gun had tried to cross an old wooden bridge just east of the Amblève's confluence with the Salm. The bridge had collapsed under its heavy weight, plunging the vehicle into the river. It would be easy for foot troops to cross the river over the vehicle, but there was no way that tanks could get across. To cross the Salm, German infantry would have to capture a bridgehead on the river's west bank and protect their engineers as they built a bridge strong enough for tanks to cross.

The farmhouse we found was excellent for observation purposes but it presented us with a severe problem. It stood on top of the hill and would be the first thing German panzers saw if or when they crested the opposite ridge. They could not help but identify it as a potentially good observation point and surely take steps to prevent us from using it. A stone wall extended to the south along our ridge for several hundred yards. We decided to set up the equivalent of some duck blinds along about two hundred yards of the wall. We cut trees and branches and put them against the wall so we would be covered when we directed fire on the hill across the Salm. We put other trees along the wall so our newly built positions would not stand out as obvious targets.

The ground was too frozen to dig foxholes. We had not yet been issued winter clothing, so we were always cold. We set up another position a hundred yards back in the woods behind our jeep and dug a sheltered fire pit that could not be seen from the east so we could cook and warm ourselves a little at night. Although the Germans were good at sending out small night patrols, they rarely launched major attacks in the dead of night, so we took turns manning the observation post to make sure we heard the panzers if they arrived in the dark.

Since there were no Germans in sight yet, we kept watch from the second floor of the farmhouse, from which we had a better view to the east. We immediately began to register our artillery on selected points on the far side of the river by firing single rounds on them until we scored a direct hit. These targets were ones we could readily identify on our rough, self-made maps. For example, we fired several rounds at a crossroad that we designated "Point A." Once we were on target, all we had to do was tell the guns to fire on Point A, and Point A would always be hit. We established a dozen such aiming points. If we needed to hit targets at other points nearby, we would use the aiming points to shift fire by saying, for example: "Fire three hundred yards over and five hundred yards left of Point A." Once this process was completed, we were confident we could accurately hit any target that might later appear within our view on the high ground on the other side of the Salm. Meanwhile, the infantry sent patrols across the river. These patrols reported that panzers were about five miles to the east and seemed to be preparing to move toward us.

The five-thousand-man panzer task force north of the Amblève near La Gleize could neither advance nor retreat, and American armored units moving down from the north would destroy it if the rest of 1st SS Panzer Division was prevented from relieving or reinforcing it. This task force was later identified as being commanded by Lt. Col. Joachim Peiper, one of Germany's most aggressive, ruthless, and successful panzer commanders. On 21 December the 1st SS

Panzer Division began the first of several strong attacks intended to drive through our positions and reach the panzers north of the Amblève. A German armored car came over the ridge at high speed shortly after 1300. Apparently its occupants were unaware we were in defensive positions along the Salm. A bazooka team destroyed it. The survivors said they were the lead reconnaissance unit of the 1st SS Panzer Division, which would defeat us very easily and quickly. The infantrymen placed mines across the road a hundred yards behind the knocked out armored car, and soon another armored car crested the hill and exploded when it hit a mine.

Panzers accompanied by *panzergrenadiers* (infantrymen who moved about in trucks, on tanks, or in half-tracks) came down the hill on the far side of the river in the midafternoon. The *panzergrenadiers* were excellent infantrymen. The positions we had prepared along the stone wall away from the house proved wise since it was only a few minutes before three 88mm tank rounds slammed into the farmhouse and it burned to the ground. It was almost impossible to hit individual tanks with artillery, so scoring a direct hit with a howitzer fired from several miles away was pure luck. The new top-secret American proximity artillery fuse (POZIT) was introduced during the Normandy campaign. This fuse allowed shells to be set to explode at a planned height, say, fifteen feet above the ground. Although they could not destroy a tank, shells with these proximity fuses accomplished two things: they forced tank commanders to take cover inside the tank with the hatches closed, severely restricting their visibility, and the accompanying infantry were either killed or discouraged from staying with the tanks.

With no infantry protection and their commanders forced to remain buttoned-up inside, the vehicles became almost blind, making them easy prey for our infantry's tank-killer teams. Our infantry had captured many German *panzerfausts* in Holland. The *panzerfaust* was a single-shot, rocket-propelled antitank weapon that was far superior to our bazooka. Without infantry to protect a panzer, a hunter-killer team could maneuver to the side or rear of the vehicle, where its armor was thinnest, and destroy it. Our POZIT fire was very accurate that day, killing or wounding many of the *panzergrenadiers* who were protecting the tanks and driving the rest away. Our hunter-killer teams knocked out many panzers. By dark, the first attack had been repulsed.

The next day, the commander of the infantry battalion we had been supporting visited us at our observation post. He thought we had done well and was interested in getting a better view of the other side of the line. The visit was almost a celebration since our success against a crack German panzer division had left us all feeling exhilarated. Mostly, though, our feelings were of relief that the attack was over—at least for a while. We had survived, and we felt an enormous sense of accomplishment.

The colonel was also elated that the battalion's 57mm antitank guns had knocked out two panzers. Costly experience had shown us that these weapons were no more effective against the heavy panzers than rifles or rocks would have been. Worse, once an American antitank crew fired a round or two at a tank without effect, it usually found the antitank gun. It then would fire a single cannon round in return, killing or wounding the crew and destroying the gun. Being almost immobile, these guns made easy targets, so using them against panzers was almost suicidal.

The colonel explained that they had kept a few of the 57mm sabot rounds the British had issued them in Holland, where we first learned of them and their effectiveness. Sabot rounds had a more powerful propellant charge, so they reached a much greater velocity than the high-explosive antitank rounds designed for the gun. It was a kinetic-energy round, meaning it employed an eight inch-long rod made of hardened tungsten steel instead of explosives to penetrate armor. This penetrator was surrounded by a discarding shoe called a sabot (hence its name). After the round was fired, the sabot fell away and the tungsten core continued on to the target. The rounds were not available to us through normal supply channels, so many American units would barter almost anything in order to obtain a few of them from the British, then carefully hoard them.

On 22 December the 1st SS Panzer Division attacked the positions

(handwritten in left margin) 57mm anti-tank knocks out panzers

of another 82d regiment to the south of us. It was also repulsed. On the twenty-third, the remnants of the American force at Saint-Vith, about fifteen thousand men, withdrew through our positions and we learned that the panzer spearhead to our north had run out of fuel and was hopelessly surrounded.

10

Captured by the SS

On the nights of 23 and 24 December there were developments on both sides of the line that radically affected our observation team. However, we were sitting fat, dumb, and happy at the time, and had no idea of what was going on. The problems began during the day on the twenty-third. The Germans were jamming our radio frequencies, and our radio was not holding up well in the near zero weather. To make matters worse, our telephone line went out at about 1700. We had laid about two miles of line from the location of the battalion fire control center near Basse-Bodeux to our observation post near Trois Ponts. There was no choice but to trace it and fix or replace the line. As soon as it began to get dark, Corporal Hancock and I set out on this mission. There was about a foot of snow on the ground with deeper drifting, burying the wire in snow. We lifted it and passed it through our gloved hands as we searched for the break.

After going about two thousand yards we finally found the break. We went down on our hands and knees to search for the other end of the wire. After ten minutes we still had not found it, and, even worse, we discovered we had lost the other end, too. Both of us had become completely disoriented during our search. By then it was very dark and we had no idea which way to go to get to the fire control center or the observation post. We feared using a flashlight to read our compass since it was likely that soldiers from either side would fire at a light. There was nothing to do but move over into the bushes and sleep out the night.

I had an eiderdown-lined, mummy-style sleeping bag that was very warm. I slept with my rifle and pistol in the bag. Jim's sleeping bag was much less protective than mine. When we awoke in the weak light before dawn we discovered it had snowed all night, covering our sleeping bags. Only a breathing hole above my face gave any sign that I existed. During the night, Jim had suffered frostbitten fingers, and his feet were numb and cold. We saw the right way to go as soon as we could see the compass, so we set off immediately.

When we arrived at Battery A headquarters, we explained the situation. They had been in intermittent contact with the observation post (OP) by radio, but it was clear that communications were unsatisfactory. Staff Sergeant Russell H. Burton Jr. had been sent out to replace me. Jim was sent to the aid station to have his frostbite treated. I said I wanted to lay a new telephone wire to the OP as soon as I could, but was told to wait until afternoon when the weather was predicted to be bad enough to give me some cover. I left at about 1500 and was certain I could find the way through the falling snow as long as there was some light. The going was slow since the roll of wire was heavy and awkward. With the aid of the compass I was able to finish laying the wire into the OP at about 1600.

Christmas Eve 1944 was my 591st day in the army. After all these years, I still intensely recall that night as my most confused and most personally dangerous of the war. Even with the substantial help of Captain Alley's log, with which I do not always agree, it has taken an extreme effort to write about this night with the accuracy it deserves. I only hope that most of the events and details as I describe them are close to what happened and that no one who participated has been left out or slighted.

When the 82d arrived in Belgium its mission was to engage the German panzer divisions and—with the help of other divisions that had been rushed to critically threatened points—stop them. Holding the key defense line along the Salm River would frustrate their efforts to drive west and north. The 82d was a lightly armed division, so we knew it would be difficult to compete with the heavily armed panzer divisions, but we had a high skill level and the ability to take advantage of strong defensive positions. After halting the Germans on our front, we extended our positions toward Saint-Vith to assist in the recovery of the American troops surrounded there. That maneuver resulted in the formation of a six-mile salient extending southward from the otherwise straight defensive line on the north shoulder of the bulge.

The 82d once again came under the operational control of Field Marshal Montgomery, who commanded all Allied troops north of the bulge. Seeing the salient the division held along the Salm as far south as Salmchâteau as an irregularity, Montgomery ordered us to fall back four to six miles to the north to eliminate it and thus shorten our lines—or in his words, "tidy things up a bit." Orders were issued for this move to be made during the night of the twenty-fourth, with the part of the 505th positioned below us in Trois Ponts moving about two miles to the west to form part of the new defensive line.

Lieutenant Cameron, who was without communications to the battery, was dependent on the infantry for information. The team was located about a half-mile from the nearest soldiers in the infantry battalion it was supporting, and the infantrymen apparently forgot to inform Cameron of the impending move. They did not learn about it until I arrived with the news.

Also on the twenty-fourth, SS Lieutenant Colonel Peiper decided his position behind our lines was untenable. There was no way to save his tanks because they were out of fuel, and the American defenses around his positions were too strong to fight through without tanks. He then ordered his units to break up into groups of about a hundred men, slip through the American lines, and attempt to link up with German troops. They began their escape attempt as soon as it became totally dark. Neither side was aware that their decisions meant many troops from both sides would be moving in all directions over the same terrain.

That night, after I rejoined the team, we followed our normal routine going back to the jeep and fire pit about an hour after dark, leaving one man, Pfc. Delbert L. Ehinger, at the OP to watch the valley below. I had brought orders that we were to move at midnight. Ehinger observed what he thought was our infantry bringing some of the men in from their outposts, but he saw no men being sent out to replace them. This worried him, but he did not have enough information to draw any conclusion. Nevertheless, he thought it looked like they were preparing to pull out ahead of us. He came back at about 2200 and reported that he had seen unusual movement in the valley. He said the infantry were acting as though they were making some kind of a move, but figured it might only be one battalion replacing another. While we were talking about a dozen Germans wearing black leather and armed with Schmeisser machine pistols rushed up to our position out of the darkness and surrounded us. The five of us were surprised and helpless against their number. In the flickering light of our campfire we could see the silver death's head on their caps and Nazi runes on their coats, so we knew they were SS rather than Wehrmacht (regular German army) troops. Since their headgear was not the typical coal-scuttle-shaped steel helmet of the German infantry, we concluded they were probably tankers from a panzer unit.

That they were exhausted and hungry became apparent by the way they wolfed down all our food in minutes. Those not occupied with questioning us dropped to the ground to rest after they ate. After disarming us and stealing our watches, compasses, food, and anything else worthwhile, an officer who spoke poor English asked us if there was a nearby footbridge over the Salm or Amblève. At first we answered with only our name, rank, and serial number, as required by the Geneva Convention. But this did not satisfy them. They were desperate to get back to the safety of their own lines. They proceeded to beat all of us severely. Lieutenant Cameron was a small man, standing about five-foot-six and weighing about 130 pounds. He received the worst of it when an SS man held him off the ground by the shoulders and two others took turns punching him in the stomach. The whole incident was like a nightmare to me. After all, only eighteen months before I had been an eighteen-year-old freshman at Purdue, and I still thought of myself as a college student on some kind of a military sabbatical. Now, some big Nazi bastard was trying his best to beat the hell out of me with his fists.

Soon, things got a lot worse than a mere beating. It was clear they did not want to be burdened with five prisoners. After identifying Cameron as an officer and Burton and me as sergeants, they decided we might be able to help them. They shot Pvt. Ralph G. Adkins in the hand, then changed their minds and kept him with us. Next they seperated us from Ehinger. Then they told us to talk it over and decide if we wanted to help them or be shot.

The three of us were angry and scared, and we estimated our chances of survival were mighty slim no matter what we decided to do. Since we did not expect to survive, we decided to try to lead them into a trap; at least that way we would take some of them with us. We told them about the self-propelled antitank gun in the Amblève about a mile to the north in hopes that our troops were still guarding that point. We knew if these SS tankers concluded we were leading them into a trap they would shoot us, but we hoped we might be able to find a way to escape before we reached the crossing site.

They did not give us enough time to work out a detailed escape plan. We told them about the antitank gun, and when they asked if our troops were guarding the crossing, we told them they probably were but that we knew of no other easy crossing. They apparently had better information than they had wrung from us. As we left we saw Ehinger standing against a tree with a German holding a gun to his head. We later learned they did not execute him but left him sitting there after shooting him in the thigh. Several of the Germans tried to use the jeep but gave up and fired some rounds into it when it would not start. The reason the jeep did not start was that Ehinger had removed the distributor rotor and put it in his pocket. This was standard practice after our own paratroop infantrymen in Holland stole several of the battalion's jeeps. After they left him, Ehinger crawled to the jeep, replaced the rotor, and drove back to an aid station.

The Germans set off in a single file, keeping the four of us together. After about twenty minutes the column halted and the officers obviously were discussing their next step. We had about a minute to talk together in whispers, and quickly worked out a simple escape plan based on their marching habits. Already being wounded, Adkins decided he did not want to make the attempt with us, so we separated ourselves from him to avoid endangering him further. Our plan was not much, but it was the best we could come up with on such short notice. It had a slim but reasonable chance of success.

The Arty Fire Contl team is captured by SS

It is with great pride that I recall our mutual steadfastness to escape together or not at all. Lieutenant Cameron removed his belt and hooked it through the back of mine so he could hold onto it, and Burton similarly attached himself to Cameron's belt loop. In this way we could signal one another silently and not become separated in the dark. I went first. It became even darker when clouds covered the moon. Our idea was that once the column began moving I would fall back and allow a ten-yard gap to open up between me and the German soldier to my front. If that worked, we would then walk faster and try to open a gap between Burton and the man behind him. Burton would look back from time to time and if he saw at least a five-yard space behind him, he would pull the belt twice and we would make a run for it. Obviously, running fast was the most critical part of the plan. Decisiveness was also critical since any hesitation or indecision would almost certainly have led to our deaths.

About twenty minutes later the column moved to within about thirty yards of the heavy woods to the west and Lieutenant Cameron signaled me with one pull on his belt to try our plan. It worked like a charm. I built the necessary space ahead of us quickly. After we sped up and veered right, however, Burton looked back and saw the rest of the column following right behind him.

"Get back in line quick!" he whispered urgently.

So much for our first try. But, considering our situation, it was impossible for us to give up. Ten minutes later we tried again. This time the tankers behind us proved to be extremely tired and less than alert. When Burton saw the gap widen to ten yards behind him, he tugged on his belt twice. Cameron instantly relayed the signal to me and we raced toward the dark woods. For those few seconds, I doubt if the world hundred-yard dash champion could have beaten any of us. The Germans fired a few rounds from their Schmeisser machine pistols at us but did not come close as we moved deep into the woods.

Once we thought we had gone far enough into the woods, we felt we were relatively safe for two reasons. First, the Germans had enough problems of their own as they concentrated on getting back to their lines. Second, they appeared to be tankers, not infantrymen, so they were lightly armed and not trained for the job of hunting down escaped prisoners. Although the Schmeisser machine pistol was an excellent close-range assault weapon, it was not effective at more than fifty yards. A few *panzergrenadiers* armed with good rifles would have presented us with real problems. Even after escaping, our situation was still pretty bleak. We were unarmed and wore only knit caps and lightweight jumpsuits. The temperature was near zero. We had to keep moving to keep warm until we found our own people. Cold and exposure were threatening us, to the point that we would freeze to death unless we found help soon.

We decided to follow our footprints back to where the Germans had captured us. We hoped Ehinger might still be alive, but held out little hope for him. Nevertheless, we knew it was our first duty to try to find him. It took us the better part of an hour to find the place where the jeep had been, but it was gone and there was no sign of Ehinger. This was encouraging, though, since we knew Ehinger had the distributor rotor in his pocket. I was lucky to find my sleeping bag nearby. Soon we found some infantrymen from the 505th. Our first thought was to try to persuade them to send a force after the Nazis who had abused us and shot our friends. They told us they had been in a firefight with some German panzer men earlier that night but that most of them had escaped. They had no word of our comrade's fate.

The battery had moved from the position it had occupied earlier that day, but the infantry battalion commander gave us some blankets and told us where he thought our battalion was. The night had been one of those rare times when soldiers from the opposing sides could pass each other going in opposite directions without disturbing one another because they had been ordered to move and avoid being engaged along the way.

Two weeks later, the 505th found Adkins in a cellar where the Germans had left him. After his rescue, Adkins reported that the Germans had taken care of his medical needs and treated him fairly well after they crossed into their own territory. He was evacuated to a field hospital. Lieutenant Cameron, Burton, and I made it back to the battery in time for breakfast.

Lieutenant Cameron and Burton were sent off to be interviewed by the battalion intelligence officer. While they were gone I went to the supply sergeant and obtained most of the new equipment I needed.

There can be no greater bond between men than to have worked together successfully to escape death or imprisonment. The three of us forged just such a bond that night. Although the circumstances were terrible, I've seldom approached the feeling of elation I had that night when we escaped.

We learned a month later that it was members of Peiper's force that had captured us, and that his men had massacred eighty-six defenseless American prisoners and forty-three more men they had wounded were left for dead at Malmédy a week earlier. The news was sobering and told us just how dangerous our situation really had been and how lucky we were to be alive. We concluded that if we had not escaped, those callous, hard-core Nazis would probably have shot all of us when they realized we were of no further use to them.

There was a rumor that prisoners of war were sent home if they escaped. We thought this was a great idea, but it turned out not to apply to us. Apparently being a prisoner for only a few hours did not qualify.

After we returned I soon realized that our battery area was under sporadic artillery fire. A single shell fell nearby; and all around us they were coming in at the rate of one to three rounds an hour. The first sergeant said this had been going on since about 0300 and it was clear that the large 155mm shells were coming from an American battery somewhere behind us. Captain Alley was beside himself; the idea of his men being hit and perhaps killed by American shellfire was just too much. Every fifteen minutes or so he sent a message through channels reporting the friendly fire. Once he went personally to battalion headquarters to complain about it, but nothing did any good. Finally, about 1500, after twelve hours had passed and dozens of shells had fallen harmlessly nearby, this shelling stopped. We never learned where the shells came from. The important thing was that no one was hurt.

After a week of fighting in terribly cold conditions in summer uniforms, the division finally began to receive winter equipment. It took about three days for everyone to be issued what he needed. However, since we had even less than the others, Lieutenant Cameron, Burton, and I got ours on the first day. Most important were two items: overcoats and snow-pacs. Snow-pacs were boots designed for winter operations. They had rubber soles, were waterproofed and insulated,

They say "snow-pacs"; we say "shoe-pacs"

and laced halfway up to the knee. When worn with the heavy woolen socks issued at the same time, they protected us from trench foot and other foot disorders that had been a great cause of discomfort and casualties during the previous week. Somehow I lucked out and was issued a pair of 13B snow-pacs. My shoes were getting closer to the right size. One consolation after our miseries on Christmas Eve was that everything we were issued was superior to what we had lost to the Germans.

By the end of Christmas Day it was apparent that the German offensive had fizzled out because of a lack of sufficient supplies, ammunition, men, and the strong resistance of the 82d, 101st, and many other American divisions. Although Field Marshal Montgomery had been given command of operations on the north shoulder of the bulge, the Battle of the Bulge was an almost all-American battle, and the largest single one that the U.S. Army ever fought by itself in any of our wars. Besides the three days of attacks on us by the 1st SS Panzer Division, which I had witnessed personally, the 2d and 9th SS Panzer Divisions had also attacked the 82d. These strong, elite, German divisions had been intent on relieving Peiper's spearhead and then driving north to take Liège, which they hoped would threaten the supply lines that four Allied armies to the immediate north depended on for survival. All these attacks were repulsed, and the three German divisions were essentially destroyed as effective fighting units.

During the first five days after its arrival, the 82d had an unprotected right flank, and a determined armored attack against that flank might have proved disastrous. The fifteen thousand men we helped evacuate from Saint-Vith occupied this opening after the twenty-third, and it was after that when the Germans chose to attack us from that direction. It is ironic that the American troops we rescued were able to return the favor by saving us from disaster.

Between Christmas and New Year's Day, the Germans began a hasty retreat, and the 82d saw only light action. The day after Christmas, Lieutenant Cameron and I (Burton went two days later) were given passes to the Belgian town of Spa, where reservations had been made for us for two nights at the Hotel des Baines. We went to Spa, though not together, since officers did not go on leave with enlisted men. However, this protocol proved weaker than the bond we had developed on Christmas Eve, and we had an excellent meal together in a civilian restaurant one night and spent much of the other in a bar.

Spa was interesting. It is many centuries old and built over one of Europe's great hot springs. A huge building, maybe five stories high, housed perhaps two hundred bathrooms, each with a huge copper bathtub attended by two middle-aged ladies. The ladies filled the tub with sulfurous-smelling water from the hot spring and proceeded to scrub my nude body thoroughly with soap and brushes. After an hour of soaking, they emptied the tub and sprayed me with clean water. After being dried with huge, fluffy towels, I proceeded to a massage table where I was rubbed all over for about another half-hour with various oils and creams. All in all, it was wonderful.

The trip to Spa was the best two-day pass I ever had in my army career, and we returned to our unit rested and invigorated. On our return, we learned that the rest of the 456th had been trucked to portable army showers to remove the heavy layer of grime from their bodies. The ladies at the Hotel des Baines did a much better job.

Both the 82d and 101st Airborne Divisions had done a difficult job well. Both had demonstrated an unexpected ability to stop and defeat heavy armored divisions with relatively light arms. In doing so, both divisions had suffered heavy casualties. If the terrain in the Ardennes had not been so rugged it would have been even more difficult and things might have turned out differently.

11

Reflections on Fighting

One of the things soldiers occupy their time with is continuously griping among themselves about what they think is wrong with the army, the high command and its mistakes in the latest action, or life in general. Morale is usually high as long as the griping continues. However, when it stops, you can bet things are really bad. One of the subjects I recall that we discussed in Spa was the quality of the U.S. Army's ordnance compared with that of the Germans.

We certainly had a strong advantage in both the numbers of men and almost all types of weapons, but we believed that America's ordnance makers had not sufficiently considered quality when they designed some of the army's most important weapons. As an example, the best hand-held antitank weapons we used were German and British, not American. On the positive side, the U.S. M1 Garand rifle was superior to any other personal weapon of the war. It loaded easily with an eight-cartridge clip, was accurate to quite a long range, and could be fired rapidly. Our artillery had superior accuracy, better fire control, and better ammunition that was available in greater quantities. Our proximity-fused artillery shell was better than any type of artillery ammunition in the world. Our trucks were superior in number and quality, giving the U.S. Army greater mobility than any other army fighting the war. This enabled us to move troops and supplies in greater quantities more quickly than the enemy could. By this time our airplanes of all types were equal to or superior to the entire list of enemy propeller-driven types. However, we had seen a few dozen German jet-powered planes, and they were much faster than our aircraft. We were concerned that the German jets might eventually tip the balance back in their favor, overcoming substantial air superiority our air forces had achieved by the end of 1944.

In the important area of tank warfare, it seemed to us that the Allies faced far more negatives in quality than positives. In North Africa in 1942, the Germans had adapted their excellent 88mm antiaircraft gun for antitank and general artillery use. No Allied tank could survive a hit by this gun's high-velocity projectile. Soon after this innovation, the Germans adapted the 88 for use as the main gun in their heavy new Tiger tanks, which featured a redesigned chassis and a new, much more powerful engine.

The Panther tank had better armor than did our M4 Sherman medium tanks, and its high-velocity, long-barreled 75mm gun could penetrate a Sherman's frontal and side armor. The Panther was faster and more maneuverable than the Tiger.

The Germans saw the value of a heavy tank armed with an 88 early on and successfully executed a plan to produce these weapons in quantity. The British also began to develop such a weapon but moved more cautiously. U.S. ordnance experts likewise saw the need and began developing the M26 Pershing tank, which packed a 90mm main gun and heavier armor protection. However, as the first few Pershings began rolling off production lines, an unfortunate decision was made to continue mass-producing Shermans instead of giving priority to the Pershing—much to our tankers' sorrow. The Pershing was finally introduced late in the European war and helped seize the Rhine River bridge at Remagen and participated in other operations.

Our Shermans had no chance against German 88mm antitank guns or the Panther and Tiger tanks in an even fight. The Panther's 75 and Tiger's 88 opened them up like tin cans. Our tankers thus depended on our aircraft, infantry, and artillery to take out known 88 antitank gun and tank positions before they advanced.

Another problem plaguing our tankers was the inferiority of the Sherman's main gun. Earlier Sherman variants were equipped with a 75mm medium-velocity cannon that could not pierce the heavy frontal armor of the latest model panzers. Since they usually wound up dead in single tank combat, our tankers developed swarming and flanking tactics that gave them shots against the panzers' more vulnerable side and rear armor. A 76mm high-velocity cannon was introduced in later Sherman models. Although much better than the 75mm gun, it did not make them fully competitive with the best German panzers because they still lacked sufficient frontal armor.

We also had some tank destroyers armed with 90mm high-velocity guns, and these were effective weapons against Panthers and Tigers. They employed ambush tactics because, like the Shermans, they lacked the armor protection needed to engage the German panzers in open battle.

The Sherman was effective against infantry and fortified positions when it was used as an assault weapon, but during the winter of 1944–45 the U.S. Army was still at a great disadvantage in armored warfare except for having a greater numbers of tanks.

In the field of infantry hand-held antitank weapons, the single-shot German *panzerfaust* was superior to our bazooka in striking force and, if well used, could destroy any tank. Although our bazooka was light and could fire several shots in a short time, it was only effective if the gunner hit a Panther or Tiger from the side or rear. The bazooka's multiple-shot advantage paled in comparison to the *panzerfaust's* greater striking power, which was the most important thing to an infantryman facing a Tiger or Panther tank in a one-to-one confrontation.

The use of 88s as conventional artillery was common, and it was superior in all direct-fire missions. However, its flat trajectory made it harder for gunners to engage targets that they could not see directly, such as those on the reverse slope of a hill.

Excepting the Garand rifle, most of our other personal infantry weapons were inferior to those of the German army. For assault purposes, nothing we had approached the Schmeisser machine pistol; so, many American infantrymen carried them, risking summary execution if captured with a German weapon. However, the British Sten, which we did not use, was close. The Thompson submachine guns we were issued for assault purposes were awkward, heavy, did not fire quickly, were hard to aim and control, tended to ride upward when fired, and had a smaller magazine than the Schmeisser.

Our fragmentation grenades were good, although different in principle from the German "potato-masher" concussion grenades.

Both were about equal in quality and effectiveness. Their P-38 and Luger pistols were far more easy to handle and more accurate than our heavier and clumsy .45s. Our mines were fine, as far as they went, but we could not match the array of antipersonnel and antitank mines and booby traps the Germans had at their disposal.

One weapon the Germans had that we could not compete with until late in the war was the Nebelwerfer. Known as the "moaning minnie" and "screaming meemie," each weapon fired six or eight heavy rockets in a single salvo. The sound they made was unforgettable. It is hard to describe, but when you heard its distinctive sound you immediately sought cover. Although inaccurate, everything in the area where the rockets hit was seriously damaged. It was more an intimidation weapon than the more serious threat of an aimed weapon. Nevertheless, it proved to be a portent of the future effectiveness of rocket weapons.

We wondered if our ordnance people had paid any attention at all to the war in North Africa. Were they provided decent intelligence about German and British weapons employed there? If they had been, we figured the state of our arms and ordnance should have been far advanced from what it was in late 1944. Alternatively, our experts might have had a "not-invented-here" attitude (a tendency to believe anything Americans did not invent and use was no good). If so, this attitude cost many American lives, the waste of which could have been prevented by more timely attention to the realities of the war. As far as we were concerned, we could only hope that improvements would be forthcoming soon. In the meantime, we hoped our much greater quantities of "stuff" might overcome the lesser quantities of superior German weapons.

One issue every honest soldier was concerned about was whether he might grow to love war and enjoy killing. In Spa, Lieutenant Cameron and I spent some time over drinks discussing this concern. In our own recent experience, we had been told the 1st SS Panzer Division had lost about seven thousand of its more than eleven thousand men in a week fighting against the 82d. Some of those Germans were prisoners of war, but many were killed or wounded. We knew our little four-man team had contributed substantially to the carnage. We explored how we felt about killing other men. In spite of moral teachings of varied intensity, a soldier's job is to kill another soldier who is just as diligently trying to kill *him*. He eventually develops a positive obsession to perform the task well. Personally, the experience Lieutenant Cameron and I had when the SS captured us helped us to rationalize our mixed feelings about killing. The SS seemed to be evil incarnate. They had shot two of our friends and seemed intent on harming us when we were helpless to defend ourselves. In the absence of reaching a mental and emotional condition that allowed a willingness to kill, a soldier would almost certainly perish. If that can be defined as a "joy of killing," then so be it.

A logical follow-up question is: does becoming a soldier who has gained experience in killing make him dangerous in later civilian life? I think not for two reasons. First, military killing is an almost emotionless task, unlike murder, which is either an emotional, out-of-control response to some perceived slight, threat, or harm, or a calculated act done for personal gain. Second, military killing does not require a positive personal decision, whereas deciding to kill an enemy civilian is a positive decision. I have purposely excluded any consideration of psychological or professional killers. Although there are always exceptions, I think such men would find it difficult to adjust to an army's disciplinary structure.

The last thing we talked about in the wee hours of our final night in Spa was medals. I asked Cameron if he thought we might get one for escaping from the German SS men. He said he thought not. He told me that General Gavin had said in a speech he gave while we were in France that almost every 82d trooper who had seen combat in Normandy and Holland probably deserved at least one Silver Star. However, he said they would not get them because each division had a share of medals informally allocated to it by SHAEF. General Gavin said he thought this was unfair but there was nothing he could do about it.

When we returned to our battalion, we found it had been withdrawn from the line; to our surprise, it had set up a brothel. We had not heard of the army doing such a thing before, but a set of unusual circumstances led to it. Apparently a couple of soldiers had found two ladies who volunteered their services, and they set up shop. The battalion closed down the operation, but this almost caused a riot.

Then the commanding officer found an army doctor who was willing to examine the women and their soldier-customers.

An NCO volunteered to collect the fees from the customers and divide the money among the women; by then there were four of them. The brothel was set up in four adjoining tents with a common separate entry tent, and the women worked in shifts: two hours in the afternoon and three in the evening. The doctor examined the women before and after each shift, and he examined each customer as he entered the brothel. The operation lasted for three days—until an order from a higher command shut it down.

About half of the soldiers from our battalion and other units nearby used the facility. I was lucky to be away in Spa on the day it was set up or I, as special services NCO, would probably have been pressured into running it. As for using it, the whole process was just too clinical and gross for me—as it proved to be for the other half of the 456th's soldiers.

One of those who didn't use the brothel was my friend Bart, Cpl. Albert Barthelmes Jr., another ex–college student who had attended Tufts University near Boston. The battalion was resting and refitting amid a group of farms cut out of the woods near Chevron, Belgium, behind the northern edge of the bulge. This proved to be a boon to Bart, who had been slightly wounded by a shell fragment on Christmas Eve. It was a lucky wound: the fragment only cut the back of his right hand, nicking one bone slightly. Although it hurt a lot, he persuaded the doctors to let him recover at his unit instead of sending him to a field hospital.

Most of us slept in pup tents on frozen ground but everybody felt sorry for Bart, so Captain Alley had me talk to one of the farmers. The man agreed to let Bart move into their warm farmhouse. The next day I went to Spa and returned three days later. While I was away, it seems that the farmer's twenty-year-old daughter had taken excellent care of Bart, cooking his army food and probably furnishing him with other comforts.

Everyone knew we would again be involved in the fighting when we launched our huge counterattack against the bulge. Our rest did not last long. To the south, the 4th Armored Division of General Patton's Third Army had relieved the week-long German siege of the 101st Airborne and other troops at Bastogne. The Germans continued to attack Bastogne for several more days, but by 29 December Patton's troops were ready to attack to the north to cut off and destroy German forces still deep in their penetration. In an effort to frustrate our efforts and escape capture, the Germans were still fighting hard.

Although the aggressive Patton was eager to begin his attack on the southern flank of the bulge, Field Marshal Montgomery wanted to make detailed preparations before allowing any attack to begin. We were brought up to the line on the twenty-ninth ready to attack, but then sat for several days while the Germans strengthened their positions and brought up what seemed to be massive amounts of men and artillery. We watched the activities from our observation post but we were not allowed to "waste ammunition." All we could do was take notes, and you cannot kill many Germans with notes. We could not understand why our commanders allowed what would have been an easy attack to turn into a much harder and more costly one by frittering away those important days in inactivity.

After we repulsed the Germans in the bulge, Allied commanders and fighting troops contracted a "disease" that lengthened the war and resulted in more casualties. Everyone thought the German attack had been their last great effort, and many thought all we had to do to end the war was ride our trucks eastward into Berlin against no resistance. Those people forgot that we still fought a disciplined, highly skilled, and determined foe who was expert in defensive warfare. And that foe still had two naturally strong defensive lines available to him between our positions and Berlin: the Siegfried Line and the Rhine River.

This disease manifested itself differently in the high commanders and the frontline troops. The high commanders turned to politics as their principal interest. They were full of themselves in the politics of a victory they had not yet won, and they fought among themselves to protect their personal positions in history. Caution became their watchword. The frontline troops also became cautious, believing they were about to go home. They did not want to fight hard anymore or take personal risks in order to achieve victory. This wishful attitude prevented both groups from recognizing that victory could best be accomplished by going for the enemy's throat before he could recover from the pounding he'd taken in the bulge. Some American army and corps commanders like Patton, Ridgway, and others recognized this need for aggressive action. They believed that even if aggressive action resulted in a higher rate of casualties in the short run, it would almost certainly shorten the war and reduce the total number of casualties we would suffer if the war dragged on. In fact, experience showed that aggressive tactics usually brought about fewer casualties than cautious ones, so the whole idea of employing cautious tactics was faulty in the first place.

The spread of this "easy-end-to-the-war" disease meant that elite units like the airborne divisions—which were willing, able, and trained to fight—would be called on for greater effort and even more suffering. Because of their willingness to fight, these high-quality fighting divisions could be expected to carry the fight to the end. Perhaps the most dangerous period of the war lay ahead for the 82d Airborne Division.

12

The Allies Resume the Offensive

Winter conditions in the Ardennes were dreadful in late December 1944, but in early January 1945 they changed for the worse. The high temperature averaged about 15 degrees Fahrenheit, and the strong winds made it seem much colder. The snow averaged about eighteen inches deep in the open, drifting to several feet in spots, and continued to fall heavily.

On 3 January Montgomery launched his attack in his usual overly cautious style. He ordered each division to advance to a phase line, a predetermined line on a map normally keyed to a readily identifiable terrain feature, and wait for further orders. These phase lines were placed at arbitrary distances on the map with little regard to their potential to serve as defensive positions. Once we reached a phase line we wanted to take advantage of our success and, at the least, seize any stronger ground to our front. But Montgomery's system did not allow for such initiative. Our forced halts thus gave the retreating Germans time to prepare for our next attack.

On the first day of the attack, the 82d's troopers slogged through the heavy snow and captured more than two thousand prisoners as they overran the remnants of the 9th SS Panzer and 62d Volksgrenadier Divisions. With no German troops of any substance ahead, the high command ordered a halt after two days because the division had reached its phase line too quickly.

On the fourth day, the division was allowed to renew the attack, and it moved almost unopposed to positions along the Salm that had been given up on Christmas Eve. As usual, our little four-man observation team accompanied one of the 505th's battalions. From our position in the heights above the village of Vielsalm, we saw an unbelievable sight: a German column of about thirty-five trucks and half-tracks carrying infantry was struggling through the heavily snow-covered road moving toward the village below.

The 505th's regimental headquarters ordered us to prepare for a full-battalion fire mission. Every gun in the battalion was told to fire several rounds on a crossroads that was prominent on the ground and on our maps. We had previously registered fire on a nearby target, so our accuracy was certain. We were to give the order to fire as the rearmost vehicles in the column passed the crossroads. In this way, the crossing would be blocked with destroyed and damaged vehicles when our infantry, who were waiting ahead of the column in ambush, sprang their attack.

Our devastating artillery fire blocked the road as planned, and the infantry fired a mortar barrage aimed at the head of the column that stopped it and brought on general confusion among the enemy troops. The SS *panzergrenadiers* reacted like all good soldiers: they dove for the roadside ditches and began to resist, but their efforts were hopeless. The ambush was over within minutes. All the Germans—from a force we estimated at about five hundred—were either killed or captured, and many of the prisoners were wounded. The survivors told us they were being rushed forward to reinforce the 9th SS Panzer Division. Most were poorly trained sixteen-year-old boys, older men who had been drafted after the draft age had been raised, and men wounded in earlier fighting who were being sent back to the front. The veterans and noncoms among them tried to fight but the kids and older men just panicked.

Except for their difficulties with the snow-packed road and the cold, their column had been moving confidently forward, blissfully believing the front to be more than fifty miles farther west. They had been told the Amis (German slang for American troops) were still headed westward in full retreat. They did not know that the 9th SS Panzer Division had been all but wiped out. They said they had no idea that their great counterassault had been halted well before it crossed the Meuse and far short of Hitler's objective: the Belgian port of Antwerp.

The 82d renewed its attack on the eighth, moving across the Salm and establishing a strong bridgehead. Our team was with the headquarters of the 505th's 2d Battalion that day when it came under enemy artillery fire. Everyone followed the usual drill of finding the best cover available. Good cover was a relative term because no one was able to dig a good, deep foxhole in the frozen ground. Several men, including Lt. Col. Benjamin Vandervoort, were hit by shell fragments. Vandervoort began his service with the division before Sicily as a company commander in the 505th and by the time of the Normandy invasion was in command of its 2d Battalion. Vandervoort had made four combat parachute jumps and was with his unit every day that it had been in action despite suffering a broken ankle in Normandy and being hit in the shoulder by a Schmeisser on 21 December. This time he lost an eye and was sent home. He was sorely missed by all because he was an excellent commander who cared for and was considerate of his men and all others who dealt with him.

The 75th Infantry Division relieved the 82d on the ninth and we were ordered back to the rest area we had recently occupied near Chevron. The division needed to replace the heavy losses in men and equipment it had suffered since going into Holland. The 82d had received only a handful of replacements since the end of the Market-Garden operation in November, and quartermasters had as yet to finish giving everyone heavy winter uniforms to replace their lightweight jumpsuits. I was lucky, having received winter clothes, heavy boots, and an overcoat in late December, but many troopers were still cold and ragged. Many men wore German overcoats when they were safely clear of the front lines, but there was always the possibility of being mistaken for the enemy and being shot. Others made improvised capes out of their shelter halves, and captured German blankets were used for everything from scarves to face masks to body wraps under their uniforms to help them resist the effects of the extreme cold.

Once we had settled in around Chevron, we were told we would rest there for at least two weeks as long as no unusual emergencies arose. During this period commanders were to provide everyone not under arrest with a three-day pass. The lucky ones went to Paris and Brussels, and a few went to Liège or Spa. I was again made special services NCO and told to combine my pass with business. My assignment was to go to Brussels with a driver and truck and buy beer for the battalion. Brussels was only about eighty miles away over good but icy roads, so we made it in less than three hours. I selected Pvt.

Marcel C. Four, a first-generation American whose parents had come from Alsace, as my driver. He spoke fluent French and German. Our passes allowed us to stay in a nice, centrally located Brussels hotel, where we cleaned off the grime and relaxed in hot baths.

We were stopped frequently by American and British military police. They had difficulty accepting the fact that we were driving around Brussels in an 82d Division six-by-six truck even though the orders we carried clearly stated we were authorized to be there. Fortunately the hotel allowed us to park the truck in a protected area, otherwise we feared the MPs might haul it away. We ate well for two days and found an excellent Belgian brewery. They filled up our truck with barrels of good beer for $10 a barrel plus some coffee and cigarettes.

Marcel and I also arranged for another entertainment troupe similar to the one I had found earlier at Saint-Denis but with no statuesque dancers this time. We sent a truck back to pick them up the next Saturday and the troupe entertained us that afternoon in a barnyard. However, because of our primitive circumstances, they had to be taken back that night.

The day I returned from Brussels, Bart told me that he and his Belgian farm girl wanted to get married. He wanted Lieutenant Cameron to be his best man and me to be in the wedding party. It was difficult to get the army's blessing, but the chaplain performed the ceremony later that week. Bart was given a three-day pass that weekend, and the happy couple went to Liège for their honeymoon. Bart made it through the rest of the war unhurt but I lost contact with him afterward. I have always wondered what became of Bart and his Belgian bride.

Before our rest and relaxation period near Chevron ended, several of us tried to address the soldier's continuous and fundamental gripe: the food was lousy. Bart's new father-in-law told us the surrounding country abounded with large Belgian hares, so we asked for permission to go on a rabbit hunt. We were told we could do it, but only if we used captured German arms. There was no shortage of these, particularly Schmeisser machine pistols.

Four of us went out carrying an assortment of German pistols, rifles, and Schmeissers. We found that if one of us walked about five yards inside the woods along the edge of a field or past a bushy pile of rocks, the hares ran out into the field in fair numbers. These hares were large, probably weighing twenty pounds or more. The farmers preferred shotguns for hunting hares, and our pistols and Schmeissers were not very effective, especially when the latter were fired in single-shot mode. It was just too difficult to hit them. The German rifles were more accurate but the bullets were heavy and caused too much damage, leaving only large parts of rabbit. When we fired our Schmeissers on automatic we were able to walk the stream of bullets across the hare by following the impact of the bullets in the snow. This also proved less than desirable because we wound up with ground rabbit. We finally discovered that if we limited the Schmeisser fire to three-round bursts we could hit a hare and not damage it too badly. By the end of the afternoon we had bagged about a dozen hares and our cooks did a fairly good job of preparing a rabbit stew that proved to be a pleasant change from the standard army fare.

After hunting men on and off for seven months and knowing I would continue to hunt men into the indefinite future, I longed to discontinue doing so. Our rabbit hunt seemed unfair and unnecessary killing, and I decided I would hunt neither men nor animals again after the war ended.

The people in the area around Chevron and Pepinster were friendly as they were almost all loyal Belgians. They shared what they had with us, and we shared our food with them. On several occasions the locals received needed medical attention from our field hospital. Things were different a little farther east because many of the people living along the border were of German origin and sympathized with the Nazis.

Our stay in the area around Chevron was almost idyllic. It was peaceful, and many of us developed friendships with the local people, who were grateful to us for driving the Germans away. They had feared that the Germans might take reprisals against them for welcoming us. That was what happened to other Belgians when the Nazis reoccupied the territory they gained during the Battle of the Bulge. Tears were shed when we were finally ordered back into action. We, in turn, missed those kind, simple, country people.

The C-47 (Douglas DC-3) carried most of the troops and cargo that were flown in Europe. It was a sturdy, reliable workhorse that remained in commercial airline service for several decades after the war.

Taken from an open escape door, this picture shows only one of a hundred such planes that was dropping paratroopers in an exercise jump. A hundred planes could place a battalion of infantrymen deep behind enemy lines ready to fight.

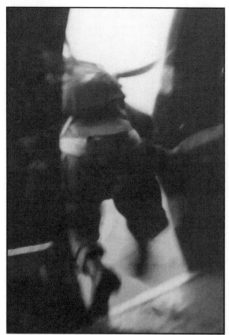

This trooper is the last of a stick of eight who jumped through the door. He had to run quickly to keep up with his comrades. A few lost seconds at 180 feet per second (125 miles per hour) could spread them out on the ground, eliminate their ability to support one another and cost lives.

This trooper is flying through the air at the speed of the plane, 125 miles per hour. When his parachute opens, he will almost instantly decelerate to zero. His position is good; otherwise he risks sprains, even a broken neck.

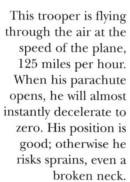

It takes 300 feet of fall, about three seconds, for a parachute to open. These chutes are not yet open, but they are deploying properly. The white dots are open chutes approaching the ground.

The 505th Regimental Combat Team of over 4,000 men made this practice jump near Reims, France, in March 1945. I snapped this picture just after I had landed. The loss of an engine at a critical time caused an accident that killed nine troopers and aircrew men.

The 75mm pack howitzer was designed to be broken down into pieces and carried by mules. These same pieces were dropped by parachute. This one is dug in beneath a camouflage canopy in Holland. (Herman L. Alley)

This is a Mark V Panther tank. Peiper's spearhead of the First SS Panzer Division ran out of fuel near La Gleize, Belgium. Not knowing they were only a mile from a U.S. Army gas dump, Peiper abandoned his tanks. While the tankers were trying to find their lines, they captured four comrades and me, but we escaped.

On the way to a camp near Reims after two months of combat in Holland, those of us who were left were a happy, if ragged, lot. I am in the center rear; Paul Swazuk is to my right; Bart Barthelmes is to my left; and Marcel Four kneels in the foreground.

The farmers around our rest-camp near Cheviot, Belgium were friendly and supportive. This couple's daughter married Corporal Barthelmes. Closer to the German border, Belgian citizens were ethnic Germans and some were sympathetic to the Nazis.

Hitler had tens of thousands of bunkers built in the West Wall and the Siegfried Line. They were almost impervious to bombs and high-angle artillery fire. To defeat one bunker, troops had to get very close to it and use flame-throwers, directly fired cannon shells, and explosive charges.

Captain Herman L. Alley stands among the dragon teeth of the Siegfried Line near Udenbreth, Germany, in February 1945. Thousands of miles of these dragon teeth were built. (Herman L. Alley)

After returning to France from fighting in the Huertgen Forest, I was relaxed and happy. The war was almost over in March 1945, but one could still die. I was crossing the Vosges Mountains on a special service mission (a boondoggle) to Alsace with Corporal Marcel Four to buy liquor while visiting his relatives.

No major German city escaped the wrath of the American and British air forces. This was Dusseldorf in April 1945.

German civilians were trying to clean up their cities as we passed through in April 1945. Buildings were being pulled down and the rubble stacked in piles in the streets. They had to use their hands to do the work since nothing else was available. People lived in the partially destroyed buildings, ignoring the threat of immediate collapse.

All of the German bridges built over the Rhine had been destroyed by 1945. This is one of many U.S. Army pontoon bridges that crossed the Rhine near Dusseldorf.

This is a 75mm mobile antitank gun mounted on a Mark IV tank chassis that broke the bridge over the Ambleve River a thousand yards east of our position. The Ambleve and the slightly smaller Salm River impeded the initial German advance. (Courtesy Jean Jacob. His father took this picture in January 1945, just after the fighting was over.)

Battery A of the 456th PFAB is on parade at Templehof Aerodrome in Berlin in 1945. The troopers are towing 75mm howitzers by hand. This was the only way they could be moved after being dropped by parachute or glider. These troopers are much neater than they would have been in battle. (Herman L. Alley)

13

Frozen Bodies Stacked Like Cordwood

Early in the morning on 27 January we boarded trucks and left the Chevron area and began moving eastward. As usual, I rode in an open jeep, which was no privilege thanks to the intense cold. Our officers and senior noncoms had attended a meeting at the 505th's headquarters the previous day. As the second-ranking man in an observation team, I was ordered to attend. Colonel Ekman, the regimental commander, led the presentation, and General Gavin, who was also present, made occasional comments. The rumor mill had been grinding hard for a week. The most prevalent rumors were that we would be going back to France for refitting or moving north to join the fighting around Aachen. The first thing the meeting disclosed was that the rumor mill was wrong: we had an entirely different new combat assignment, which meant we were all probably in trouble again.

The colonel told us that General Ridgway's XVIII Airborne Corps had been assigned the job of breaching the Siegfried Line in an area east of our present position. He said the 1st Infantry Division, another elite ETO unit, had been assigned to the corps and would join the 82d in making the assault. Three tank battalions and additional heavy artillery would support our effort to break through the German defenses and into their homeland. The 101st Airborne, which was also part of the XVIII Airborne Corps, would remain in SHAEF reserve during this operation because it was still recovering from the heavy fighting around Bastogne.

This was another example of what happened to elite units. The 82d and 101st were repeatedly given difficult assignments throughout World War II. Numerous times we took over jobs from other American divisions that had failed and usually accomplished the task with apparent ease. We always seemed to be fighting elite German units because the enemy knew only their best outfits had any chance against us. Now the 82d and 1st Divisions would reap the rewards of being elite units with a proven willingness to carry the battle to the enemy. Their reward would be casualties and perhaps betrayal by the SHAEF high command when it lost interest in our operation and focused its attention elsewhere.

Both divisions were willing and able to engage in moving firefights and hand-to-hand fighting, something that more poorly trained units were incapable of or unwilling to attempt. Except for their best elite units, which were made up of their most highly trained soldiers, the Germans were vulnerable to such tactics. Fortunately for us, they did not man their fortifications with high-quality troops at this stage of the war.

The prospect of assaulting the Siegfried Line frightened most Allied soldiers because of what we had heard about it from Nazi propaganda and other sources. In the late 1930s, when we went to the movies as kids, we had seen newsreels describing its construction. And the 82d had gained some slight experience with the northern end of it near Mook when it was in Holland. Although we did not attack any of its formidable bunkers, we sent numerous patrols through the spaces between them, and I had been on a patrol that penetrated the full depth of the line there. There was little doubt that the Siegfried Line on the Belgian-German border was far stronger than it was along the Dutch-German frontier.

We were given sample maps showing a typical portion of the Seigfried Line, although not necessarily the portion that we were going to assault, as the target area was still a secret. Thanks to aerial photographs, the maps depicted the exact location of every bunker and even the intervening infantry positions.

The Siegfried Line was a long, continuous fortification that extended along the German border from the Waal River in the north to the Rhine River just north of Strasbourg, France. In most places it consisted of two belts, each a mile or more in depth. Where they built only one belt, it was much deeper. The main and strongest belt was called the Scharnhorst Belt. About a mile behind it was Schill Belt, which contained mostly long-range artillery. Our intelligence officers reported that the Scharnhorst Belt was strongly manned, but the Schill Belt contained little more than the manpower needed for the artillery.

A few hundred yards in front of the Scharnhorst Belt were the famed "dragon teeth." These were large, solid, reinforced-concrete structures rising four to ten feet from ground level. Tanks could not ride over them, and they were too close together for tanks to move between them. Infantry positions were placed in front of, among, and behind the dragon teeth to keep our infantry and engineers from approaching them with demolitions. Mines were also sown among and around the teeth.

The Germans built numerous reinforced-concrete bunkers that were almost impervious to artillery fire or bombs from fighter-bombers. These bunkers were well camouflaged so they could not be seen easily by artillery observers or from the air. In the mile-deep Scharnhorst Belt, the bunkers were arranged so that they could support one another with overlapping fields of fire.

The bunkers in the first tier of the Scharnhorst Belt were spaced irregularly about two hundred to four hundred yards apart. Each bunker had at least one casement for an 88mm gun, which could transverse about 60 degrees to either side. These guns provided low-angle fire against tanks or groups of infantry. The bunkers also had ports through which the defenders could fire rifles and machine guns at infantrymen trying to attack them. Some bunkers had steel hatches in their roofs through which mortars could be fired at approaching enemy troops.

The Germans had also dug trenches and set up machine-gun nests and strong points throughout the first tier. Many of these were also covered with reinforced concrete. These positions were designed to cover the spaces between the larger bunkers, protecting them from teams of tanks and infantry trying to get through the gaps.

About three hundred yards behind the first tier of bunkers in the Scharnhorst Belt was a similarly designed line of defenses. The second tier could offer fire support for the first-tier defenders during an attack. The Scharnhorst Belt contained about five such tiers.

Clearly, if everything worked as the Germans intended, breaching the Siegfried Line would be a formidable task indeed.

However, some things had radically changed in our favor since the Seigfried Line had been built. Static defenses had become obsolete during the early years of the war. In 1940, German armored spearheads bypassed the vaunted Maginot Line, and the defenders were forced to surrender without ever fighting after the rest of the French army collapsed. The Siegfried Line had been breached in several places in the fall of 1944 by new and superior mobile strategies and tactics. New and effective weapons that did not even exist in 1940 when German armor bypassed the French static defenses had also been developed and were available to us in 1945.

Breaching such a strong fortified line required a complex attack plan, a process that included many steps, none of which could falter or the attempted breach would fail. The 505th's operations officer gave us a detailed explanation of how this plan would pierce the Siegfried Line. The 1st and 82d Divisions would attack side-by-side simultaneously, each holding a regiment in reserve. The first step was for artillery to drive off the German infantry protecting the dragon teeth so engineers could reach the minefields in front of and between them. Our artillery would fire enough smoke shells to shield the engineers from German eyes while they cleared mines from a selected portion of dragon teeth. Our infantry would then move up and capture the dragon teeth so engineers could again be brought forward to clear a path through them for our tanks. Infantry and tanks would then pass through the dragon teeth and establish defensive enclaves beyond them. Much of this would have to be accomplished after dark.

The operations officer pointed out that tanks and bunkers had many similarities. Both had substantial strength in weapons and were thick-skinned and difficult to destroy. However, both had limited vision because the occupants could only see out through slits, telescopes, and periscopes when buttoned up under attack, which produced blind spots. The main difference between tanks and bunkers was that a tank was mobile, whereas a bunker was stationary. If they were not well protected by infantry, both tanks and bunkers were highly vulnerable to attack by infantry supported by engineers who were specially equipped to destroy them.

He then told us how we would take advantage of these weaknesses and breach the line. The first assault would be against three carefully chosen target spaces between four bunkers. A few rounds of artillery would be fired on each bunker to drive the enemy troops into them, forcing them to button up. White phosphorus smoke shells would be fired around the bunkers to temporarily blind the occupants. Next, a heavy artillery barrage would be fired on the infantry positioned in the spaces between bunkers. Killing or driving off the infantry in these gaps would allow our infantry and tanks to move relatively freely between and behind the bunkers.

Tanks and a company of infantry would maintain fire on each of the bunkers once they were buttoned up. The artillery would shift its fires to the next tier of defenses, smothering them with a barrage consisting of a mix of air-bursting, high explosive, and white phosphorus smoke rounds. The purpose of this artillery fire was to blind the defenders in the rear tiers and to interfere with any attempts to move reinforcements forward. Protected by smoke, an infantry battalion (two companies with one in reserve) would attack each of the target spaces with the objective of killing or driving the enemy infantry away.

Once a gap was cleared, infantry flamethrower teams, tanks, and engineers with explosive satchel charges would move around the bunkers on each side of the space. The flamethrowers would blind a bunker's firing slits while a tank maneuvered to fire directly into the entry door in its rear. If tank and bazooka fire did not open the door, the engineers would set satchel charges against it and throw smaller charges through the bunker's larger openings.

We were told this process usually resulted in the surrender of the bunker's surviving defenders. We were also warned to be ready for an unpleasant German surprise once we took the positions between the bunkers: the Germans preregistered artillery fire on their bunkers and other defenses and fired on them when they surrendered. The operations officer said we either had to go into the bunker or move beyond it to avoid this fire. Once the German artillery fire stopped, we were to get the captured German soldiers to the POW cages in the rear. The engineers would then destroy the bunker before we moved on. Blowing up the bunkers would eliminate the possibility that the Germans might recapture and use them again. By knocking out four adjacent bunkers we would open a space about a thousand yards wide in the first tier of the line.

The assault battalion would continue fighting until it had knocked out four bunkers, then move back into reserve. The next battalion would either widen the breach in the first tier by flanking the two bunkers on either side of it or deepen the penetration by repeating the process on the next tier of bunkers. He estimated it would take us a week to penetrate the entire Scharnhorst Belt using these tactics.

We were also made familiar with another technology that would be available to us. A team of experts in directing counterbattery fire would set up sound equipment that could accurately determine the direction from which the enemy fired an artillery piece. Several such stations would be set up across our front and if two stations got a fix on the same battery, they could establish the exact position of the enemy guns by a simple triangulation process. It was understood that such counterbattery targets would have priority over all other targets except for a major German counterattack, which no one expected.

Colonel Ekman said this new doctrine for attacking lines of bunkers was developed by the troops who penetrated the Siegfried Line at several points before winter set in, and it had worked well. He pointed out that as our penetration deepened, German troops in bypassed bunkers would often be abandoned and that follow-up forces would need to be alert for them.

When the colonel finished, several questions were asked, and many points were discussed over a period of an hour or so. When it was over, no one was enthusiastic about the idea of assaulting such a formidable objective, but all felt better that we at least had a solid plan. We were ordered not to discuss the objective or the plan with any soldier not present at the briefing until we reached the German border.

The Siegfried Line had been designed to take advantage of natural terrain features and was situated to make approaching it as difficult as possible for attackers. One important factor compromised the design: the requirement that the line be continuous for many hundreds of miles. To maintain continuity, the designers had been forced to make terrain compromises that produced short stretches that were weaker than other parts of the line. Another compromising factor was that they had not been able to build any of their fortifications across the border in Belgium, where superior ground was available.

Our planners expended much time and effort finding a soft stretch in the general area we were to assault. Such a stretch was apparent in the line between Udenbreth in the north and Hunderfeld to the south. There, the land on the Belgian side of the border was higher than the land a few hundred yards east where the Siegfried Line had been built. Another advantage was that woods on the Belgian side approached the border so we could make our attack preparations without being easily seen.

The drive toward the Siegfried Line began on 28 January. Each of the forward observer teams was assigned to accompany an infantry battalion as we moved east, and the main body of the 456th PFAB moved a few miles behind the infantry, keeping pace. The snow on the roads was too deep for wheeled vehicles, so tanks, a few with blades on them, broke trail for trucks carrying troops.

Resistance was sporadic and light as we moved east but occasionally the infantry had to stop and attack small pockets of defenders. When this happened we would have to set up our guns and provide supporting fire. On 29 January Battery A fired on such a group of resisters and then remained in position overnight. The next morning we received a few rounds of counterbattery fire, which killed my friend Pvt. Thomas F. Boyce and seriously wounded another friend, Cpl. William N. Needham.

We moved east from Malmédy toward Losheim on the same road the Germans had taken in the opposite direction in mid-December. There was still a great assortment of American and German wreckage scattered about—tanks, trucks, artillery pieces, just about everything that two defeated armies could have left behind.

It was cold, and the ground was too frozen to dig graves. Back from the road a hundred yards or so we saw several stacks of bodies. The dead soldiers had been stacked like cordwood in piles that were about six bodies high and maybe a hundred feet long. From a distance, the frozen bodies appeared undamaged. They looked more like soldiers sleeping uncomfortably one on top of another than dead men. However, the long hair blowing in the wind made it seem much more personal. Most of the stacks were German as indicated by the gray uniforms, but at least one was olive drab. This was a vivid mortality check for every one of us.

The stacks of dead brought my attention to a change in the air I had not yet noticed. In June in Normandy and in Holland in the fall, the battlefield was overwhelmed by the stench of death until the graves registration people collected and removed the dead for burial. In frozen Belgium, the rock-hard bodies did not smell at all. Although it was still horrible, the intense cold made the deadly conditions of battle seem clean, almost sterile.

As we approached the German border we were told we would attack what appeared to be a weaker stretch of the Siegfried Line just south of the German hamlet of Udenbreth. After we breached the line, an armored task force would pass through and drive eastward to the Rhine. This is not to say that the Siegfried Line was intrinsically weak in this area, only that the point our intelligence people had selected for our attack was a little weaker than it was elsewhere.

Tiny Udenbreth was the only hamlet of any size in the twenty miles between the larger towns of Monschau to the north and Losheim to the south. This pastoral, wooded area was one of Hitler's favorite vacation spots. What few roads there were amounted to narrow forest trails through woods that were an extension of the Ardennes. Much of the German land across the border behind the Siegfried Line had been cleared for farming while most on the Belgian side remained undisturbed woods.

We completed our morbid drive through eastern Belgium, arriving in our assembly area west of Udenbreth in the early afternoon on 30 January. We moved into an open area about two miles west of the border and set up our artillery batteries. The 505th PIR was in hilly woods between our position and the border. Many of the 456th's officers and the observation teams went forward to check out the target area. We were careful not to be seen, but what we saw did not encourage us much. As far as we could see from north to south, there stretched an endless ribbon of dragon teeth. Although we could not make out any of the well-camouflaged German fortifications behind them, we knew they were there. The Siegfried Line looked even more formidable and threatening than we had expected it to be.

14

The 82d Airborne Breaches the Siegfried Line

The mere title of this chapter seems ridiculous. Airborne divisions were made up of lightly armed troops, organized to establish airheads behind enemy lines so that attacks could be made in depth, contrary to the concept of only attacking the crust of the enemy's defenses. The forces assigned to attack the crust were designed and provided with the heavy weapons to do so. Coordinated assaults by both of these forces had proven effective. Now, the lightly armed 82d had been ordered to attack the enemy's strongest defenses, the Siegfried Line.

Beginning shortly before dawn on the morning of 31 January 1945, we laid a heavy barrage on the dragon teeth and fired numerous smoke shells at the bunkers behind them. These bunkers were invisible to us but they had been carefully plotted on our maps. The maps clearly showed all the terrain details around the bunkers, with the locations of the German fortifications depicted in red. Aerial infrared and plain photography had been used to identify the carefully concealed positions. The many people who carefully analyzed millions of such pictures over thousands of hours did a wonderful job and missed very little.

As our infantry moved toward the dragon teeth, we lifted and shifted our fire to the bunker locations and the spaces between them. This fire cloaked the activities of our infantrymen. Our intelligence officers had selected a choice location that placed us on higher ground than the Germans manning the defenses, giving us a terrain advantage against them. We could observe their defensive positions in front of and among the dragon teeth and fire down on them, whereas they could not see our positions well. The superiority of our

Map 5: 82nd Airborne Division Major
Battles in Germany:
The Siegfried Line and Beyond

☆ Breaching the Siegfried Line

★ The Huertgen Forest

★ Crossing the Elbe River

0   50   100

Miles

position forced the Germans to abandon their prepared defenses in the dragon teeth.

The first attacking infantrymen to reach the dragon teeth found many antipersonnel mines in front of and near them, and a number of men suffered serious wounds. They held their ground but could advance no farther until the engineers, who were expert at disarming mines, were brought forward. While we fired smoke shells to try to protect them, the engineers cleared a path a hundred feet wide and laid out strips of white tape to identify the cleared area. This took over an hour and cost them a few casualties. However, their efforts allowed the infantrymen to move through the dragon teeth and push out about two hundred yards beyond, where they dug in as best they could using timber and whatever else they could find to help protect them on the frozen ground. At the same time, the engineers set about widening the area cleared of mines. Then they began to blow up individual dragon teeth to make three passages for tanks and other vehicles to move through.

One advantage we had in this situation was that we were not fighting first-class German infantry who would have immediately counterattacked the position we had gained to try to drive us from it. These troops were fortress troops who were trained only to defend bunkers, and they were usually made up of young boys, overage men, and veterans recovering from wounds. Almost all of these men were in poor physical condition. This is not to say that they were helpless. They were well armed and held superior defensive positions. They were quite capable of killing many of us as we tried to drive them out of their strong, relatively comfortable fortifications. However, they were not capable of fighting with us at close quarters on anything close to even terms. Thus, I was clear to all that this fighting would be different than any we had encountered previously.

By the end of the first day our infantry had occupied a strong position in and beyond the dragon teeth, and we all spent the night bringing up logs to strengthen the position against fire from rifles, machine guns, mortars, and artillery. Up and down the two-division front similar penetrations had been successful. Our four-man observation team built a lean-to against a dragon tooth using several six- to eight-inch logs we had cut. This gave us some protection against shell fragments from above. Underneath the forward part of the lean-to we built a wall three logs high and two deep as protection against incoming small-arms fire. We always had the option of moving behind the concrete tooth itself, which offered far better protection from enemy fire. From this position, we referred to our map to see where the target bunkers were supposed to be. We thought we could identify three out of four of those that should be in our view. However, the fourth bunker was too well camouflaged for us to find with our binoculars, so we had to assume it was where the map showed it to be.

During the night a number of infantry patrols scouted the enemy positions. They took advantage of the fortress mentality of the troops facing them, finding only a few enemy soldiers in the open outside the warmth and protection of the bunkers. They killed most of these men. The patrols confirmed that all four bunkers were in the exact positions shown on our maps. The patrol leaders recommended an attack be made a few hours before dawn since they believed the German soldiers would not man the positions between the bunkers much before daylight. Throughout the war, few German soldiers showed any desire to fight in large numbers at night. These bunker-bound Germans liked night fighting even less. Although night fighting was difficult and unpleasant, our infantrymen were well trained in it and used their skill to advantage.

The Germans were familiar with our tendency to lay down heavy artillery barrages just prior to an infantry attack. Therefore, if the intelligence gained from our patrols was correct, a prolonged artillery barrage would only alert them to our intentions. Our commanders decided to delay the barrage until the infantry reached their jump-off line about a hundred yards from the German positions. An hour before dawn, the infantry crawled toward the jump-off line. When they reached it their commanding officer fired a flare. We responded immediately with a three-minute barrage from three artillery battalions that hammered the German positions between the bunkers. At the same time, tanks began to fire at the bunkers from the higher ground west of the dragon teeth to keep them buttoned up and hold the attention of their occupants. After our short barrage, we again shifted our fire so that it would hit the German positions to the rear of the targeted bunkers with a mixture of smoke, high explosive, and POZIT shells. Within ten minutes our infantry had captured all the positions between the four target bunkers without taking any casualties. They waited there until tanks, flamethrower teams, and engineers carrying explosives moved forward to support them at first light, and then the combined force moved beyond the bunkers as our mortars and artillery fired smoke rounds at the bunkers in the second tier to blind the occupants.

About this time enemy artillery rounds began to fall among the dragon teeth. Apparently an enemy observer had deduced that someone in the dragon teeth was directing our artillery fire. One of the counterbattery fire-direction units was about twenty yards to our right. I worked my way to their position only to find that they had been hit. Two of the men were slightly wounded and their radio had been destroyed. However, they had managed to get a good bearing on the guns firing at us. Their officer, who had not been wounded, crawled back to our position with me, and we dispatched some medics to take care of his comrades. By means of a roundabout radio routing we were able to pass their information to their headquarters. This data was combined with information obtained from another station and the coordinates of the enemy guns were given to the artillery battalions in our rear. They fired more than a hundred rounds at the German artillery positions. All this occurred within about five minutes of our arrival back at my team's position. The counterbattery fire was extremely effective; we suffered no more from such a concentration of enemy artillery fire upon our positions that day.

We developed great respect for these sound-direction experts. Throughout the rest of this campaign we always made it a point to know where they were, and we no longer begrudged giving their targets preference over our own target priorities. After our initial easy success, the bunkers themselves proved harder and more costly to capture than we expected. Two of our tanks in the immediate front were destroyed, although the tankers escaped with minor wounds and burns, and enemy artillery fire killed two and wounded a dozen infantrymen and engineers attacking the two bunkers immediately to our front. Nevertheless, all four bunkers were captured by noon. The occupants were quickly rounded up and sent to the rear as prisoners of war. As soon as they were cleared, the engineers began rigging charges to destroy the bunkers—except for one the battalion commander planned to use as his temporary headquarters. They finally blew the charges later that night. The loud explosions woke up everyone on both sides.

In the early afternoon another infantry battalion moved into the forward attack position. As we fired smoke rounds at the next tier of bunkers, the troops with us withdrew behind the dragon teeth into the woods at the top of the rise. Our little team went back with them and was replaced by another observer team for the attack that was to be made on the second tier that afternoon. We went back to the battalion position, exhilarated by the success of the day. We were pleased to tell everyone just how effective the artillery fire had been during the attack.

The next afternoon, after two other battalions had taken four bunkers in the second tier, we were brought back to the front with orders to take six bunkers located to the south in the first tier. It was thought that these would be easier than the first ones we had captured since these bunkers could be taken in the flank and rear from the more advanced positions we held. This proved to be true. Two of the bunkers were empty and three of the remaining four surrendered when smoke shells were fired behind them and the tanks fired at their fronts. Rather than waiting for us to attack the rear doors, the occupants of three of the bunkers opened the doors themselves and showed white flags. However, the occupants of the other bunker offered heavy resistance and had to be forced to surrender.

Since we had been ordered to stay in the line that night, the infantry battalion commander invited us to stay with them in the bunker he had kept intact. The engineers had blown a hole on the side toward our line so everyone could escape in either of two directions in the unlikely event the Germans counterattacked. The covered bunker was a comfortable change since the Germans had equipped it with a stove that kept us all warm during the night. They even had a toilet. We were not too impressed with the sausages, black bread, and sauerkraut the Germans had left behind. Unlike most of the others, who chose to eat their U.S. rations, I decided to try the German food. The bread felt and tasted like sawdust, and the sausages had a rank flavor but did not make me sick. My curiosity was satisfied and I stuck to our rations thereafter.

The 82d always sent out patrols at night to gather intelligence about the enemy immediately to our front. This practice proved particularly effective during the Siegfried Line campaign. That night in the bunker I talked with an infantry platoon sergeant named Smith who was an old acquaintance. He had led the patrol that escorted our team behind German lines in Holland. Smith was a four-jump man who twice had been offered a battlefield commission. He refused each time saying he did not like officers and did not want to deal with them any more than he had to, particularly on a social basis.

Night patrols were usually made by volunteer groups of two to four men. To be effective and survive, they needed four main attributes. They had to be able to move silently, see well in the dark, sense the presence of other men nearby, and kill quickly and quietly with a knife. Only a few well-trained infantrymen—maybe one in a hundred—had these qualifications, and they volunteered to go most of the time. As a reward for this duty, they were not required to take part in the action the next day. Although there is no such thing as safe duty in war, some men thought patrolling was less risky than assaulting an enemy force in well-prepared positions or other battlefield actions.

Smith pointed out a baby-faced nineteen year old who always volunteered for patrols. He said that since Normandy the man had been on fifty or so patrols and that he seldom came back without killing two or three Germans. Smith said he thought the man enjoyed killing. We wondered what he would be like if he made it home, which we both believed was an unlikely possibility. Most men who went out on patrol felt they were going into danger. However, Smith said that when "baby face" went on patrol he *was* the danger. On reflection, we were all killers. My artillery observation team had probably killed many times the number of German soldiers that "baby face" had. Was there really any difference between those who killed up close and personally with a knife and those who killed remotely by ordering long-range cannon to fire on enemy soldiers?

Frequently a patrol was asked to capture a German soldier for interrogation. This meant one of our patrols had to silently pull an enemy soldier out of his foxhole and bring him back to headquarters, where it was hoped he would disclose valuable information. This kind of overt action on a patrol increased the risk manyfold. When the order was to bring back an officer, it made things even more difficult and dangerous because officers were seldom alone and usually occupied more secure positions than did common soldiers.

While I was in the bunker that night four men, including "baby face," were sent out to bring back an officer. They left at midnight and three of them returned at about 0500 with an SS *panzergrenadier* captain, which indicated some new and unexpected development might have occurred. The patrol had encountered a three-man German patrol led by the SS captain. A silent knife fight ensued and they killed the other two Germans but lost a comrade, whose body they also carried back. "Baby face" had survived again.

One of our intelligence officers was a Jew who had fled to the United States from Germany before the war. His German was fluent and idiomatic, and he was expert at persuading prisoners that Germany could no longer win the war. He also tried to persuade German captives that they would be safe and would sit out the rest of the war in comparative comfort if they cooperated. He was able to convince many prisoners, including the SS captain, that they should cooperate in order to get better treatment and maybe to be sent home sooner.

The SS captain gave us much valuable information. He told us he was from the 9th SS Panzer Division and that he had fought for four years in Russia, Holland, and now Belgium and that he knew their cause was lost. It turned out that he spoke fluent English, so after an initial exchange in German, he spoke English. All who were nearby overheard the exchange. He told us he felt lucky to be safe. He said his unit consisted of about four hundred survivors of the fighting in Belgium and that most were still recovering from minor wounds. They had been sent to give some infantry backbone to the fortress troops in the sector we were trying to break through. However, he could not see what four hundred tired and injured men could do against two elite Ami divisions, especially since the fortress troops were hopelessly inadequate as soldiers. The *panzergrenadiers* had been told to concentrate on laying antipersonnel mines to slow us up. He also told us we had only two more tiers of bunkers to take and that the bunkers in the Schill Belt were not well prepared for defense.

He was defensive about being a member of the Waffen SS. He tried to persuade us that they were no different from the Wehrmacht, the regular German army. He said officers, particularly generals and colonels, were interchanged between these forces and that they often fought side-by-side. We were not persuaded. We later found that most German soldiers and civilians tried to distance themselves from the Nazis. They tried to tell us that they knew nothing of the evil Nazis were doing; they always said they personally had never done anything wrong.

The next day we followed the same routine. In four days of hard fighting we had advanced two miles, breaching the entire Scharnhorst Belt. However, we soon learned we had little to celebrate since we had been ordered to turn the breach over to the 99th Infantry Division, which in turn had orders to hold in place. In spite of our success, there would be no armored drive through the breach to the Rhine. Meanwhile, we had been ordered to go to another vicious hot spot of the war: the Huertgen Forest. Everyone from General Gavin down felt this failure to follow up our successful breaching operation was a betrayal of the good men who became casualties. It surely seemed like the high command had wasted our time and our lives in a very difficult and futile effort.

Many men wondered why we had been asked to fight so hard for these bunkers. Attempting the breach was utter foolishness if there was no intent to follow it up once we broke through. And if the decision was made *after* the breach was actually accomplished, the decision to do nothing further seemed even more foolish. These questions, among other things, made us think that our senior generals thought little about the consequences of their decisions. Was this callous betrayal the result of their attention being focused more on the army politics that would determine the rank they would hold after the war was over?

15

The Huertgen Forest

By the time we arrived in Germany's Huertgen Forest it was a huge graveyard of unburied corpses. After the war, I read some military history and found many references to battles in forests, most of which were disastrous. In the fall of 1944, fighting in the Huertgen Forest had cost seven American divisions thirty-three thousand men killed, wounded, or captured. The small German town of Schmidt was adjacent to the Roer River dams. These dams gave the Germans the ability to flood the river downstream and disrupt the planned American drive across the Roer, the last obstacle to moving up to the west bank of the Rhine. If our forces were only partially across the Roer when the flooding occurred, those not yet across would be unable to support them. This would make the men already across the river vulnerable to being surrounded and captured.

In September 1944 most soldiers and generals were convinced the war would be over by Christmas. There was a short time before the Germans had a chance to organize their Siegfried Line defenses when the Allies had a real opportunity to breach it easily and reach the Rhine. Unfortunately the general euphoria, overconfidence, and logistical and intelligence failures caused the effort to make many breaches and destroy large parts of the Siegfried Line to fail. This failure extended the war and cost many lives.

Commanders and intelligence officers had failed to grasp the importance of the Roer dams earlier, when they could have been destroyed or captured easily. Then, to compound this failure, an inadequate force—the U.S. 28th Infantry Division—was given the mission of driving through the Kall Valley in the Huertgen Forest to capture Schmidt. An infantry corps of three divisions might have completed the task successfully, but a single division had little chance in terrain where a few well-trained defenders had a great advantage. To make matters worse, the Huertgen was part of the Siegfried Line and had its full share of bunkers and pillboxes. In spite of all these impediments the 28th Infantry Division succeeded in capturing Schmidt. Still, army intelligence did not recognize how important Schmidt was to any future U.S. advance across the Roer. Thus, they did not call for the additional reinforcements the division required if it was to have any chance to hold its position in Schmidt. The Germans launched a fierce counterattack, and the 28th Division lost six thousand men in just ten days as it was driven out of Schmidt and back across the Kall Valley by German troops under commanders who understood the critical nature of the ground over which they fought. After this failure, the U.S. high command sent division after division piecemeal into the meat grinder of the Huertgen Forest in vain attempts to recover the town the 28th Division had placed in their possession in November. Their repeated failures in the bloody debacles in the Huertgen represented the greatest defeat the U.S. Army suffered in the ETO.

Our trip from Udenbreth to the Huertgen Forest town of Vossenach took about eight hours in a cold, driving rain. About a mile across the Kall River from Vossenach was another small town, Kommerscheidt. Schmidt is a mile farther south. The intervening valley was 450 feet deep and heavily wooded, with only the steep, winding, dirt and gravel Kall Trail connecting the towns. The slopes of the ravine were steep, and another rough road wound through the valley floor along the banks of the Kall River. This was part of the ground that soldiers from six American divisions had fought over before our arrival. Spring was early that year, and in early February the heavy snow from the bitter winter was beginning to melt. There was mud everywhere. This was the scene that greeted the 82d Airborne's 505th RCT when it pulled into Vossenach on 7 February.

When we arrived we learned that a special unit called Task Force A had been formed. It consisted of the 505th PIR and 456th PFAB from the 82d, the 17th Airborne Division's 517th PIR, and other artillery and armored units. Task Force A's mission was to cross the Kall

Valley and capture Schmidt, other nearby towns on the far ridge, and the Roer River dams.

The day before we arrived, General Gavin and his aides had personally scouted the Kall Trail. Based on his reconnaissance, the 505th's 2d Battalion was ordered to make an immediate reconnaissance-in-force down into the valley and then up the other side to determine how far it could go before enemy resistance became strong enough to stop its advance. Our observation team accompanied the battalion's headquarters section.

In the early spring of 1945 the Kall Valley was a nightmarish place. Thousands of dead men from both sides seemed to be rising up from the melting snow. These bodies were in various stages of decay and many were so grotesque that they were almost unrecognizable as human. As the weather warmed, the stench became overwhelming. Along the road and the stream at the bottom of the valley were dozens of bodies of men whose wounds plainly had not been serious enough to kill them. The bodies were on litters and cots in a large abandoned aid station. The men had been left behind and died a slow, painful death as a result of exposure when their doctors, attendants, and comrades fled. What a terrible way to die.

This panorama was the most bizarre and horrid that I saw during the war. Part of the basis of the 82d's élan stemmed from the fact that we were convinced the main difference between a civilized army and a callous mob was how it cared for its own and its enemy's wounded and dead. The 82d had always been meticulous in its care for its wounded and dead. We had been forced to leave a few dead behind enemy lines, but the thought of abandoning wounded in mass was so revolting to us that many of our men had great trouble dealing with what they saw there. We also blamed the First Army command, which could have negotiated a truce with the enemy so that both sides could recover their dead and wounded. Such callousness was appalling, and the First Army Command lost our respect for allowing this terrible thing to happen. To be wounded was bad enough, but to be left to die by your commanders, doctors, and comrades was unthinkable.

The battalion set out down the ravine from Vossenach at dawn. Most of the column of about a thousand men began walking down the Kall Trail with scouts and engineers leading the way looking for any sign of the enemy, especially mines. They frequently halted the column while they disarmed mines. Next in the column was a platoon of infantry. The battalion headquarters, which included our four-man team, followed in six jeeps. The rest of the battalion completed the column. The trail was in terrible shape wherever the sun could reach it. The shady areas were icy and snow-packed, but where the sun shone on the road the surface quickly turned to slush and eventually to six-inch deep mud as the day grew warmer.

The American divisions that fought in the Huertgen Forest in the fall of 1944 had performed one important task that helped us to make our move easier and far more safely. Whenever they captured a bunker, their engineers immediately destroyed it. Thus, we did not have to face Germans in strong defensive positions during our trek through the ravine. Part way down, the jeeps began having great difficulty even staying on the slippery trail. The colonel stopped his vehicle and all but the driver got out and walked. We quickly followed his example. We would have sent the jeeps back but it was impossible for them to make it up the icy and muddy trail back to our starting point.

The lighter load did make the jeeps a little more able to deal with the problems of the road. As we continued down we observed that about a dozen tanks had slid off the road and down the 60-degree slope. The hatches on the tanks were open, so we figured the crews got out safely, although probably with dirty drawers and bad headaches. Numerous jeeps and trucks had also fallen into the untidy heap on the valley floor. When we reached the bottom the drivers parked the jeeps along the river road and everyone began climbing the steep, winding trail that ran up the other side of the gorge. The sun did not reach the north-facing slope as well as it had the route down, so the road up was still covered with ice and snow. It was a narrow choice, but I recall we preferred the ice and snow to mud. We were used to the convenience of the jeep, and we struggled up the steep trail carrying forty-pound packs that contained our food, bedrolls, dry clothing, and other personal items. In addition, we carried personal weapons and ammunition. We took turns carrying the sixty-pound radio, which was our only link to the guns at Vossenach because it was impractical to lay wire given the conditions. If ever the extremely strenuous physical paratrooper training helped us to perform difficult physical tasks, it did on that day.

Except for occasional halts while engineers removed mines, we made good time. In addition to being dangerous to us, exploding mines would announce our approach and alert any defenders who might be on the ridge overlooking the ravine. We were also anxious to reach the top in order to attack quickly and take full advantage of surprise.

We reached the top on the far side in late morning. Although we had been told that a large German force held Kommerscheidt and Schmidt, by noon we had moved into Kommerscheidt, encountering only minor resistance along the way. Kommerscheidt was held by only about a hundred Germans and our infantry captured it in less than an hour. The prisoners they took told us they thought the Amis had had enough of fighting in the Kall Valley the previous fall, and they had not expected another such attack. They also said their main defenses were west of Schmidt on the road to Lammersdorf. This meant that our force had gained a very threatening position well behind the main German force. We were on high, open ground, and Schmidt was only another mile away. We could not believe that it, too, was weakly defended, so we ordered a heavy artillery barrage on the town, after which a platoon-sized patrol was sent toward Schmidt to evaluate the town's defenses.

The patrol returned an hour later. The patrol leader reported that they had entered Schmidt and encountered only token opposition from a few ineffective snipers. We radioed regimental headquarters with word that Schmidt seemed ready for the taking, and two more infantry battalions were sent to join us. By 1430 the snipers had been killed or driven off, and we had captured the town with ease. By dark the entire regiment was in Schmidt. However, we soon found ourselves in the same situation a 28th Division battalion had faced when it captured Schmidt the previous fall: we could not receive any supplies by the route we had taken to get there since no vehicles could get through the Kall River gorge. Like the 28th Division men in late

1944, we were in danger of being surrounded and destroyed. Nevertheless, we were all confident. Being surrounded was nothing new to us. We had been surrounded several times in our earlier war experience and survived. Our reaction was to build a strong defensive perimeter around the town. We were certain the rest of the division would not allow us to be trapped anywhere, much less in Schmidt.

V Corps headquarters was in Lammersdorf, six miles west of Schmidt, and a hard road over high ground connected the two towns. After we spent the night unsupported in Schmidt, V Corps sent a combined tank-infantry force to assist us. It drove down the road against moderate opposition while more Task Force A troopers crossed the Kall Valley to join us.

After the war, General Gavin wrote a paper questioning the attack on Schmidt through the Kall Valley the previous fall. In his opinion, an army skilled in maneuver and having substantial superiority in men, armor, and artillery should choose its fights in areas where it can best take advantage of its superior skills and numbers. It was foolish to become bogged down in rough forests where these advantages were canceled out by terrain in the hands of skilled defenders. It was also a waste of the U.S. Army's most precious commodity: its skilled manpower.

That the high ground approach to Schmidt was practical was demonstrated by the comparative ease with which V Corps units moved into the town in February 1945. This should have been done the previous fall. Had we done so, the German troops in the valley could have been bypassed and destroyed at our leisure.

The 82d reached the huge Schwammenauel Dam too late to capture it intact; the Germans had already blown it. Although this flooded the Roer River, the flooding would soon subside. The division quickly advanced through the hills and woods to the Roer River below the broken dam. There we were ordered to prepare for an assault crossing by boat. After we secured the far shore and the engineers built a bridge, V Corps could drive down the hill into Duren, a town on the Roer's east bank, thus outflanking the German defenders. The river was swift and running high, making such a crossing dangerous to an extreme. All preparations were made for the crossing, and we were ordered to be ready to go on 16 February when the floodwaters were expected to have subsided. Luckily for us, we received orders on the fifteenth to abandon our plans for the river crossing, turn the enterprise over to another division, and prepare to return to France on the seventeenth. The winter war was over for the 82d. We were all delighted.

16

Back to France

By 19 February we were back at Camp Suippes near Épernay. As it had been previously, our first problem was to replace our old, worn, personal equipment and uniforms. After our service in the snow and mud, almost everything was in hopeless condition, so this process took most of two weeks.

Since the battalion had no need of forward observers while it was in barracks, I again became a special services NCO. Private Marcel Four, who had previously served as my driver, told me he needed an excuse to visit his relatives in Alsace and that he thought we could trade things only U.S. soldiers had for local food stuffs and liquor. Alsace is a province in France that has a mixed French and German heritage. Alsace and another province, Lorraine, had changed from French to German control in 1870. In 1919 the two provinces were returned to the French under the terms of the Treaty of Versailles. Germany reclaimed them in 1940.

Most of Alsace had been liberated during the fall of 1944, and Marcel was anxious to visit and help his relatives in any way he could. The Germans only recently had been driven out of the Colmar Pocket west of the Rhine in Alsace, and he did not know whether his family had been in the area controlled by the Germans or only close to it. We sold the idea to the battery commander and set off for Alsace with a jeep and trailer on the twenty-fifth. We took five days' worth of personal rations in cans and other containers, extra sugar and coffee, cigarettes, and medical supplies such as aspirin, iodine, stomach remedies—simple things that we knew were in short supply in France. We also took fifteen empty five-gallon water cans, which we hoped to fill with wine.

Our destination was a small village east of the town of Saint-Dié across the Vosges Mountains in the Alsatian farmlands. We drove southeast for a short distance before being stopped by 82d Airborne MPs. However, our papers were in order, so they allowed us to proceed. Military policemen stopped us several more times along the way, but the most serious delay was in the old fortress town of Nancy. There we were led to the MP headquarters and our jeep was searched while they called our battalion headquarters to verify our status. After apologizing and releasing us, the duty officer explained that there were more than fifty thousand American deserters scattered throughout France. Some of them possessed stolen U.S. Army vehicles, so they were searching all vehicles that were not part of an organized convoy. He said they had picked up more than a hundred deserters or soldiers who were absent without leave (AWOL) that week.

After the war it was reported that a hundred thousand American soldiers were classified as deserters or AWOL in the ETO by V-E Day. If a man was away from his unit for less than thirty days he was considered AWOL; after that he was considered to be a deserter. Although deserters were subject to death by firing squad, only one, Pvt. Eddie Slovik, was shot during the war. Usually they received prison sentences of six months to a few years. An AWOL soldier usually received unit punishment of thirty days or more of extra duty or was confined in the local guardhouse.

From Saint-Dié we drove south to Fraize, where the road turned east through the Vosges Mountains. The steep, primitive road twisted and turned through the beautiful mountains. We went through a high pass, the Col du Bonhomme, and down into rolling, hilly country, reaching Marcel's relatives' farm in the late afternoon. Although we were not expected, Marcel's relatives—there were about twenty uncles, aunts, and cousins—warmly received us. None of them were healthy males of military age. All the males of military age had been taken away to serve in either the French or German armies. The first thing we did was give them our rations. Next we divided up the coffee, ten cartons of cigarettes, and medicines we carried among the four households with no strings attached. The women took the bounty to their homes and in about two hours we sat down to a sumptuous meal made from local staples and part of our rations. As usual, we were impressed with how good a French cook could make army rations taste. After dinner, they offered us their best beds. It was my first experience sleeping in a foot-thick feather bed.

The next day they provided us with clean farm clothing while they laundered our uniforms. We had a huge breakfast consisting of fresh eggs, excellent ham, homemade bread, and fresh milk—things we had not eaten for months. We toured the four family farms, which together were quite large. They had a dairy operation, a chicken and egg business, and a variety of orchards and fields where they grew wheat and vegetables. Although the area had been liberated during the fall, it was near the Colmar Pocket, from which the Germans had been driven only a few weeks before we arrived. They feared and respected the German army, and the threat of the enemy returning was very real for these people. They had sold some of their previous year's grain and fruit crops to the American army, and French markets were beginning to open in a few nearby towns. Nevertheless, economic conditions were still terrible for French civilians. As frugal farmers, these people were able to supply most of their own food if only they could prevent the occupying armies from confiscating it.

Every farm actively canned fruits and vegetables, and each had at least one still. They produced schnapps—a concoction that is something like white lightning—from cherries, apricots, and apples, and a vodkalike liquor made from grain or potatoes. At the time we arrived, they were distilling from a cherry mash that had been fermenting for several months. They had a number of large bottles of various types of finished schnapps on hand.

That day, while Marcel and I played with the children and otherwise loafed, they butchered a calf, something they had not done for months, and served us a truly wonderful evening meal. When I told them I liked liver, my portion turned out to be about a pound. They prepared the liver in thin slices with a bacon, apple, and onion sauce, and it was close to the best I have had—before or since. They also served an excellent soup made of cabbage and probably a dozen other ingredients.

On our second full day in Alsace, Marcel and I drove a few miles to the east to see the Kayserberg castle. Situated atop a hill, it had been one of Kaiser Wilhelm's favorite lodges before World War I. It was beautiful from a mile away, and up close it looked like something out of a fairy tale. The castle was deserted but the doors were locked, so we could not go inside.

When we returned, they asked us if we wanted to take some schnapps. We said we could take sixty gallons but we wanted to pay for it. They said we had paid enough but after some negotiation we gave them everything we had left: $150 in American invasion money and five more cartons of cigarettes. They also gave us fifteen gallons of heavy cream, thirty dozen fresh eggs, and four cured hams. They said all of it would keep during our daylong trip back. All of us were highly satisfied with the bartering.

We were sorry to have to leave these kind people, but the next morning we loaded everything into the jeep and trailer and, after another wonderful breakfast, were on the road by 0830. Strangely, no MPs stopped us on the way back until we were near Camp Suippes, where 82d Airborne MPs gave us a cursory inspection and passed us through. Back at our unit, although the schnapps was well received, it was the cream, ham, and eggs that were most enjoyed. The first sergeant placed guards in the kitchen to watch the cooks prepare the eggs. If they had their way, they would break them all into pots and scramble and overcook them. Everyone wanted the eggs fried sunny-side up, and it took the guards' full attention to make sure the cooks prepared them that way. Most of us had not had delicacies such as ham and fried eggs for almost a year. Our trip to Alsace was a success—especially for Marcel and me, who had lived like civilians and tourists for two days and three nights in the middle of a war.

During the short four days we were gone rumors had run wild. The most persistent one was a "good news, bad news" story: the 82d would be going home on the *Queen Mary* on 1 May. However, after thirty days' leave and forty-five days of training, we would parachute into Japan. After one to two years of intermittent combat, everyone wondered how many would come back to the army from such a leave. All of us thought we had done enough, but most said they would continue the war. Variations of this rumor continued until the Japanese surrendered in August. Fortunately we never had to make up our minds whether to come back from leave and participate in another airborne assault.

By this time a point system had been developed to determine the order in which men would be sent home. Points were awarded for time in service, time in the ETO, and for each battle, assault, and medal. As an example, I had 94 points, which eventually got me home in December 1945. Most of the soldiers in the 82d had over 90 points, but many had 140 or more. Another persistent rumor was that everyone with over 100 points would go home and be discharged, independent of the need to fight Japan. This would amount to 40 percent of the division, or about seven thousand men. Many thought this was a great plan and would have been disappointed if it did not happen. However, since this would have taken the best and most experienced soldiers from the division, common sense said it would never occur.

It was also rumored that the British and American airborne divisions would jump into Berlin in an effort to beat the Russians into the enemy capital. It turns out there was a detailed plan for such an operation, but the idea was abandoned in April. The plan involved three American and two British airborne divisions. Two regiments from the 82d and two from the 101st were to seize Templehof Airport, and British paratroopers would make battalion-sized drops on key strong points. The remainder of the five divisions would be airlifted into Templehof. Once the airhead was secured, British and American armored and mobile infantry divisions would race to link up with us in the German capital.

It was an ambitious plan that might have worked given the weakness of the Germans at that time. However, it was politically oriented rather than a military necessity, and it was abandoned because the high command decided it was not worth the projected casualties—which everyone thought would be substantial.

In March we began to see the seeds of another intriguing scheme. The expectation was that the Nazis would abandon northern Germany and concentrate their remaining armies and government leaders in the Bavarian Alps, using this mountainous region as a "national redoubt." The airborne response that was being considered to this enemy move was to have the 82d and 101st parachute into the area in small groups of three to a hundred men, depending on how well individual targets were thought to be defended. All of us were relieved when we heard no more about this idea. Scattering us over thousands of square miles of Germany to fight small-unit actions everywhere just did not seem like a good idea. This plan also turned out to have had a basis in truth.

The news from the front was positive. On 7 March, the 9th Armored Division captured a railroad bridge over the Rhine at Remagen intact and a bridgehead east of the river was being rapidly expanded. We all knew that Field Marshal Montgomery was planning a huge assault crossing of the Rhine in northern Germany. Throughout the ETO, the feeling that the war was almost over had a negative effect on morale. After all, no one wanted to be the last soldier to die—especially when the war was won and one's actions and death would not affect an already destined outcome. We in the 82d were not immune to this feeling. However, with the èlan and pride of excellent all-volunteer units, excellent leaders, and an organization that had been through a lot together, we were probably less affected by these considerations than were most U.S. Army divisions. Besides being made up of mostly draftees who never wanted to fight in the first place, many of these divisions tended to fight poorly because they had been formed late in the war and the best officers were already in the divisions that had been formed earlier. Good leadership was by far the most important requirement for a division to be effective as a fighting unit.

In the second week of March it was announced that the 505th RCT would make a practice parachute jump. Even in practice, parachute jumping was serious business. An average of about 2 percent casualties were suffered on each jump. These consisted mostly of sprains, bruises, and a few broken bones; deaths were infrequent. Very few men welcomed this jump, which at this stage of the war seemed to be an unnecessary risk. However, from the standpoint of our commanders, the division had not jumped since September, and making it was an important part of our preparation for possible missions.

About five thousand troopers made the jump on 15 March. It was uneventful for me, although I made my usual poor landing. However, disaster struck elsewhere. One of the troop-carrier planes lost power—some said it lost a propeller—just as the mass of troopers jumped. The plane fell into a stick of jumpers from a plane ahead of it. Five paratroopers were killed, either hit by the other propeller or by being snagged on the falling plane's wing. The stricken plane crashed and burned in full view of us all, killing its crew. This terrible incident cast a pall over the entire division.

I was summoned to battery headquarters the next day. Lieutenant Cameron was the acting executive officer, replacing another officer who had been wounded. He closed the door and asked me to help him with a problem. I agreed even without knowing what it was because I fully trusted him and respected his judgment. He told me that a mutual friend had refused to jump the previous day and would face a general court-martial for disobeying a direct order unless he promptly made up the jump. I was surprised to learn that the man was Cpl. Jim Hancock, one of my oldest friends in the outfit.

Cameron and I talked about Jim's record and agreed he did not deserve this treatment. We both had been on frequent observation missions with Jim, and we knew he was a good and brave man. He had joined the battalion in Sicily and had fought in six major battles. Along the way, he had been awarded the Purple Heart for wounds and a Silver Star for gallantry in action. He was one of the few doubly decorated soldiers in the battalion. We agreed we had to try to do something to remedy the situation since we knew the court would sentence him to a long prison term followed by a dishonorable discharge. I asked Lieutentant Cameron what he had in mind.

"We'll try to talk him into jumping, and if that doesn't work, we'll throw him out of the plane!" he replied.

Although this was a sign of Lieutenant Cameron's dedication to his men, it was a highly illegal and dangerous plan. He had already enlisted the support of Jim's platoon sergeant, S.Sgt. Russ Burton, so there were three of us in on the scheme. Our biggest concern was that we might become obsessed with getting Jim out of the plane and as a result get tangled up and all fall to our deaths.

The four of us took off in a C-47 from an airport near Reims. If the whole thing had not been so stupid, risky, and serious, the exercise would have been comedic. At first Jim agreed to jump. As we approached the drop zone the first time, Jim was in the door, I was second, Cameron was third, and Russ stood beside the door acting as jumpmaster, ready to follow us out. The idea was that if Jim faltered, Cameron and I would get on either side of him and Russ would move directly behind him. We would then all push him as hard as we could.

Russ followed the routine required of a jumpmaster, and when the green light came on yelled, "Jump!" Jim froze, and when we moved around him he put his feet and hands on both sides of the door and resisted our efforts to push him out. We used all of our strength and were surprised at how strong Jim was. However, after a minute of effort, we knew we had failed.

Cameron told the pilot, who was a drinking buddy, to take a fifteen-minute flight and then return to the drop zone for another try. In the meantime, we tried to get Jim to cooperate. He finally agreed to follow me out the door. This time, when the green light came on I followed Russ's order to jump. After my chute opened, I looked up to see if Jim had followed but I could not see through the canopy. I made a textbook landing: knees bent, a forward roll over both shoulders, and then onto my feet. It was the only perfect jump I ever made, and there was no one else around to see it. I was happy that this one turned out to be my last.

After landing, I looked up and saw the sky was empty. We had failed again. I watched the plane circle and another pass. Finally, after two tries without me, it flew away to the north. It was strange being the only jumper on the drop zone. A truck was supposed to be waiting for us but it had gone back to the airfield following our first attempt after seeing no jumpers.

I gathered my chute together and began to walk to what I thought was the road to Reims. I expected Lieutenant Cameron to send a jeep for me, so I sat beside the road and waited. An 82d MP jeep came by first. To my surprise, the MPs did not give me a hard time and they agreed to take me back to the airfield when I asked them for a ride.

The next day, Jim was given a final chance to jump with a planeload of men who had missed the practice jump due to illness and other reasons. This time he hit the quick release on his harness and dropped his chute on the tarmac. No one could persuade him to put it back on, so he was led away to the division stockade. His trial was scheduled for the following week.

Before the trial we tried to get a doctor to declare Jim a victim of combat fatigue and therefore unfit for duty. This idea also failed. It was obvious the division command was determined to make an example of Jim. Captain Alley, Cameron, Burton, and I testified as to Jim's record and character, but we both also had to testify that he had directly disobeyed Cameron's order when he refused to make the first jump. We left out the details of our subsequent efforts. If we had told them what we had done we probably would have gone to the stockade, too. The court was made up of airborne officers, and they were in a tough spot no matter how much they might have sympathized with Jim's plight. He was technically guilty, and if they did not give him a stiff sentence there was no telling how many other soldiers who had had enough might refuse to follow orders. On the other hand, they all knew the war would soon be over, so they might at least have considered a lighter sentence.

As it was, Jim was sentenced to two years of hard labor at a disciplinary barracks. After serving the sentence, he would receive a dishonorable discharge. Based on his knowledge of Jim's record, one prosecutor told us Jim would probably spend only a couple of months in the stockade and then be sent to another division as a replacement. The whole affair left Lieutenant Cameron and me disgusted with the army and army justice. I wrote a four-page letter to General Eisenhower, and Cameron said he would write or see General Gavin, pleading Jim's case in hopes of his receiving clemency. We heard no more about Jim, and I attempted to contact him a few years later in his hometown, Indianapolis, to no avail.

After the war, Richard Mote, another Battery A comrade who lives in Indianapolis, met Jim on the street. Mote said Jim told him he spent six months at a disciplinary barracks in Italy and it was hell. He returned to the states in November 1945 and was given a dishonorable discharge. Mote said Jim was bitter about the army and everything in general.

Jim Hancock's case was a difficult one for all concerned. His offense was blatant disobedience of a direct order. He was given several chances to cure the problem but did not do so. This left our commanders little choice but to try and convict him. In fact, some clemency *was* granted when his two-year sentence was reduced to six months. The thing that bothered us, his loyal comrades, was that no credit was given him for his outstanding combat service—for which he received two decorations, including the nation's third highest award for valor. It seemed to us that a single transgression wiped all of this out, and we thought that was unfair. On reflection, I conclude there was no good way to handle this bad situation. All things considered, the army did as well as it could have under the circumstances.

On 25 March Field Marshal Montgomery led a successful crossing of the Rhine near Duisburg in northern Germany. The U.S. 17th and British 6th Airborne Divisions made a daylight jump into drop zones on the east bank to secure a bridgehead. They suffered substantial losses from antiaircraft fire during their approach. As was his inclination, Montgomery had spent so much time in meticulous preparation that he disclosed his intentions to the Germans, giving them plenty of time to prepare for the crossing. This was yet another serious intelligence failure. It also seemed foolish to route the flight paths used by the two divisions right over concentrations of antiaircraft guns that were positioned to fire on the streams of Allied bombers headed toward central Germany and the major cities there.

We were glad to leave Camp Suippes on 31 March. All the rumors and doing nothing had sapped our energy, and we looked forward to doing something useful again.

17

On to the Rhine

On 1 April 1945 the 82d was ordered to move to positions on the Rhine's west bank between Cologne and Bonn, centered on the small town of Weiden. Our battalion headquarters was to be located in the nearby town of Bruhl. We were assigned to defend the river so German troops surrounded in the Ruhr Pocket could not cross and escape to the west. Although this was an unlikely prospect, it was our stated purpose for being there. Technically we were still in SHAEF reserve, and we were not expected to see any heavy action on this assignment.

The 82d moved northeast from Camp Suippes near Épernay in two serials, one of vehicles, the other by train. Each group in the vehicle serial had slightly over two hundred men. I again rode in a jeep. The French countryside was beautiful in the springtime. As we crossed the German border south of the ancient city of Trier, we observed a huge change in our surroundings. The French countryside had suffered relatively little damage except in areas just south of the border where General Patton's Third Army had made its preparations to breach the Siegfried Line at one of its strongest points. We saw some damage around Trier, where Patton's men had driven the German defenders out quickly, but the city itself had not been heavily bombed or shelled and thus was in fairly good condition. The roads to the Cologne area ran through woods and some vineyards and were pastoral and pleasant.

When we reached Cologne, moving through it was slow and tedious. There appeared to be no commercial activity; it was a city of women, a few children, and old men. People were living mainly in the intact parts of buildings that had escaped total destruction. Many lived in basements. However, some buildings had been struck in such a way that part of them still stood. The people who lived in those buildings seemed to accept the constant threat of further collapse. There were many rotting corpses in the rubble, so the stench of death was everywhere. The few people we saw on the streets walked with their heads down and looked defeated and haggard.

Even though the war was not yet over, these people had begun the cleanup process. Very few automobiles survived German confiscation or Allied bombing. Many of the wider streets had streetcar tracks down the middle. The tracks were kept clear while they and the streetcars were being repaired. The portions of the roads normally used by automobiles were covered with huge piles of rubble. There was no heavy equipment available to clear the wreckage, so everything had to be done by hand. All able-bodied people living on each block spent their days cleaning it up. They moved from building to building, pulling down damaged walls with ropes and carrying the rubble to the piles in the street.

Clearly, the Germans in the cities had little left of their prewar lives, especially their valuables and property; they had merely survived. Many of these same people had lost sons, fathers, and husbands killed in their five-year war of aggression, and many more had returned with wounds of varying severity. They were forced to rely on their American and British conquerors for food, fuel, and water. Fortunately for them, we proved to be generous in these desperate circumstances.

As we spent more time in Germany, we found that many of the once-proud German women turned to prostitution to support their children and other family members. Soon, large numbers of released German POWs would be returning home—but to what? At least the soldiers who returned would be able to provide the manpower, management, and leadership needed to rebuild their shattered cities.

Our battery set up about ten miles south of Cologne and about two miles from the riverbank. Between the riverbank and a railroad running closely parallel to it was a large grain elevator. It was about twelve stories high and had not been damaged. On top of a structure consisting of eight huge storage bins was a large area that had been used to distribute incoming grain among the bins. Offices with large glazed windows overlooked the river, offering a beautiful view of the Rhine and the countryside beyond. A large, multitrack railroad yard was located directly across the river. The grain elevator seemed like an ideal observation post, and we decided to use it. We immediately broke out all of the windows so there would be no flying glass if the enemy fired at us.

At the same time we were moving into the Cologne area, the British were driving east from their Rhine crossing site near Duisburg in the north, and American troops who had crossed at Remagen farther south were doing the same. These two spearheads had completely surrounded the Ruhr Valley, the industrial heart of Germany. Within the pocket thus formed were 325,000 German troops whose position had become hopeless. Forcing the surrounded enemy troops to surrender as quickly as possible would save many lives for both sides.

Since there had been no interference from our side of the Rhine as yet, the railroad yard was still active when we arrived. To place additional pressure on the Germans in the Ruhr Pocket, we had been ordered to aggressively fire on any targets of opportunity we identified east of the Rhine. We did not expect to find many targets close to the river, so we were straining our eyes through binoculars and a telescope trying to find good targets farther beyond it.

Early in the morning on our second day on the Rhine we were shocked to see several trains moving into the rail yard across the river. There was much switching, loading, and unloading activity going on. We discussed the situation with our battalion fire control people and we all agreed we would have only one really good chance to engage targets there. After that, the Germans would probably stop using it. Our battalion command decided to wait until two additional artillery battalions could be committed to the initial barrage. They also decided to wait and see if any more trains might show up.

At about 1000 we were told that all three battalions (thirty-six guns) were ready. About thirty minutes later we saw three trains moving in the yard area, along with a high level of other activity. It seemed to us to be the right time. We had given the fire direction center the coordinates of the target and the bombardment began promptly on our signal. Three salvos of airbursts were fired rapidly in a spread pattern over the target area. They were followed by three salvos of high-explosive shells. The surprise bombardment lasted for two minutes, with the 216 shells falling in a pattern that covered the entire railroad yard. The results were devastating. After the firing stopped, the only activity we saw in the yard was salvage crews working to pull the wounded, dead, and anything else of value from the wrecked trains.

After spending two days in the grain elevator we were replaced and sent back to our battery. There we learned the battalion had been ordered to contribute guards for a Russian POW camp that the Germans had abandoned nearby. Most of the ten thousand Russians in the camp had been undernourished but they were still strong enough to function. They hated the Germans with a passion. The Russian camp commander and a few of his officers spoke broken English, and a handful of others spoke German. No one in our outfit spoke any Russian, so communication was extremely difficult. The camp commander had organized the camp well, with subordinate officers commanding company-sized units of about two hundred men. Their officers were political activists who wanted to protect their men from any influence that might erode their communist ideals. Both the Russians and the Americans discouraged fraternization.

It is interesting to note that the Soviet government did not warmly welcome Russians returning from German POW camps. It considered them to have been tainted by Western ideas, and some thought they were traitors for having surrendered. Some returning Russians were executed without trial on the word of a comrade who might have been a personal enemy. It is ironic to think that some of the dedicated communists in the camp we guarded may have encountered such a fate.

The day after we rejoined the battalion I was assigned as sergeant of the guard. I was given a hundred troopers from the battalion to guard about one-fifth of the camp for an eight-hour shift. This was my first contact with Russians. We were in a quandary. We did not want to waste our time guarding our allies. They believed, however, that they had earned a right to raid the German cities, steal whatever they could, and rape the women. They were high-spirited and could not understand why we did not want to do the same things. We supplied them with food and other needs, and plans were made to ship them east as soon as possible. I was glad when my eight-hour shift ended. Fortunately we had not been forced to shoot any escaping Russians or, even worse, allow them to escape to perform subsequent crimes. None of us liked the idea of shooting allies.

About 8 April we went back to the grain elevator. Late in the morning we directed fire on a few trucks moving along a road about a mile east of the river. Some alert German officer had come to the obvious conclusion that our artillery was being directed from the elevator, and he called up two tanks or tank destroyers armed with 88s. We did not know they were there until a couple of 88 rounds were fired at our windows. I saw the guns fire and yelled a warning, but the shells struck before anyone could react. The first two shells hit the outside of the grain elevator, and the explosions were deafening. We were fortunate. If a shell had entered the room through a window and exploded while we were in there, it is almost certain we all would have been killed.

All four of us ran from the room, down ten flights of steel stairs, and into the basement. We were shaken but unhurt. We heard four more rounds hit before the firing stopped. When we finally recovered our nerves, we were more angry than frightened. We quickly climbed back to the top, where we discovered that a shell had exploded inside the office we had occupied. Most of our things, including our telescope, were ruined. We searched for the German guns in the vicinity of the position where I had last seen them. We thought they were still there, so we called for fire on them. I don't know if we hit them or not, but we received no more fire.

The 82d sent several patrols across the river but nothing much came of it. On the fourteenth, American troops moved up the east bank of the Rhine opposite our positions and there was no longer any need for us to maintain combat conditions. That same day, the 456th PFAB was attached to the 505th PIR for military government duties in the area south of Cologne.

On 21 April the 325,000 Germans in the Ruhr Pocket surrendered. All of us were bored. We were not trained to govern civilians. We wanted to get back into the fight, end the war, and go home.

18

Under Monty Again

American armies continued to drive deep into central and southern Germany against weakening German resistance throughout the month of April 1945. At the same time, British, Canadian, and American units under British Field Marshal Montgomery's command were moving across northern Germany with the goal of reaching the Baltic Sea. This would prevent the Russians from entering the Danish peninsula and perhaps keep them from gaining political control of the Scandinavian countries. Despite Montgomery's objections, General Eisenhower had decided to leave the capture of Berlin to the Russians. Thus, the Anglo-American Allies were no longer racing them to the German capital. However, in his usual meticulous fashion, Montgomery continued to move slower than did the Americans to his south, and soon his armies were stalled on the west bank of the Elbe River, where they remained for over two weeks.

The SHAEF high command, impatient with Montgomery's slowness, assigned General Ridgway's XVIII Airborne Corps to reinforce the British Second Army and force a crossing of the Elbe by 29 April. This time the corps consisted of the U.S. 82d Airborne, 7th Armored, 8th Infantry, and British 6th Airborne Divisions. All of these divisions were experienced and had a reputation for success and aggressiveness. This was what was needed in the circumstances.

On 22 April the 82d boarded trucks for the move to its planned positions on the Elbe. We drove north through the Rhineland and crossed the Rhine at Dusseldorf. Next to the military bridge was a large steel and concrete road bridge that had been destroyed by the retreating German army. Like Cologne, Dusseldorf was a major German city that had been almost totally destroyed by British and American bombers. The scene there was like a replay of what we had observed in Cologne.

In 1962 I paid an unexpected visit to Dusseldorf. This time I was with a business associate, Morris Irving Cohn, who graduated with me from Purdue and became one of my best friends after the war. We were flying from Geneva to Copenhagen on business and made a brief stop in Dusseldorf to change planes. The stop lasted four hours because of a mechanical problem with the aircraft. Being Jewish, Morris did not want to see any Germans or any part of Germany, so he moved a chair into the corner of the waiting area and said he would stay there, facing the corner, until our plane was called.

Knowing that Morris was too intellectually curious not to come with me, I explained that I had been in Dusseldorf in 1945 when it was a bombed-out wasteland and that I wanted to see what changes had occurred since then. Morris seemed to like the idea that the city had been destroyed, so he relented and agreed to accompany me. We hired a car with a driver who was Aryan in appearance in the classical Nazi sense. He even wore a green uniform complete with a high-peaked officer's cap that made him look like a parody of a German World War II soldier. I laughed, but our guide made Morris feel uncomfortable.

The first thing we noticed were two steel-and-glass skyscrapers of typical American design, each over forty stories high. Numerous other tall buildings formed a modern emerging skyline. I assured Morris that no major buildings had survived back in 1945. The other general feature that was most noticeable was that the wide streets had been laid out in an American style square grid. There were still many open spaces where rebuilding had not yet been completed, and there were numerous parking lots. Then we went to the shopping area in the middle of town, which was beautiful and prosperous. One could not tell that a war had ever occurred there.

We had a very pleasant lunch in the Old Town, which had been totally destroyed during the war. However, it had been restored to its prewar condition and mideival design. As we drove back to the airport, Morris asked the driver if there was a synagogue in the city. The man said that all the Jews had "moved away" and that there were none in the city. His reply was typical of how the Germans swept their evil Nazi past under the rug. Morris and I were very offended by his answer, but we realized it was unreasonable to expect a confession. After all, the Germans were struggling with a huge burden of personal guilt over their treatment of the Jews and other minorities. Pretending the holocaust never happened was possibly one way to keep their sanity.

In 1945, the poor condition of the cities and their internal roads made moving through them very slow and tedious. However, since European road grids were not square but were based on a city-to-city pattern, we could not avoid driving through the cities. Along the way we moved through the large cities of Essen and Dortmund, as well as many smaller towns in the Ruhr. Since the huge Ruhr industrial area was one of the most important targets in Germany, all of its cities had suffered numerous bombing raids. Because of the destruction, it took us more than two days to make the trip from Cologne to Hannover—a 540-kilometer trip that takes less than three hours on today's autobahns. Whenever we stopped, German women offered us their services as prostitutes, and children begged for chewing gum, candy, cigarettes, and food. The once-proud people of Nazi Germany had fallen to their knees; moral principles had become secondary to survival.

We stopped and camped at an airfield on the outskirts of Hannover. The wreckage of about two hundred Luftwaffe planes of all types and sizes destroyed by our fighter-bombers was scattered all around. The next day we moved to the vicinity of Lüneburg, twenty-five miles south of Hamburg, where the various units of the 82d assembled and prepared to force a crossing of the Elbe on the night of 28 April.

The 505th PIR was assigned to accomplish this mission near an old ferry crossing at a hamlet called Bleckede. Our observation team moved up to the river in the late afternoon. Even at this late date in the war it was obvious the enemy planned to contest the crossing since we could see a number of men digging in and bringing defensive weapons up to the other side. Once again it did not appear we would be facing first-rate German troops when we attempted our crossing. In this case, we had an additional advantage in that the Germans on the other side of the river must have known that if they fought hard they would die for a cause that was now clearly lost.

At 0100 on the twenty-ninth, the 505th began to cross the river in collapsible boats. The troopers encountered little resistance. Even so, about ten men were killed or wounded. It was a tragic thing to have happen so late in the war. A bridgehead was quickly established and then enlarged during the day. Engineers began to build pontoon bridges, which were completed on the thirtieth. Heavy enemy artillery fire and the engineers' hesitation to expose themselves had slowed construction. About noon on 30 April we crossed the Elbe in force. Earlier that same day we received word that Hitler had committed suicide. German resistance seemed to evaporate after the announcement of Hitler's death. For all intents and purposes, the war was over.

As the 456th crossed the Elbe in the early afternoon of the thirtieth, my friend Russell Burton was shot in the knee by a sniper. Russ had been promoted to first sergeant about a month earlier and was looking forward to returning to his home in Rhode Island. A knee wound was bad since repairing it was difficult. There was also a chance the leg might have to be amputated above the knee. Fighting fell off to nothing the next day, making Russ the battalion's last combat casualty.

The 82d moved east to Ludwigslust and captured it on 1 May. As we approached the city, we began to encounter large numbers of German troops moving toward us from the east. They offered no resistance, and their officers asked, "Where do we go to surrender?" It took two days to round them all up. After taking a count, we found we had captured about 125,000 men—remnants of the German Twenty-first Army trying to escape from the Russians. We talked to many of these prisoners as we took their pistols and military decorations as souvenirs. Almost to a man they encouraged us to join them in fighting the Russians.

At about noon on 3 May, an 82d Airborne reconnaissance platoon contacted elements of the 8th Brigade of the VIII Russian Mechanized Corps at Grabow, Germany, and by midafternoon the final cease-fire order was given. Almost immediately our responsibilities changed from being fighting soldiers to taking care of the tens of thousands of German POWs in our pens.

We were now south of Schwerin, and other elements of the XVIII Corps had reached the Baltic coast. The Danish peninsula was safe from an incursion by Russian troops. The German civilians greatly feared American paratroopers because Nazi propagandists said we regularly committed atrocities against civilians. General Gavin ordered the mayor of Ludwigslust to continue to manage his town until a formal military government could be established. That night, the mayor shot his wife and daughter and committed suicide. At the time we thought this act was a sign of devotion to the Nazi cause. However, on our second day there we discovered it was the result of his guilt concerning events at the Wobelein concentration camp.

As German concentrations camp went, Wobelein was a minor affair. It had only four thousand inmates, no gas chambers, and only about 25 percent of its inmates were Jews. Most of the inmates were political prisoners from France and Holland, but there were at least a few from all of the Nazi-occupied countries. Their offenses seemed relatively minor. Many had merely complained about food supplies, minor rules, or other people's problems. Some were city officials who had refused to collaborate with the Nazis. However, the Germans considered these serious offenses. They were unwilling to accept even a minor breach of their authority. Still, Wobelein's inmates were comparatively lucky; many others like them were sent to much worse camps or executed outright.

The reason the mayor killed his family and himself was concerned with the camp's food supplies. The SS allotted food on a per capita basis to each of the large number of camps they administered, and the food was shipped to the mayor of the town closest to each camp. The mayors were in turn ordered to deliver the food to the camps. However, the SS apparently did little to police the process. Food supplies were at a minimum sustaining level for the civilian population of Ludwigslust, so the mayor decided to distribute most of the food allotted to the camp among his constituents and starve Wobelein's inmates. No one in the town was willing to acknowledge the existence of a concentration camp near their town or the atrocious conditions and starvation that existed there.

On 3 May the division's Jewish chaplain came to the battalion to insist that our Jewish soldiers go to the camp to help the inmates, and invited those of other faiths to help if they wished. Only about a third of our battery could go because most of the men had duties to perform. Having no regular duties, I volunteered to go with about

sixty others. As we approached the camp we could smell it from over
two miles away. The conditions there were terrible. The camp only
held men, some of whose normal weight would be 160 pounds but
who weighed only half that. Human intestines were strung on the
barbed-wire fences surrounding the camp as a warning to those who
might try to escape. Inmates who had been in the camp for over a
year were in the worst condition. However, those who had been recently detained there were strong enough to exact revenge.

Most of the camp's guards had been executed, and their bodies
were still hanging from nearby trees. The camp commandant, still
wearing his dress uniform and high-peaked German officer's hat, was
hanging from the camp's gallows. Since the commandant and the
guards had been executing about ten inmates per day for various offenses before we arrived, we did not think the execution of some
guards by inmates was an unreasonable action. In any event, they
happened before we arrived. Some townspeople suggested we bring
the inmates to trial for murder, but that was far from what we had
in mind. It was obvious to us that the inmates had been the only real
victims there.

We tried to give the inmates food and water but many were too
close to death to take either. Almost all of the division's doctors were
in the camp trying to do whatever they could to help. Intravenous
fluids were often not effective due to shrunken veins, and we soon
realized that those who could not drink any water were probably beyond help. This proved to be the case; within five days most such inmates were dead. Within a week of our arrival about a thousand inmates, roughly 25 percent of the population, had died in spite of all
the medical and personal help we could give them. However, most
of the remaining three thousand had gained sufficient strength to
ensure their survival.

After fighting German soldiers for at least a year and seeing the
atrocities they committed, all of the members of the 82d were angry
with Germans as a group. Wobelein accentuated this anger and directed it toward the civilian population. We could not understand
how any country could behave toward fellow human beings as the
Germans under Hitler had. General Gavin's response was to make
the citizens of Ludwigslust and all our German officer POWs help

dig the graves and attend the burial services for the thousand in-mates who died after we came. Three chaplains—one Jewish, one Catholic, and one Protestant—conducted a one-hour service as the bodies were buried in a mass grave. At the same time, the service was translated into German so the civilians and POWs could understand the enormity of the situation. We expected that some Germans who attended would accept a certain amount of personal guilt, but we were shocked when about fifty townspeople killed themselves within a few days of the service.

On 5 May the main forces of the Russian army reached Grabow, a small town about five miles southeast of Ludwigslust. We initially greeted the Russians in friendship, exchanging cigarettes for vodka, among other things, and eating in each other's mess halls. Our first meetings were casual and often developed into drunken brawls. The Russians were extremely heavy drinkers, and many of us found our-selves prostrate while they still seemed fairly sober. We soon learned that they were an undisciplined bunch whose main occupation now was to find German women to rape and houses to rob. If they did not find what they wanted, they often burned the houses. Their com-manders did not discipline their soldiers but instead joined them in committing such atrocities. Within ten days we were forbidden to fraternize with the Russians, and the victory parties came to a quick halt.

Although we were not supposed to fraternize with German civil-ians, one of our duties was to protect our former enemies from Russ-ian soldiers. This proved to be futile, however, since the area we were in eventually became part of the Russian Zone of occupation. Nev-ertheless, while we were there we did our best to protect the civil-ians, which allowed us to see how much they, too, had suffered un-der the Nazis during the war. Our anger against Germans began to recede the more we recognized that the real enemy in Germany had been the relatively small part of the German population that had been fervent, fanatical Nazis. The others had fallen prey to Hitler's political rhetoric and promises. Thereafter, they were inescapably held under control by his raw power. It was also true that many Ger-mans were willing to climb on the Nazi bandwagon as long as the regime was successful and victorious. Still, our most skilled enemy in Normandy, Field Marshal Rommel, as well as many other German officers and civilians, died as a result of efforts to overthrow Hitler and his henchmen—a fact that is to the German people's credit. However, the details concerning attempts to overthrow Hitler were not fully known until well after the war. In any event, it is still difficult for me to understand why the Germans followed Hitler as long and as devotedly as they did.

One reaction we had to all the suffering brought on by this dictatorial demagogue and his evil cohort was to ask the question: "How can we avoid this kind of evil in the future?" With communism shown to be a failure by the early 1990s, the chances of humanity answering this question satisfactorily seem greater than ever before.

19

A Nice Furlough in Nice

The day of Hitler's suicide marked the transition between the shooting war and its aftermath. Huge armies were still moving across the face of Europe. Millions of German servicemen had to be relieved of their weapons, imprisoned as POWs, and examined in order to determine whether they should be prosecuted as war criminals or sent back to civilian life. The Allied governments were searching for Nazis, war criminals, collaborators, and traitors. Furthermore, the Western Allies and Russia were deeply at odds on many points. The dictatorial communist form of government was offensive to the Western democratic countries, especially after their experience with a German dictator. Nevertheless, some kind of peaceful coexistence had to be forged between the East and the West.

In many ways, the transitional period of the next six months was more difficult than the last three months of the fighting. During that time, the occupied countries devoted their energies to finding and prosecuting collaborators, many of whom were executed or imprisoned. Partisan forces in France, Italy, Belgium, Holland, Norway, and Denmark had been helpful and effective in bringing about the Nazi defeat. However, in many of these countries the partisan forces included groups dedicated to opposing ideals, either democratic or communist. These groups now fought one another, contrary to their efforts during the war when both were somewhat coordinated resisting the Germans. Where these political struggles were not peacefully resolved, the affected countries soon found themselves in a prolonged and much more dangerous conflict. In many ways American soldiers occupying a defeated and struggling Germany were less at risk than they would have been in a Western country that was sorting out its political future—sometimes violently.

I lost a number of friends, acquaintances, and comrades to death, wounds, and mental or emotional problems between June 1944 and May 1945. After the three who were killed on that dreadful night in Holland, I stopped counting the casualties, but a later review of unit casualty lists showed the final tally to be seventeen. Russ Burton was the last of my friends to be physically wounded, but others suffered from mental and emotional problems later as a direct result of the war.

After the deaths of my three friends that night in Holland, I changed my attitude toward making friends. I remained kind and friendly to all and helped a number of men write letters home and with other things, but I was no longer willing to get really close with anyone else. Only those who were my friends before Normandy remained so; I added few new ones. As was common among surviving soldiers, I could not understand why I had survived unhurt when so many others in the same circumstances had not. I was no better or worse, morally or otherwise, than those who were killed or wounded. My feelings of guilt about surviving had begun some months previously, but with the end of the shooting and thoughts of going home, these feelings intensified. I really believed that being my friend had contributed to their harm in some strange way. For five years after the war, making close friendships continued to be a substantial problem for me.

When the war ended I was just a month away from my twenty-first birthday. Twenty is usually an age when men feel strong, confident, and invincible. They do not respect any personal risk to themselves. However, the war and its repeated demonstrations of man's mortality had stolen those years of invincibility and confidence from us.

Overlaying all other considerations was the question: "Will *I* have to go to Japan to fight?" Note that our fear was now for ourselves. The signals we were getting were mixed. Rumors had sometimes been reliable in the past, and at that time it was rumored that we were going to Japan soon. Countering this was the point system. Those with sufficient points were told they would soon be going home to stay, with no more army obligations.

All believed that since we had won the war in Europe, it was time to go home. Nothing short of being loaded on the next boat could satisfy us. I was lucky that I had a more predictable future than most of my comrades; I was single, and since I had been a college student before the war, I could go back to Purdue University and resume my engineering studies as soon as the army discharged me. Many of my comrades had much more uncertain futures. Many had received devastating "Dear John" letters from wives or sweethearts telling them they had found another mate. Others wondered how civilians would receive them. With millions of American soldiers returning home, many wondered if they would be able to find good jobs. If they were unable to find decent work, would they be able to get into college? Postwar crowding would surely increase the competition for admission.

Great things were going on around us in May 1945. The Russian government had begun its systematic looting of German factories, museums, and banks, taking everything of value. They stated that this looting was in reparation for the cost of their war and what the Germans had stolen from them. Russian soldiers were looting everything of value they could find in private homes, and trying to rape every German woman they could, sometimes many times.

More than 25 million people had been displaced by the war, and most of them were attempting to return to their homelands. The inmates of liberated concentration camps were being cared for in preparation to sending them home or to some other country. The Western Allies were sending Russians home from German POW camps, and German POWs were being released to return home. Soldiers from eastern European countries who had fought with the Allies had to decide whether to remain in the West or return to a Russian-occupied homeland. While these things went on around us, we were no longer a part of the action. We were stuck in a small German farming community near Schwerin in an area that was an antiquated backwater of civilization.

Discipline had been necessary to win the war, and sometimes such discipline was rigid, poorly directed, and unreasonable. Many thought the way the army had treated Jim Hancock was a case in point. Now, it seemed that discipline was even more arbitrary and unfair. With the war over, the army was easily able to control those men who dearly wanted to go home to a reception or a purpose they knew would be good. However, it had a much harder time dealing with those who knew they had little to look forward to back home. By the time the fighting ended, peace had become such an unnatural concept that we really did not know how to handle it. We settled down to wait for whatever would happen to us next as occupation troops.

On 6 May I was informed that I had been granted a week's furlough to Nice on the Mediterranean coast of France. The next day about twenty of us from the 82d were trucked to the huge American air base near Bad Godesberg, where we spent the night. After a good breakfast in a superior air force mess hall, we were loaded on a C-47 that would fly us to Nice. The plane was still set up for jumpers, with seats along the sides facing inward. There was no door, just an open portal such as the ones through which we had jumped. They had not had time to convert all of the troop carriers to a more comfortable configuration. As we flew high over the French Alps, the temperature in the plane fell to well below freezing. Three heat registers ran down the center of the cabin from which a minimum amount of heated air came out. We stood huddled around these inadequate heat sources until we encountered rough air and the plane began to bounce all over the sky. There was no "fasten seat belts" sign, and the plane's crew did not care what happened to us since they were in the warm cabin up forward. For our part, the most important thing was to avoid freezing. Luckily no one fell out the open portal. Ever since that terrible ride I have never failed to appreciate the comforts of modern airliners.

Nice was a beautiful city with palm trees and a great beach looking out on a deep blue sea. From the horrors of Wobelein to Nice in just two days was almost more than I could handle. The day I arrived we learned that the Nazis had formally surrendered the previous day, 8 May. We all joined the French in Nice in celebrating V-E Day. That night my French was stretched beyond its limits when I engaged in an argument with a French communist in a bar. He tried to convince us that Russia would soon conquer Europe and America, and everyone in the world would be living happily under communism within five years. I described what I had seen of the Russians in northern Germany and expressed serious doubts about their capabilities. My argument was that the Russians were overextended with what they had conquered in the past three years. I also questioned the ability of any country to recover easily from the enormous loss of more than 20 million people and the huge losses in material goods and infrastructure. Russia clearly seemed to be in too bad a shape to attempt to conquer the world. I told him the Russians would have their hands full at home for many years, by which time we would figure out how to handle them. The argument became quite heated. We were lucky it was V-E Day or we would probably have been arrested.

While we were near Cologne I had found a large reel of unexposed 35mm black-and-white movie film among some items that had been abandoned by the retreating Germans. In Nice I found a French camera shop where I hoped to sell the film. After testing it, the Frenchman paid me the equivalent of $400 in francs and gave me a dozen cassettes of film for my camera. Along with my ample supply of cigarettes, this made me a rich American in Nice. Since the army furnished my hotel room and I could eat free in mess halls when I wanted to, I ate and drank well. I wound up spending about half of my money in six days, all on recreational activities. On the second day I rented a sailboat and four of us spent the day sailing along the beautiful Mediterranean coast and among the nearby islands. The captain landed us on a small island where we feasted on the local shellfish and other seafood in a tiny fishing village.

The next day three other troopers and I decided we needed better transportation than our feet. We saw an opportunity to "borrow" an MP jeep and took advantage of it. We drove into the mountains and up and down the nearby coast to see more sights, making sure we stayed out of the city. We used the jeep for two full days without being disturbed, but got caught late on the third night. We were coming out of a bar somewhat under the influence when four armed MPs surprised us. The MPs were angry, threatening, and abusive, and they took us to their headquarters in an old French police station. Fortunately for us it was not a jail, so it had no cells. They wound up locking the four of us up in a second floor room while they waited for an officer to come deal with us. It was a major error on the MPs' part to choose such a place in which to keep paratroopers. When we found the second floor window unbarred and open, we simply jumped out of it into the courtyard below. They had not yet taken our names, so we got away clean. I made my usual poor landing and scuffed my nose and forehead on the cobblestones. We were otherwise unhurt. After six days of sun and fun, I was glad to return to my unit even though it meant another scary plane ride, this time to Hannover. From there we were trucked to Schwerin and I was dropped off at our nearby farm.

Almost immediately on my return to my unit, I sensed that our morale had tumbled. There were several reasons for this severe problem. For one thing, we no longer had anyone to fight. An army with no one to fight has little of value to do, so our self-esteem tumbled. Another problem was that we hated the Germans and were stuck in their midst. Finally, the specter of being a spearhead division for the invasion of Japan was aggravated by news of enormous casualties in the fighting on Okinawa, which was to be a staging area for the planned assault on the Japanese homeland. Our future was extremely uncertain.

Conditions were ideal for mischief, and sometimes GIs attempted stunts that were beyond mischief, becoming criminal. I came very close to becoming involved in such foolish activity. Everyone was annoyed with the officers because they seemed to have abandoned their duties and left all control and discipline to the noncoms. Meanwhile, they had chosen the best available house in which to live. It included an upscale mess, so they rarely ventured out. They played cards all day and well into each night. The officers had gone from sharing everything with us and doing their portion of the work to isolating themselves and giving themselves the best of everything. Two other sergeants and I decided to play a trick on them to get their attention. They played cards around a table in the living room in front of a large window under a small chandelier. The plan was that after dark on a clear night one of us would shoot the light out over their heads. Because I had qualified "expert" with the M1 rifle we agreed that I would fire the shot.

A few days later the conditions were right, but by then I had begun to have second thoughts. What if I missed and killed one of the officers or the window deflected the shot? After all, we did not hate these men. They had faced the same dangers we had and had performed well. In fact, we respected and admired them as they did us. None of us wanted to hurt anyone, no matter how annoyed we were with them at the time. There were other questions. If we were caught, could we satisfactorily explain that it was only a prank? Would this interfere with anyone going home? As the would-be shooter, I had another special question: would I alone be blamed if we were caught? Fortunately for all concerned I came to my senses and refused to fire the shot. I was not willing to take the chance that what was intended to be a mischievous prank might be viewed as a criminal act, or worse, result in someone's serious injury or death. The reason we even considered such a prank was that we had nothing to do and had lost perspective concerning the relationship between officers and enlisted men. Since no one else wanted to shoot either, the plan was aborted. We later had a discussion with the officers that led to their resuming most of their responsibilities.

Mischief was the key word of those times. No sooner had I escaped my own desire to make mischief than I was innocently drawn into another's more serious protracted scheme. In this case, mischief was an inappropriate description of what was a mad, criminal act. Most of us were no longer angry with the German populace, but a few men still felt an obsessive rage against them. I was told that while I was in Nice, someone had burned a barn killing the six dairy cows it contained. It was believed that an American had done this but there was no evidence that could identify the culprit. My sleeping quarters were in the attic of our headquarters, which I shared with the chief cook, Sgt. Jack McNabb. Jack had been with the 82d since before the invasion of Sicily. At one time he had been a staff sergeant, but he had been busted to private twice. He had been wounded twice and decorated once for valor. After Normandy he no longer sought active, dangerous assignments and became a cook. Then, he was wounded in Holland when a shell struck the kitchen. He also developed a severe drinking problem. No one blamed him for this as we all thought he had done enough for the cause. Now, he appeared content simply to have survived. However, underneath this peaceful facade was a bitter, angry man.

One morning we learned that a farmer's draft horse had been shot shortly after dark the previous night. Since only American soldiers were armed, it was obvious one of us had done the deed. That night I went to sleep early. Later, probably about midnight, Jack, who held a .45-caliber pistol pressed against my head, awakened me. He told me he knew that I knew he had shot the horse, and he planned to shoot me to keep me from telling on him. I asked him how that would help him since it would be pretty obvious to everyone that he had shot me. That made him pause to think things over a bit. I lay there helpless, zipped up in my sleeping bag and unarmed. I knew I was dealing with a deranged man. I reminded him that he had more discharge points than almost everyone else in the battalion and that he would be going home soon if he did not screw up anymore. Most of his words were incoherent, and he was not responsive to anything I said. I was convinced he was really crazy because he did not smell of alcohol. Since I was getting nowhere talking to him, I told him I was tired and was going to sleep, and he could do anything he wanted. Nothing more happened. Within a few seconds he pulled the gun away from my head. Feeling a little safer, I was asleep within five minutes.

The next morning I was awakened by reveille, pleasantly surprised to be alive. There was no sign of Jack. After cleaning up, I went to breakfast. Jack was serving, acting as though nothing had happened. I was tempted to forget all about the incident but, on reflection, I realized he was far too great a danger to himself, others, and me if he should have another similar episode. He might actually kill someone. After breakfast I met with the battery commander and my long time friend, 1st Sgt. John Donahue, who had been promoted from supply sergeant to replace Russ Burton.

They were not surprised. They said they suspected that Jack had burned the barn but could not prove it. They also thought they had seen some erratic behavior on his part, but at this time they were questioning everyone's sanity, including their own. They accepted the truth of my story and agreed with my conclusion that Jack was crazy. When they asked me if I wanted to file assault charges against

Jack, I refused, explaining that I thought he was sick and needed help. We all ignored the criminal aspects of destroying German property; Germans were too recently our enemies for this to be very important to us at the time. Two things worried us. First, Jack was sick and in need of the kind of help that a criminal prosecution could not give him. Second, if given another chance, he could end up killing someone if we ignored the situation. Captain Alley told the two of us to keep an eye on Jack while he went to the division hospital to seek advice from a psychiatrist.

Captain Alley returned later that morning with a doctor and two MPs. As they took Jack away he raved at the three of us, calling us Nazi-lovers, traitors, and many other odious things that did not fit at all with the reality of our situation. We heard little more about Jack, but we knew he was never court-martialed since we would have been called to testify if he had been. Jack had become another casualty of the war, driven to madness by the stress, danger, and everything else that he had experienced during the previous two years. We could only hope that he was eventually cured of his affliction and that he did not spend the rest of his life in an asylum. Although we were far from experts, we did not rate the chances of a cure very high.

On 22 May we received word that we would be going back to France to refit and receive replacements. After that the division would move to Berlin and become part of the American military government there. We began the move back to Camp Chicago, a huge tent city near Sissonne, on 3 June. Berlin was less than a hundred miles east of Schwerin. Only the U.S. Army would choose to route us there by way of Reims, hundreds of miles to the west.

20

Berlin Occupation Duty

The trip to Camp Chicago took five tedious days. We were trucked to the Rhine across the river from Cologne, where we marched across a military bridge. We boarded boxcars at Cologne for the slow train ride to Reims. The French army had taken over the old barracks at Camp Suippes, so we were installed in the nearby tent camp.

The eight-man tents were comfortable in June, and a large, battalion-sized mess hall was located in a building nearby. The food there was an improvement over what we had been eating in the field. While we waited for orders to move to Berlin we were given useless, make-work activities to perform. Naturally, morale plummeted again. It is quite likely that only the common desire to go home kept the U.S. Army in Europe from mutiny in the summer of 1945.

Many of the old rumors and some new ones abounded. We were leaving France next month to fight Japan. Everyone who had a hundred points or more as of V-E Day would soon go home to be discharged. We were leaving for Berlin in a week to join the occupation forces there.

Since I had only ninety-four points, the hundred-point rumor depressed me and the many others who fell short of that mark. At least duty in Berlin sounded more interesting than the make-work projects we were given in France. We also liked the idea of going to Berlin a lot more than moving to the Pacific theater.

An exchange program involving the 82d and 17th Airborne Divisions was begun about this time. Our men with a higher number of points were being sent to the 17th, and their men with a lower number of points were being sent to the 82d. The conclusion we drew was that the 17th would move to the Pacific earlier than we would. Some of the officers with the most points were given an opportunity for promotion and transfer to the 17th. The rumor mill proved to be only partially correct. The 17th Airborne Division was shipped back to the states, destined for early deployment to Japan. However, the high-point men who went with it were given the choice of being discharged or continuing to serve.

After two weeks in Camp Chicago we were moved to another camp near Épinal, where all of the 82d's artillery battalions were concentrated. It became clear that these would be the units and soldiers going to Japan when training intensified.

After four weeks of boring camp duty we finally received orders to proceed to Berlin in early July. However, the move was postponed several times because of the Potsdam Conference, which dealt with the occupation of Germany. The Berlin problem was one of the more difficult for the politicians to solve. Finally, on 1 August, we were loaded into boxcars at Reims for the move. They were the same "forty-or-eight" cars designed to carry forty men or eight horses that the doughboys had complained about in World War I. My group was lucky. A layer of barracks bags was spread over the rough, splintered wooden floor and only about ten of us were in our car. There were no windows, but the doors were not locked, so they remained open most of the time and several of us climbed out and rode on top. We soon realized this was unsafe and quickly abandoned that idea. We had field rations and plenty of water, and we were able to exercise during the frequent stops the train made. These were also the same type of boxcars the Germans had used to ship prisoners to concentration camps. It was easy for us to imagine what a weeklong ride with fifty or more other people in a sealed car on hot, sunny days would have been like with little or no food or water and no toilet facilities.

Since there was as yet no railroad bridge over the Rhine, we marched across, camped for the night, and then were loaded onto another train. We spent a week on trains, finally arriving in Berlin on 7 August. German women offered themselves to us in exchange for cigarettes or invasion money every time the train stopped. It was obvious they were not professional prostitutes but housewives who were desperate for money to help their families survive.

"Hurry up and wait" was now the army motto since there were no longer any objectives that required fighting and dying. The high command had lost interest in us "grunts." Our efforts were no longer required to meet the top-ranking generals' goals. Some generals' interests were now channeled toward other things, such as quarreling with other commanders over who got what credit or blame. They were more worried about who would be given promotions and important commands in the coming invasion of Japan, or what permanent rank they would hold when they retired. Some dreamed of running for civilian political office. Then, of course, there were memoirs to be written and documentary support to be gathered. Some generals, concerned about their place in history, looked for ways to publicize their accomplishments, sometimes enhancing them.

The 456th was the first 82d battalion to reach Berlin, and we were directed to a suburb in the southwest part of the city called Saaleck Platz, Lichterfeld, Steglitz. The area had been damaged very little. The battalion occupied a block of houses from which the residents had been cleared. Most had been forced to move in with their neighbors in the next block. The morning after we arrived, I saw a man of about sixty wearing a well-made suit, a clean white shirt, and a tie rummaging through our garbage. The U.S. Army was so well fed and wasteful that our garbage was the best food-source the residents had seen in months. This incident again illustrated the depth to which these once proud people had sunk.

There was almost a complete absence of civilian men between twenty and fifty years of age in this prosperous area. Almost immediately, our main duty became protecting the German women from marauding Russian soldiers. The border with the Russian zone was only a mile to the east, and at that time most Allied soldiers were free to move among the various occupation zones. Although we were under orders not to enter the Russian zone without permission, there were no checkpoints at the border. If we did cross, we risked being subjected to our own army's discipline. The Russian army had no such rules governing the movement of its soldiers, and they roamed about at will, usually in small groups.

Until we arrived, the prosperous appearing area we occupied was a favorite hunting ground for the Russians. It took about two weeks for us to drive the Russians out of our area. They continued their marauding activities in their own zone, but there were fewer targets and more competition for them. During this process, we lost all respect for those brutal and callous men.

At the time, all American and Russian soldiers carried loaded weapons. One little game the Russians liked to play was similar to an Old West shootout. Sometimes when they encountered a single GI or a small group of American soldiers, they would draw their pistols like gunfighters. Our problem was that we could not tell whether it was a bluff or a real threat since we could not understand what they were saying. Rather than wait to see if they were bluffing, we simply shot them. It did not take the Russians long to lose interest in their little game. By 20 August we had gained control of our part of the American zone, and unruly and criminal Russian soldiers no longer bothered us. Later on 15 September a friend, Pvt. Beryl L. Sizemore, was shot in the arm by a Russian soldier.

The first time I went into central Berlin I was struck by the devastation, which seemed to be far worse than in any other German city through which I had passed. The smell of death still pervaded most areas. The smell came from the thousands of Berlin citizens killed by the many bombing raids. Their bodies were still buried in the rubble. The smell of burnt flesh was also sometimes present. Additional damage had occurred when the Russians shelled the city heavily and randomly during the last few weeks of the war. With the small exception of a few major buildings that might be restored, it was clear that if Berlin were to be rebuilt they would have to clear out virtually everything and start from scratch.

We often saw large numbers of Russian soldiers wandering around or performing various duties. They were a pretty sorry lot. Most were short and scrawny, their uniforms were dirty and fit poorly, and they smelled as though they spent most of their time rolling in a pigpen and had not bathed in months. With the exception of their honor guard, I never saw a Russian enlisted man or officer under the rank of major who was over five-feet-six inches tall, and none looked to be in good health or in strong physical condition. Even many of their younger men had missing or rotten teeth.

Occupied Berlin was an enclave completely surrounded by the Russian-occupied zone of East Germany. Berlin itself was divided into four occupation zones, one of which was occupied and controlled by the Russians. Similarly, the French, British, and Americans each controlled a zone. The four countries operated a central Berlin joint command, and the Allied armies took weekly turns providing a company-sized unit as an honor guard for its headquarters. When it came to be their turn, the U.S. command simply rotated the duty through all the companies and batteries in the 82d Airborne Division. I do not know for sure, but I believe the British and French followed a system similar to ours.

The Russians employed a very different scheme, however. On the several times that I saw them, their honor guard consisted of two hundred of the most magnificent physical specimens I had ever seen in a group. They all appeared to be between six-foot-two and six-foot-four, between 190 and 210 pounds, and very healthy and fit. Their uniforms were spotless, and their buttons, black leather belting, and their knee-length boots shined like mirrors. There seemed to be no individuality in their honor guard; it was as though they had all been cloned from some perfect model. Where the Russian army found these specimens is difficult to imagine. Perhaps these were the only such men in their army of many millions. One thing seemed certain, these same men always came back whenever the Russians had the duty. Their goose-step style of marching made them look like the Nazis they had helped defeat.

I missed out on honor guard duty because I was attending the Biarritz American University when our battery's turn came around. All of the French, British, and American honor guards were made up of fine looking men, but none could compete with the Russian unit, which had clearly been handpicked. This proved to be another facade similar to many others we eventually identified concerning the Red Army and its political leadership.

There was a booming black market in items that had become scarce in Nazi-occupied Europe, but nowhere were there more black market activities than in Berlin. As the Nazi government and its banking structure collapsed, one problem for the population was the lack of a trusted currency. The French had not trusted the invasion currency we introduced in the spring of 1944 because they feared the Germans might yet drive us back into the sea. However, by 1945, the currency backed by the Western Allies was the only reliable money on the continent.

These chaotic economic conditions led everyone in the Nazi-occupied countries to try to convert whatever money and paper assets they had into hard assets of intrinsic value such as gold or silver bars or coins and jewelry—preferably things they could easily carry. Things that had been missing from the European markets for months assumed much higher than normal value. These scarce items included hundreds of things but primarily cigarettes, coffee, tea, many food items, medical supplies, and pharmaceuticals. One of these scarce items, cigarettes, offered special opportunities for common soldiers, whereas most other items had to be stolen from army stores.

Under U.S. Army regulations, every GI was allowed to buy one carton of cigarettes a week at the PX for fifty cents, and when he was on a combat assignment his supply sergeant issued him a free carton. Soldiers' relatives were also allowed to send him a standard-sized parcel each week. The parcels my mother sent to me usually contained five to seven packs of cigarettes, a can of some specially desired food, chocolate, chewing gum, and a paperbound book. This meant I averaged about seventeen packs a week. Back in England I had given my cigarettes to my smoking buddies since I was never a smoker, but once I learned about the black market, I hung on to them and sold or traded them.

Cigarettes soon became the common currency for trading with communities outside of the army. Many of the men who had smoked a carton a week cut back to one pack or two so they could barter or sell the rest. Bartering was easiest. One pack of cigarettes would usually get you something that cost four or five dollars in our invasion currency. Although I had no commerce with prostitutes, my friends said the price for a single act of straight sex was five cigarettes, and a pack would get them a full night. To my knowledge, all soldiers were willing to sell their cigarettes, but doing so was difficult because the black market tended to move about and it was illegal. Finding a civilian to sell them for us was bothersome, and some civilians cheated soldiers.

These practicalities caused a wholesale market to develop, and someone in every unit somehow became its cigarette trader. We sold our cigarettes to him for $20 per carton in our invasion money, and he sold larger quantities to black marketers after marking them up. It was a convenient and easy arrangement, and everyone held onto a few packs for bartering.

My army pay as a "buck" sergeant was $93, plus I got a $50 monthly bonus for being a qualified paratrooper—a total of $143 per month. Selling my cigarettes more than doubled my pay. The army encouraged soldiers to send money home to their wives, children, and other relatives. When we went to the pay table every other week, we could send home all or part of our total available cash, even if it amounted to more than our pay. I made arrangements to send most of the cash I had to my parents, who put it in a savings account for me.

Things became sticky when the soldiers of all ranks in the 82d collectively sent home significantly more than 200 percent of the money they had received at the pay tables on their first payday in Berlin. By the next payday, a regulation was in effect that limited the amount an individual could send home to 110 percent of his pay. This regulation changed nothing since it was easy to find a proxy, usually a confirmed smoker who did not want to sell his cigarettes. I found a friend who sent $3,500 of my money to his father over six months in exchange for $1,000. His father sent my father checks totaling $2,500. Throughout this period I continued to send home 110 percent of my pay.

When I left Berlin in December 1945, the black market in American cigarettes was still thriving, and prices had not deteriorated significantly. I eventually received a degree that included a major in economics, but my cigarette experience was a really practical lesson in economics, money, and banking. It was also a personal lesson because when I finally returned home my savings account had about $6,000 in it. This allowed me to buy a car and helped with my education, although the GI Bill provided most of the funds I needed to obtain my bachelor's and master's degrees.

Just being able to observe the problems of ordinary people in an economic world that had crumbled around them was a valuable lesson. All these people found themselves in terrible economic conditions that they were absolutely unable to influence. As has frequently happened in history, paper money became worthless. Those who had exchanged all or some of their currency for gold or silver early, before the situation became critical, had valuables they could exchange for needed goods in a society without currency. However, holding gold and other hard assets was not without risk. Many people were robbed and some were killed for their assets. Still others wound up trading their gold for their lives. Those who did not see the crisis coming soon enough to act had nothing of value to exchange, and they became destitute, regardless of how wealthy they had been. Huge numbers of refugees, many of whom had previously been rich, were streaming into our sector of Berlin from the Russian zone, and we saw numerous examples of people who lost everything regardless of what choices they made.

The chaos in Europe brought on by the war was only beginning to clear. Being part of and observing it made all of us realize how fortunate we were that it had not been visited on the United States, and we hoped such terrible forces would never affect our country.

21

We Kill Three Russians

Soon after our arrival in Berlin two batteries from our battalion were assigned to furnish guards for the Steglitz railroad station. This was the first station in the American zone on a track coming from Russian-occupied East Germany to the south.

We were required to post twelve guards at a number of widely dispersed guard posts; another six guards were assigned to rove about. I was the sergeant of the guard in a fifty-nine-man guard detail that had the duty every third day. Three corporals worked eight-hour shifts. Each was in charge of the twelve stationary guards, who manned their posts for two-hour shifts and then were off for four hours. They were allowed to rest in the station. This cycle continued for twenty-four hours. I had an office in the station with a cot on which I could occasionally nap, and I had a corporal assistant whose main duty was to keep track of the roving guards, who also worked in two-hour shifts. Both my assistant and I had to be awake most of the time during our twenty-four-hour shift. Every day the battalion assigned an officer of the day who was responsible for the guard details at three such railroad stations. I was able to reach him or his clerk by phone at any time.

In the summer of 1945 the station was crowded with refugees trying to escape from the Russians and enter into the comparative safety of the American, French, or British occupation zones. Most of these pitiable people were older men and women, some with children. They came from all over eastern Europe. Most had lost their homes and almost everything they owned. Some were former slave laborers who had been released from Nazi concentration camps or who had worked in factories, on railroads, clearing ruined cities, or on fortifications. When the Nazis abandoned them, they and their families had nothing, and many were in poor health. Whatever material goods they had were carried in pitiful bundles, boxes, or suitcases.

When the trains came in people were clinging to the sides, and some rode on top of the cars, in addition to those inside the cars. Designed to carry two hundred people, these trains frequently had more than three times that many on board. The only food and water they had was what they carried. Many of them were malnourished, dehydrated, and near the point of collapse. Except for keeping them running, no maintenance was performed on the trains in the Russian zone, so working facilities like toilets were often nonexistent.

Besides taking care of these sick people, the problem that plagued us most severely was the criminal and callous behavior of the Russians. Russian soldiers boarded almost every train at the last station in the Russian zone and systematically robbed the refugees while the train was moving into our zone. They stole what few things of value they could find: gold, rings, jewelry, money, combs, attractive clothing, scarves, everything. They went so far as to examine the refugees' mouths and crudely pulled out any gold teeth they found with pliers they had brought with them.

If a refugee put up a fight or even protested verbally, the Russian soldiers either beat or killed him. It did not matter to them if the offender was a woman, an eighty-year-old man, or a child. When the trains stopped at the Steglitz station, our job was to inspect them. On almost every train we found a few refugees who had been murdered, and several dozen more who had been hurt.

When we began our guard shift we were under strict orders not to challenge any Allied soldiers we found on the trains. This meant we could do nothing if we saw a Russian soldier kill an old woman or commit some other terrible crime. Every day I received a dozen or more complaints from angry corporals and guards about the situations they faced. I passed these complaints, along with my own anger, to the officers above me, but they could do nothing about it except complain to higher authority. Clearly, the officers felt the same way we did about this intolerable situation.

After listening to a week of our griping, General Gavin and two other officers visited the Steglitz station on the day we were taking our turn. When he asked me what had happened so far that morning I told him two trains had come through with a total of one dead and about four dozen injured. He asked me whether our guards would shoot Russians if they had permission and if the Russians did not stop when ordered. I told him I had no doubt that they would. I pointed out that the present situation was turning everyone's stomach, and we were losing respect for commanders who allowed such things to continue. We both agreed that the Russians were laughing at us and did not respect U.S. authority in our own zone. He said he would go with me to inspect the next few trains when they came in.

Within a half-hour a train came in, and we went out to inspect it. If anything, that train was worse than most. We found five dead and three dozen injured, including six people who had their gold teeth pulled. Four Russians were running through the train toward its rear as we pursued them. When we reached the last car, the Russians jumped off and ran. The angry general reached for his pistol and was prepared to shoot them. His aide and I were forced to restrain him since this action would have been a military crime, even for a general. General Gavin expressed his appreciation to me for giving him the tour but he was a very angry man when he left our station.

On our next tour of duty, several days later, we found that our orders had been changed. If any guard found anyone of any nationality robbing or assaulting refugees, he was to challenge and arrest that person. If the person failed to stop or resisted arrest, a warning shot was to be fired over his head. If all that failed, the guard was authorized to shoot the person as he fled. We greeted these new orders with enthusiasm. At last we could do something about this dreadful situation; we would no longer be impotent observers.

An hour later we had our first chance. One of my guards came upon two Russians, catching them in the act of extracting the teeth of a woman refugee. They ran when he challenged them. Unfortunately, he was not one of our best marksmen. He fired a warning shot and then fired at them but missed. They got away clean. A few hours later another guard, this one an expert marksman with his M1 rifle, went through the same procedure when he found three Russians roughing up some old women on the next train that arrived. He did not miss when he fired at them, however.

Someone called out, "Sergeant of the guard!" I heard the call and ran to the train, through it, and into the rail yard beyond. The three Russians lay dead in the yard. I was appalled to see that they were officers: a captain, a lieutenant, and some kind of a noncommissioned officer. I posted three guards with the bodies, then ran back to the station and called the officer of the day to report what had happened. He said he would be right there and that he would bring the regimental commander.

When they arrived, I took them out into the rail yard. They looked at the Russians and said, "Yes, they're Russians and they're dead." I was to hear that remark at least ten times before the day ended. General Gavin arrived an hour later and, after he looked at the Russians, he remembered our earlier conversation.

"Well, Sergeant," he said, "it looks like we got our wish. How does the guard feel about this?"

He talked to the man and decided that he was not too shaken up. The general explained that there would have to be an investigation but there was no doubt this was a justifiable act, so he was sure the man would be cleared and sent home promptly. When I asked what we should do with the bodies the general said to cover them up and that he would contact the Russian liaison officer to arrange for them to be taken away. After another two hours, the general returned with the Russian liaison officer, a Colonel Oleg. (His last name was hard to pronounce and more difficult to remember, so I will take the liberty of calling him "Oleg" here.)

The colonel wore a beautiful full-dress Russian uniform, much like those worn by members of their honor guard. His English was perfect, with a slight British accent. When we took him out to see the bodies, which were getting a little ripe in the hot sun by then, he said, "Yes, they are Russians and they are dead." With that, he began to walk back to his American jeep, which was probably one that we had given to the Russian army. He was completely unconcerned and acted like a man with something much more important to do elsewhere.

We all protested his leaving. He pointed out that since we had shot them, we should bury them. General Gavin said we could not bury anyone, much less Allied soldiers, without authorization.

Colonel Oleg said he authorized us to bury them and began to walk away again, finished with it all. We pointed out that we had to have authorization from our army to bury anyone, and there was no way we could obtain such permission under the circumstances. Oleg seemed amused by our concern and suggested we should have thought of such problems before we shot his men. This did not seem to be an angry statement; he was merely pointing out the irony of our situation.

Gavin asked Oleg how the Russian army would report the deaths of these men to their families. Oleg said they would not tell the families anything at all about the deaths. He pointed out that they wasted no manpower on records or death reports. They only kept records on officers above the rank of major. He said they had beaten the Germans because everyone had fought; there were no clerical jobs. He said it was his understanding that only half of our army was engaged in fighting while the rest was keeping track of the fighters. Of course, this was true in a way. The U.S. Army did have more than one man in rear areas supporting each fighter. However, it clearly would do no good to argue the point. Still, we believed our system was both more efficient and humane than theirs. Oleg went on to point out that when a Russian left his family to fight, they considered that he was dead as of that moment. If he came back, it was looked upon as a lucky surprise.

The argument continued for another hour. Finally, Oleg suggested we take the corpses to a Russian hospital and leave them there. He said we should not wait around for any paperwork in exchange for the bodies. He told us simply to dump them on the receiving dock and leave as promptly as possible, with no conversation. I arranged for one of our trucks to haul the bodies away and then went along to make certain everything was done as Oleg had directed.

The next day, six marauding Russians escaped from the guards who had taken over for us. However, two more were shot the day after that. Our rotation came next, and this time two Russians stopped when challenged and submitted to arrest. We turned them over to the Russian authorities. As far as we knew, anything might have happened to them from being shot to being released without punishment.

A week after the first shooting, a court-martial was convened to try the guard who shot the first three Russians. It was plain to all concerned that he had been following orders and had acted properly. Nevertheless, the trial was important to him because if he were found not guilty he could not be accused of the same crime or tried again in any other court, military or civilian. Also, the army would have to send him home promptly if he were found innocent of homicide. The basis for this rule was sound; some relative or friend of the deceased might not agree with the verdict and decide to seek revenge.

Colonel Oleg came to the trial, which seemed to him another example of American foolishness. He told us that Russian justice was far simpler. If a Russian commander concluded that a soldier faced with similar circumstances had done something seriously wrong, he would immediately have the man shot. If he thought the action was justified, no further action would be taken and no record would be kept. Thus, the soldier had nothing further to fear. Oleg also told us he had informed most Russian unit commanders of our new policy to shoot Russians caught robbing people on trains, and that he expected the practice would soon cease. It was clear that neither Oleg nor the rest of the Russian high command placed any importance on the misbehavior of their soldiers or in our shooting them. To my knowledge, no complaint was ever made about the shootings.

In 1945 it was difficult to form an opinion about the Russians in spite of the close contact we had with them during the six months after the war ended. What the Russians showed me in Berlin was that they were callous, brutal, undisciplined, in poor physical condition, technically unsophisticated, and operated under a cruel system. It was hard to understand how they managed to accomplish anything. Yet we knew that the Germans had sent two-thirds of their divisions to fight the Russians, and eventually, the Red Army had thoroughly defeated them. We all recognized that without the Russian army's contribution, defeating the Nazis by ourselves would have been extremely difficult, if not impossible.

Their callous disregard for human life, even their own, did not seem consistent with the feelings we attached to American, British, and most German combat soldiers. Of course, the Soviets we saw may not have been of the same caliber as the soldiers who defeated the German armies in the east. They certainly did not look like high-quality combat veterans to us. Perhaps the Russian political officers had kept their best, most intelligent troops out of Berlin and away from the political contamination they feared might occur if they came into close contact with other Allied soldiers.

It is even more difficult to understand the achievements of the Russians in World War II when the handicaps with which they began the war are recognized. Russia had existed under one form of cruel despotism or another for at least a millennium, and the communists were only the latest in a long series of dictatorships. They stifled all forms of individual initiative. In 1937, Stalin felt his absolute power was threatened by the Russian military, so he ordered the execution of 80 percent of the armed forces' high-ranking leaders. Russian society was largely agrarian, made up mostly of peasants who worked primitive farms with horses pulling plows. On the eve of a war in which mechanical mobility was becoming more and more important, only about 2 percent of Russian men knew how to drive an automobile. Their heavy industry and technology were far behind the capabilities of Germany and other western nations. How did they overcome these and other handicaps and find a way to accomplish what they did?

The Soviets called World War II the "Great Patriotic War." The key word is "patriotic," and this gives some insight into what happened. The invasion of the Russian homeland by a brutal and insensitive enemy brought on a wave of patriotic fervor that resulted in the vast majority of Russians joining the effort without reservation because of their love of Mother Russia. Others fought to avenge the excesses of the Nazis, who continued to perform new atrocities. This combined effort was essential for Russia to produce an effective defense. Throughout the war Stalin maintained his despotic control. Every soldier, from the lowest private to the most senior general, knew that if he complained or failed to perform well he would be taken to a wall and shot. Many were.

In 1939 many of the Red Army's generals were useless political sycophants. Only a few able senior officers had escaped Stalin's deadly net, and many men from the lower ranks had ability, but few had experience at the highest levels of command. Nevertheless, the Red Army found in the ranks of this unlikely group more than a thousand marshals and generals capable of commanding army groups, armies, corps, and divisions, and they did it in only a few years.

In spite of his need for capable generals, Stalin continued to demand "political correctness." The Red Army had two separate hierarchies: one made military decisions; the other kept everyone in line politically. Every headquarters had a political officer of the same, or nearly the same, rank as the military commander. These political officers frequently interfered with a commander's ability to make military decisions. The most successful Russian marshal, Georgy Zhukov, was both brave and patriotic. He was one of the few effective generals to escape Stalin's purge, and during the war he made decisions contrary to Stalin's dictates yet still escaped his wrath. After the war, Stalin degraded Zhukov and sent him off to insignificant assignments, but he at least survived.

The Russian success in training millions of peasants to be effective soldiers fighting a mobile war was remarkable. Starting with almost no men who were mechanics or even capable of driving, the Russian military organized a number of tank armies that drove the very effective panzer armies from the field in many battles. Their numerous infantry divisions were also effective. To accomplish these positive results they had to train hundreds of thousands of company-level commissioned and noncommissioned officers to be effective combat leaders, starting mostly with uneducated peasants of great ethnic diversity.

Unlike the United States and Britain, Russia had no huge automobile and aircraft industries that could be converted to arms production relatively easily. They concentrated on tank production to meet what they correctly thought were the most threatening Nazi units, their panzer forces. Early in the war they began to produce the T-34 tank in great quantities. The T-34 proved to be the best medium tank of the war, far superior to our Sherman. It stood up well in one-on-one confrontations with the best German tanks. In 1944 Russia produced more T-34s than we did Shermans. Their secondary concentration was on aircraft, but even though these helped the cause, they were never as effective or of as high a quality as the planes developed by Germany or the Western Allies.

The Germans and we seem to want to credit the Soviet victories on the eastern front to huge "human wave" attacks (a tactic the Soviets had abandoned by mid-1943). However, the reality was that Russia's marshals and generals beat the Germans by making sound strategic decisions and by using the same tactics the Germans had employed so successfully earlier in the war: mobility and the concentration of firepower.

A fuller discussion of how the Soviets defeated a very effective German army is far beyond the scope of this book. The fact was that the motley men I met in Berlin on numerous occasions failed to fit Russia's great accomplishments in the war. Based on my experience with them, this discussion forms the basis of my efforts to come to grips with my quandary. Most of the Soviet troops we saw in Berlin were European—from Russia, Belorussia, and the Ukraine. We saw few soldiers from the Arabic or Asian republics. To a large extent they remain a mystery to me.

22

Biarritz American University

August 1945 was an extremely important month for me as a person; it was the month when I was given the opportunity to become an individual again. While we were guarding the Steglitz railroad station on the outskirts of Berlin, our most dire fear was put to rest when the air force dropped two atomic bombs on the Japanese cities of Hiroshima and Nagasaki, which resulted in Japan's surrender. If the United States had been forced to invade Japan to end the war, we knew that we of the 82d Airborne were likely to be called upon to help spearhead the effort. We all recognized that the Japanese army was a formidable foe and that the Japanese civilians would probably fight us, too. All were convinced that many of us would die or be seriously wounded if we had to invade the Japanese homeland. If the Pacific war continued, a reasonable expectation was that we would have to perform two or three more years of army service with all the inherent risks and deprivations.

There was no doubt in our minds that the atom bombs had saved hundreds of thousands of American lives, including many of our own and those of our children and grandchildren to be. They may also have saved an even larger number of Japanese lives since in all likelihood an invasion followed by a fight to the finish would have been far more costly to the Japanese than the casualties caused by the bombs. However, this consideration was of no importance to us at that time. Learning that the atom bomb was a reality made all of us very thankful that the Germans or Japanese had not perfected it first. They surely would have used it against the Allies with no reservations. The most dreadful possibilities in our future had disappeared almost

201

overnight. We suddenly had realistic hopes of returning intact to our homes and families. A happy future beckoned us, so we were much more able to withstand the boredom of waiting to go home.

The army also had begun to use its collective brain in a more constructive fashion. Instead of saddling us with make-work projects, the army began to come up with ideas that were designed to provide bridges between our army lives and the civilian lives we would soon be leading at home. It organized trade schools for men who were interested in a number of job areas and offered literacy and foremanship classes. It also organized and managed several "universities" designed to give ex-college students and men who were interested in beginning college a head start in their fields of interest.

The service universities were located at Oxford in England, at the Sorbonne in Paris, in Biarritz, France, and in a few other choice locations. Many leading American professors were brought in to teach courses. Besides saying that I planned to return to Purdue University and that I wanted to attend one of these schools, it was necessary to pass an entrance examination. Since my college experience fit the profile of those people the test was trying to discover, it proved easy for me. The result was that in early September I was on one of three planeloads of 82d troopers bound for Biarritz.

My freshman year at Purdue University was devoted to general engineering studies. After finishing that year I was required to select the engineering specialty I wished to pursue. Since I had decided to become a chemical engineer, my principle academic interest was to refresh my chemistry knowledge and take qualitative and quantitative chemical analysis courses. When I arrived at Biarritz, I was disappointed to find that these courses were not offered in a form for which Purdue would give me credit. I decided to take physical chemistry, psychology, and accounting—useful subjects in which I was interested but for which I had no immediate need. In the long run, I was awarded credit for all three courses.

The rules at Biarritz were far from military but they were reasonably strict. We attended classes three hours a day, five days a week. Missing even a single class without a medical excuse was grounds for immediate dismissal. We were also cautioned that off-duty misconduct would result in our arrest, and classroom misbehavior or laxity would result in our being sent back to our units. There was no military organization, nor were we required to make formations or perform military duties of any kind. We lived in pairs in luxurious hotel rooms in Biarritz. No one checked us in or out of our hotels, so we were on our own each day after class and from 1500 on Fridays, when our last class adjourned, until our first class on Monday, which began at 0900.

We ate in the hotel dining rooms. The army, which also bought some local meats and produce, shipped in most of our food, which the hotel chefs prepared in an excellent fashion. We were issued meal tickets weekly, and we could choose from among several dining rooms, although there was little difference between them. A PX was set up in the city center where we could buy necessities, which were available in plentiful supply. They also sold us cigarettes, still a common currency in France, at a low price. However, the black market in rural France was not as large or well organized as in Berlin or the large French cities. Because of this, we were allowed to buy as many cigarettes as were available, and there were no restrictions on sending money home. I knew we would be going back to Berlin eventually, so I gambled that the black market there would still be going strong and bought about two dozen cartons over the two months we were in Biarritz. In the meantime, I sent home what money I could.

Biarritz had been Winston Churchill's favorite European beach resort—he called it his favorite "watering hole"—and it fully lived up to his recommendation. The town remained relatively unspoiled by the war. The Germans had maintained only a small garrison there, and the nearest American units were hundreds of miles away. The university was relatively small, with only about four thousand students, most of whom were serious about taking advantage of the opportunity. Our ranks included soldiers ranging from colonel to private, but the school's policy was that rank had no privilege. There, amid palm trees, beautiful beaches, and nearby mountains, I was able to make an idyllic and wonderful transition between the horrors of war, the dismal wreckage of Berlin, and the happy civilian life I hoped to enjoy in the near future.

France was in a serious economic depression after the war, and Biarritz American University benefited the local people substantially by bringing in close to six thousand students, teachers, and support staff who poured money into the local economy. The university also purchased great quantities of local goods, rented space in tourist hotels, and employed hundreds of French citizens. This helped Biarritz, nearby Bayonne, and the surrounding countryside begin an economic recovery.

It was difficult for me to concentrate on schoolwork after almost three years away from it. The idea of doing homework was just too much. A term there was two months, and in order to stay for a second term one had to have at least two As and one B. However, grades did not motivate me very much because the school seemed unreal. Moreover, my ninety-four points would most likely allow me to go home in late November or early December, shortly after my first term ended. I was satisfied with two Bs and a C, which I accomplished by concentrating in class but doing almost no homework and very little extra study beyond reading the course texts.

I flew to Biarritz with Sgt. John A. Price. Although both of us were from Battery A, 456th PFAB, we had not known each other well previously. Price had been a gunner, whereas I was a forward observer, so our paths had seldom crossed. We got along well on the plane and decided to room together. Although I had had no previous success in approaching girls, Price was an expert. We registered at the university late on the day we arrived and received our room assignment. The second day we were there was a Saturday, and while I settled down to read a book, spend some time on the beach, and rest, Price disappeared and came back to the hotel very late.

The next morning he explained that he had met a fine lady. He said she was about twenty-nine and was a countess. I did not believe him until I met Countess Jeanne the next day in her villa overlooking the beach a mile northeast of town. The villa was complete with a swimming pool and servants' quarters, but both had been empty for five years. The Moorish-style villa was dilapidated. It had several broken windows and a door that had been forced in by robbers. None of these things had been adequately repaired. There was a formal garden, which was overgrown, but it showed signs of having been beautiful at one time. Jeanne's mother lived in a separate part of the house but we never met her.

John told me Jeanne worked as a telephone operator in Bayonne, a larger town than Biarritz, about six miles to the northeast. She rode her bike to work every day. Later, when we had gained her confidence, we learned that Jeanne was a wealthy woman, although she had little ready cash. Her husband, a colonel, had shared General de Gaulle's belief that only a mobile, armored French army could defeat Germany's panzer forces. He believed the French fortress system would not be able to resist all-out assaults by the German army's mobile forces. Their doubts about future French economic stability caused her husband to act early before most people saw the oncoming crisis. He had converted most of their wealth into gold and other valuables, which were stored in a vault in Toulouse, the nearest major city. Jeanne was afraid to remove any of those things for fear they would be stolen. In early October she told us that their family attorney, who had worked with her husband to arrange the safe storage of their assets, had returned from a German POW camp. He promised to work with her to obtain some of the valuables shortly, as soon as he got his own business affairs in order.

John said Jeanne had a friend who worked with her, and when he told her about me, she offered to introduce me to her. It sounded good to me, so I accepted John's offer. That Sunday evening we all met at Jeanne's villa and then went to dinner at a nearby seafood restaurant. Her friend's name was Gilbertre, and she was about twenty-eight and a very attractive brunette.

We learned that both women were married. Jeanne told us her husband had been captured in 1940 but that she had not heard from him for more than two years. Gilbertre's husband was a captain whom she had not heard from since 1940, which pretty much convinced her that he was dead. Neither had returned, and since the Nazi prison camps had been liberated as much as four to six months earlier, their survival seemed highly unlikely. Nevertheless, they retained a scant hope that their men had been in a German POW camp liberated by the Russians, who might still be holding them.

Jeanne was a tall blonde who spoke almost perfect English with a British accent but Gilbertre did not speak a word of it. We had a very pleasant evening and dinner, and before John and I left to walk back to our hotel we agreed to meet again late Wednesday afternoon since both of them got off work early that day. Although their difficult situation must have been common among French women, knowing them and discussing their circumstances made us personally involved and more sympathetic. Besides the likelihood that they had both lost their husbands, like almost all the French they were nearly destitute and depended solely on the income from their jobs to survive. The people in the area had to depend on what they grew themselves for food, and although they were surrounded by fertile farmland, the occupying Germans had taken much of what they produced. Malnutrition was a serious problem in most of France. The great advantage this region enjoyed over others was that eggs, farm products, and fresh fish were almost always available locally. The only other thing that had always been available throughout the war in the region was wine, and it ranked among the best in the world. However, because France's commercial and shipping infrastructure had broken down, the wine could not be shipped or sold elsewhere. There was also a shortage of workers to pick grapes and make wine, resulting in much lower production than before the war. These problems eliminated one of the most lucrative sources of regional commercial income and employment.

Jeanne and Gilbertre were fortunate to have jobs with the telephone company. However, many of their relatives remained unemployed and relied on them for assistance. Anything beyond basic medical services was nonexistent during the war because most French physicians between twenty-five and fifty-five had been in Nazi POW camps since 1940 and had only recently begun to return. Both women had suffered from a virulent form of influenza the previous year and Gilbertre had lost her only child, a boy of six, to that disease. By the fall of 1945 there were signs that things were beginning to return to normal. Some new jobs were being generated, the railroads were working again, food and medical supplies were being shipped into the region, able-bodied men were returning, and that season's wine production was the best in years.

By Wednesday we were both eager to see the young women again. We had dinner together, and then spent the night with them at the villa. On Friday afternoon, John and I bought bikes and, since the girls were off for the weekend, the four of us rode up to a small town in the nearby hills where we spent Saturday night in a quaint little inn. It had good food and comfortable beds. This was my first intimate experience with a woman, and I thought it was wonderful. Gilbertre and I got along well and enjoyed one another, but we both knew ours was a short-term relationship. She was a dedicated French woman, and I was determined to return to a normal life in America. We remained loyal to each other until I left Biarritz in November. During that time my French improved greatly. There is truth to the old saying that the best way to learn a foreign language is from a native whose head is on an adjoining pillow.

The four of us spent many evenings together, and every weekend we explored the area around Biarritz and Bayonne trying the local food and wine, all of which was great. Just a few miles southwest of Biarritz, close to the Spanish border, was the beautiful little fishing village of Saint-Jean de Luz. It was located on a sheltered bay along the coast, giving the fishing boats protection from the violent weather that frequently came in from the Bay of Biscay. The seafood there was superb, and we were able to rent a boat and captain for a day's fishing and sightseeing.

We visited a pleasant inn there run by a fine French woman who cooked magically and was very kind to us. John and I wanted to cross the border into Spain and spend a weekend there, but the country was off limits to GIs because its government, although remaining neutral, had been sympathetic to the Nazis. We regretted that there was no opportunity to see the nearby Spanish city of San Sebastian. This part of France and Spain just across the border was known as Basque country. It had its own unique food, language, and people, and was quite different from metropolitan France.

Several times we were invited to have dinner with the women's extended families. The second time we went they asked us to bring along four of our friends. We thought coffee was the best thing to bring as a gift, along with chocolate and chewing gum for the children and a few other odds and ends. They had about twenty local relatives, only one of whom was a man younger than fifty. He was Gilbertre's thirty-year-old brother, Jean, who had lost his left hand when the Germans invaded France in 1940. He managed a small farm and orchard in the country with his wife and two children. It was the main source of food for the whole group.

The feast consisted of ducks, mussels, fruits, and vegetables. We had brought a few cans of Spam, which they fried and served with mustard sauce. It, too, was excellent. The girls had also suggested we bring chocolate if possible. I gave them the chocolate I had brought early, and they transformed it into excellent French pastries. Although we got by far the best of the exchange, the coffee we had brought was the first most of them had seen in four years, so it was a great hit.

Jean and I had several long conversations in a mixture of English and French. Rommel's division had overrun his unit when it broke through the French army on the Meuse River in May 1940, and his fleeing comrades had left him for dead. The German doctors took good care of him, amputating his ruined hand and treating three other less severe wounds. After he had sufficiently recuperated the Germans trucked him to Paris with a number of other seriously wounded French soldiers. There they were discharged and allowed to make their way home.

Jean's greatest concern was that the stump of his left arm was useless. I told him of advances the U.S. Army had made with prostheses, and he asked me if I would write a letter to an American hospital asking them to help him. I told him I certainly had no influence but that I would do whatever I could. I planned to see a university doctor the next day, so I suggested he meet me the following Monday and we would visit the clinic there.

After dinner we asked if there was anything they needed from the PX. The list was pitiable. Since they were concerned about staying warm during the coming winter and avoiding the deadly influenza of a few years ago, sweaters headed the list. They also asked for toothbrushes, toothpaste, Band-Aids, iodine, pencils, gloves for the children, and more coffee. We were able to purchase everything on the list except coffee and the sweaters at the PX. John and I each had a sweater in our barracks bags, and we were able to find another two dozen by going from room to room and making deals with other students. Most of the time we were given the sweaters freely. We gave cigarettes to the cooks in exchange for coffee, so we were successful in all of our efforts.

I found the doctor to be sympathetic, so Jean and I visited him three days later, He said he did not have anything like the patient load he had previously in field hospitals. He measured Jean for a prosthesis and ordered it from one of the main American medical supply centers. Jean was surprised at this generosity, but we told him that the army probably had fifty thousand such prostheses left over from the war that it would never use. Nevertheless, the doctor and I hoped that no medical warehouse administrator would want to know how one of the Biarritz students lost a hand. No such inquiry came, and the prosthesis arrived a few days later. Within a week the doctor had taught Jean how to use it properly.

To show his gratitude, Jean invited the doctor and the rest of us to his farm for dinner. He had made a special effort to find fresh escargots. We all enjoyed the snails except for John, who could barely look at them, much less eat them. He dutifully ate a few and gave the rest to the doctor and me. They also served a roast goose, which Jean carved proudly, using his prosthetic hand to hold the fork. The doctor and I were pleased. It seemed symbolic of what well-meaning people could do for one another. The wonderful melons he served for dessert were new to us. They were the size of large honeydew melons but had a leathery, dark green skin. The meat was yellow and very sweet. Jean said he grew hundreds of them. He identified them as Moroccan melons and said they were his best cash crop.

My Biarritz interlude came to an end with the month of October; ten days later I returned to Berlin. I was sad to leave Gilbertre. We had been very good for one another. She had begun to adapt to the change peace brought to France, and together we had made the first key adjustments following the brutalities of a very horrible war. Our parting was final; we never communicated after that day. My hope is that Gilbertre found a good French husband and raised the family she wanted so much.

For me, it was a great learning experience that could not have come at a better time in my life. After spending two years in the company of men in difficult times, Gilbertre introduced me to the kind and gentle companionship of an intelligent and honest woman. I came to see women as being naturally tender, caring, and loving, whereas a man usually had to work at developing these characteristics. Thanks to our short affiliation I saw clearly the benefits I could expect from a good wife and family. The roving life never had much attraction to me, and Gilbertre helped me make a final determination to pursue a mutually loyal, long-term relationship with a fine woman. Fortunately I succeeded. In 1999 I celebrated my fifty-second year happily married to just such a woman.

My contact with the people in Reims, Alsace, and Biarritz was closer than many American soldiers experienced. I knew I would soon be going home and would probably spend no more army time in France. As I flew back to Berlin I thought a great deal about the French people. I was consistently impressed with their honesty, toughness, and optimism.

Their situation from 1940 to 1945 was terrible. Their problems began before 1940, when their politicians and generals developed a fortress mentality while the Germans developed a mobile army. Although by 1940 the French had more soldiers and arguably better armor and airplanes than the Germans, they were quickly and shamefully defeated. Being a proud people, that defeat was a huge burden for them. In the years that followed they were underfed and had inadequate medical services. Most of their younger men had been killed, wounded, or captured in 1940. Some of the rest were forced to serve in German construction brigades or to fight in their army against the Russians.

Liberation brought a new set of difficulties. For six months the various political factions conducted what amounted to a civil war. These factions included the Gaulists, Nazi collaborators, communists, and Vichyites, among many others. For months these factions fought viciously against each another. Many collaborators were executed or imprisoned. Women had their heads shaved and were shunned.

In World War II both American and French families suffered the loss of many sons. Beyond this, the sacrifices and deprivations suffered by American civilians were miniscule compared to those of the French. However, faced with a similar level of deprivation, I believe Americans would be just as tough as the French were. My observation was that the French were similar to Americans in work ethic, determination, and ambition. The only major differences I saw between our peoples were the language and their ancient culture.

As I flew eastward toward Berlin, I wondered what I would find when I arrived. After an idyllic two months in Biarritz, I fervently hoped there would be no more killing in the rail yards, and that the stench of death in Berlin had subsided in my absence. Most of all, I wished for a plane to be waiting to take me to an Atlantic port and a ship that would take me home.

23

Back to Berlin

After the hot sun and clear, blue skies of Biarritz, Berlin was gray, cloudy, rainy, and dismal. When I checked back in at the battery, Captain Alley told me I could be on the list to go home for discharge, leaving soon after 1 December, but he said he had another offer he thought I should not refuse.

In the reorganization of the entire army, two things concerning the 82d had been decided. Unlike most other divisions, the 82d would not be disbanded but would instead become one of a few divisions remaining in the Regular Army. In addition, the 82d had been selected to represent the ETO in a victory parade on New York's Fifth Avenue planned for March 1946. The entire division would sail to New York on the *Queen Mary* and spend a week in the city, after which it would march in the big parade. Everyone who elected to stay through the parade would immediately be promoted one rank and then given the option of being discharged promptly afterward.

Although I did not like disappointing a man I greatly respected, I asked that he put me on the list of men going home to be discharged in early December. Becoming a staff sergeant held no charm to me because I had never wanted to become a soldier in the first place. Besides, my father had told me the next Purdue semester started on 4 March 1946, and I just could not fit a parade down Fifth Avenue into my busy schedule. As it turned out, the 82d sailed for New York on the *Queen Mary* on 4 January 1946, and the parade was held a few weeks after its arrival. Either way, I would have made it to Purdue on time. Nevertheless, I never regretted my decision.

In the two months I had been gone, Berlin had changed a great deal. All parties on both sides of the war just finished were beginning to emerge from the chaos that had existed. Unpredictability had been the norm previously. It is one thing to live not knowing when one is to die as long as the long-term probabilities are good. It is quite another to have serious and real doubts about living out the day or the week. German civilians did not know if their apartment building would be blown up by Allied bombs or if the Gestapo might arrest them on any given night. Soldiers on both sides faced the threat of violent death or being badly wounded daily. Most continental European civilians wondered where their next meal would come from, and the millions of refugees had few prospects for the future. The worst parts of this chaotic condition were improving rapidly, although it would take years for the bloodied Europeans to recover fully. Still, it was a beginning, and it was at least possible for some of the people in western Europe to make plans.

Germans living in the areas of Berlin governed by the British, French, and Americans were showing signs of dealing with the need to develop a new system of law, order, and commerce. Most of the city's streets had been cleared, and many damaged buildings had been razed, resulting in much open space. Many Germans slept in our tents while we slept in their houses. At the time this seemed fair given their actions during the war.

Berlin began to have a commercial life again. Some nightclubs and theaters had reopened, markets were stocked with farm produce being trucked into the city, busses were running, and some banks were open. The stench of death disappeared after more than thirty thousand corpses were found and removed as the buildings were demolished. Prosperity was not yet there, but we recognized that the deep strength of the German people would soon bring about a strong economic recovery. The veterans returning from Allied POW camps would provide much-needed manpower with a strong work ethic, no doubt with the same determination they had shown in their fight against us. They would make the things happen that were necessary for recovery. While our POWs were shipped back to Germany in 1945 and 1946, many of the German soldiers captured by the Soviets were not allowed to return until 1955, and over half of those captured by the Russians were executed or died in captivity.

The Russians had changed radically. When I left Berlin, their soldiers had been swaggering around, apparently believing that their callous acts of cruelty were proof of their manhood. At that time they were totally out of personal or organizational control. We were convinced that their commanders supported acts of revenge against individual German civilians as a matter of policy. By the time I returned, however, the Russian soldiers had become sullen and withdrawn. There were three principle reasons for this turnabout. First, all of them had been convinced by communist propaganda that they were far better off than they would be in a western democracy. When they first saw soldiers from Britain, France, and America, they thought we were all part of some privileged aristocracy. They soon learned otherwise: that we were just ordinary citizens. When they compared their own situation to ours, two things happened: they became jealous, and they began to disbelieve what their communist masters told them. Second, they saw that we, as representatives of the western democracies, trusted and respected one another. The Russian soldier trusted none of his comrades because he could be executed at any time for making an unguarded remark that was reported to his superiors. Despite the fact that they might call their commanding officer, "Comrade," they knew that he had absolute power over their lives, which he could end without trial at his personal whim. These were the same conditions of power that their political leaders had told them existed in the West. They saw that our officers had no such power over us, and that our relationships with our officers were far more open and friendly. The idea of self-discipline, which our army relied upon to maintain discipline in the ranks, was unknown to them. Finally, Russian soldiers suffered from the same problems that we did. They had won a war but now had nothing useful to do. We all were anxious to go home, but where we believed a pleasant, prosperous, and peaceful future awaited us, they had no idea what to expect. None of the simple prospects we looked forward to were attainable for most of them. Because of these new ideas of freedom that they learned from us, contact was the contamination their communist masters feared most and did everything they could to prevent.

The day after I returned I sold four dozen cartons of cigarettes I had brought from Biarritz to our man who dealt on the black market. He told me the Russian with whom he had been trading cigarettes for vodka had disappeared but that another Russian trader quickly took his place. The Russian soldier said his predecessor had been arrested. When asked what had happened to the man, the new Russian said he had been shot for black marketeering. My friend said the deceased soldier had been one of the few decent and honest Russians he had met. Oh, well, so much for decency and honesty in Russians. Apparently such men could not last in their system. From what the Russian contact said, we surmized the real reason he was shot was that he had failed to offer a sufficient share of his profits to his commander.

The new Russian was engaged in the same activity that had resulted in his predecessor's execution. What better illustration is there of their total disinterest in life or death? Or, was this Russian more able to adapt to the corrupt rules? They were only interested in the pleasures of the moment, which were now being seriously interfered with by the brutal discipline of the Red Army's political officers. They were forbidden to fraternize with American, French, or British soldiers and their contact with German civilians was seriously restricted. Rumors, which I am sure were close to being true, said that thousands of Russian soldiers had been shot after the fact for fraternizing with Allied soldiers or German girls and for breaking various rules during the two months I had been gone.

This iron discipline had left only one legal pleasure available to the typical Russian grunt: drunkenness. All the others—which included rape, robbery, and trading or fraternizing with the Americans—were now illegal, and soldiers violating the new rules risked death if they were caught. This callous attitude toward the possibility of their own deaths meant that the new rules could be only partially successful.

Many of the Russians we saw after the new rules went into effect were so drunk they were barely able to walk. This state reduced their inhibitions, and a number of them were armed and dangerous. We were forced to go about in armed groups because drunken Russians sought out single Western soldiers to rob and shoot. Russian drunks had no consciences and were completely out of control, their anger fueled by jealousy. Their communist philosophy made them believe they were entitled to whatever we were carrying, and since we did not share their philosophy, they believed they had the right to steal from or even kill us.

At the time of my departure, the Soviets had begun to set up guard posts on the major roads leading out of their zone. They were placed there to keep Russian soldiers from leaving their zone and coming in contact with American, French, or British troops. It was certainly clear that theirs was not a society of trust and openness.

I spent the last weeks of November 1945 on boring guard duty. I had missed the day our battery had honor guard duty, which might have been interesting. Everything else the officers thought of to occupy our time was tiresome and of no redeeming value. Finally, on 28 November, I received word that I would be relieved of duty with the battery in two days and that I was to report to the discharge officer at division headquarters on 1 December. There, I would be given my orders to go home at last.

Many of the men I had fought beside for a year had already gone home, and about half of the division was by then made up of replacements who had seen little or no action. Nevertheless, a number of my old friends were still waiting for their point number to come up or had volunteered to stay and march with the division in the big parade. This made our parting a bittersweet occasion.

24

Going Home

The group I was in was informal and its members were unrelated except that all had one thing in common: we all had close to ninety-four points, the number needed to go home for discharge. Otherwise, only a few of the 202 men knew each other, in spite of the fact that we all were from the 82d Airborne Division. There were soldiers from all branches, including seven of us from the 456th PFAB, although I knew none of the others well. There were no commissioned officers in the group, which had one first sergeant and four other sergeants, including me, and about ten corporals.

The discharge officer organized the 202 men as an ad hoc company with the first sergeant in overall charge and each sergeant in command of a platoon of about fifty men. We did not have to worry much about the normal disciplinary problems such as men going AWOL or disobedience since none of us wanted to do anything that might interfere with our trip home. Our only responsibility was to keep track of everyone and keep them from wandering off, as soldiers were likely to do. We had to discourage men from chasing women and drinking—two other things soldiers are prone to do— but cooperation was excellent, so the problems we faced from our charges turned out to be minor.

The five sergeants met to plan the trip the day before we were to leave. We were lucky to have 1st Sgt. Ray Jones in charge. Ray had accumulated more than 120 points but had stayed behind at the request of his battalion commander. He had participated in several large troop movements by train. He pointed out that we would be isolated from the train crew and each other once we were on the train and moving, and unless we established a relationship with them in advance, we would be at their mercy at stops for food, water, and going to the bathroom. He explained that we needed to coordinate with the crew in advance or they would simply stop, do whatever needed to be done, and then move on, possibly without some of our men. We had to know what was going on and be able to hold the train until we were certain everyone was aboard. There was concern about how well we would survive the cold, five-day trip to Antwerp, where we were to board a ship scheduled to sail to Boston on 10 December.

Ray put a corporal in charge of arranging to pick up our C rations, which would be drawn from division stocks. We needed enough for at least six days per man. We also required a few portable stoves per car in order to prepare the food, and some men had to be trained to use the stoves carefully to avoid setting the old wooden cars afire. We would occupy twelve "forty-or-eight" rail cars, so each car would carry about eighteen men along with all their personal gear. We met the train commander, a quartermaster captain, the day before we were to leave. He said the train had a Belgian crew that made the trip from Berlin to Antwerp and back about three times a month. The captain and the crew occupied a control car that was just behind the engine. This car was set up with offices and bunks and had telephone contact with the engineer. The captain said he was neither capable of, nor interested in, commanding the troops, so it would be up to us to handle them. He said the train would stop every four to five hours for water and fuel and there would probably be many other stops due to traffic delays. He said we should remain on board during short stops but that we would be able to get off at the longer water stops, which were usually made near stations. At these stops we would have time to replenish our canteens and go to the toilet. Occasionally when long stops were necessary, we might even have an opportunity to take showers. When we stopped at major supply depots we might also find a mess hall where we could get a hot meal.

We suggested that Ray ride in the control car and serve as our liaison with the captain and the crew. A sergeant or corporal would be in control of each car and make certain it was supplied with adequate food and water, and a sergeant would be responsible for each group of four cars. When the train stopped, the NCOs would also check off each soldier as he left and returned to his car. At stops, Ray would get off the train and raise both arms as a signal that there was time for the rest of us to leave the train. When it was time to board, each of the four sergeants would check with the NCOs in his group. If a soldier turned up missing, the sergeants and corporals would track him down. When a sergeant's four cars were ready, he would wave to Ray indicating that everyone was accounted for. With Ray in the control car, we figured the crew could be prevented from moving the train before everyone was back on board. It seemed like a system that would work.

We had none of the normal tools of authority with which to enforce our wishes, such as threats of fines, reduction in rank, or being sent to the stockade. But we didn't really need them. Ray simply carried all of the men's personal travel orders. They could not get home without them. That was all the motivation they needed. Before we loaded the train, we told everyone we were all due to board Liberty ship 1291 (it had a name and another number, but I can no longer remember them), on 10 December. We also told them that if anyone became separated he would be alone in Europe without orders, and it might take months to get on another ship headed home because the army would not have much interest in him. There were still many deserters loose in Europe, so we also warned them that they could wind up in a stockade for some time while the MPs sorted out their situation. We advised everyone that if they got separated, the best thing would be to hitch a ride on another train to Antwerp and try to find and board our ship. If that failed, they would truly be on their own. None of us intended to stay behind to look for them.

Everything went smoothly. We made three stops at major supply depots where we had meals in large British or American mess halls and were able to take showers. At one point a bearing failed on the engine tender and we had to limp into a repair yard, where we sat for six hours. That was our worst stop because there was nothing to do. When it was time to go we discovered we had lost three troopers who managed to hook up with some prostitutes. The train had to wait another hour while we tracked down the three missing men and got them aboard.

We were unloaded on the Antwerp docks a half-mile from Liberty ship 1291 during the midafternoon of 8 December. After marching to the ship and waiting two hours on the dock, we were allowed to board. All of us were assigned to above-deck cabins that were usually reserved for officers. The cabins were very comfortable compared to the crowded troop quarters in the hold below deck. Each cabin had four double-deck bunks, four chairs, a closet, and a small desk. The cabins lining the outside walls had portholes that could not be opened but from which we could see the surrounding land or sea.

We knew from experience that about a quarter of the men would become seasick the moment the ship began to move, and another quarter would become seasick if the ship moved into any kind of rough weather. We questioned everyone to try to learn who had tendencies toward seasickness and who did not, since the only thing worse than being seasick was to be surrounded by others who were. Putting all the men who were prone to seasickness together in one group of cabins was agreeable to all, and the sergeants agreed that one of them would visit any seasick men at least four times a day. Except in a few of the more serious cases, seasickness usually passed in two or three days, and those who did not get over it in that time required special treatment to avoid dehydration and other complications.

Our group occupied twenty-five of the thirty-four cabins, and twelve unrelated commissioned officers occupied three, leaving six unoccupied. The ship's captain told us the senior ranking commissioned officer would command all of the troops on board. We five sergeants visited the senior officer, a major. He was a lawyer from SHAEF headquarters, and he had never commanded anything but a secretary. The other officers, four doctors and seven quartermasters, had never commanded troops either. He introduced them all to us but they were a sorry lot as far as being soldiers was concerned. They were probably efficient in their specialties and seemed pleasant enough, though. They asked us about our experience and how we had made it all the way from Berlin without any officers to su-

pervise us. We answered their questions forthrightly, describing how
we had planned and handled the move.

After that, the five of us went back to our dining room to discuss
our situation. We decided we could not depend on these officers for
much and that we would have to take care of ourselves, ignoring their
orders if necessary. About fifteen minutes later, the major came in
and said he wanted to talk to us some more. He said the twelve officers had discussed their own backgrounds and concluded we were
more qualified to command the soldiers on the ship than any of
them were. They asked us if they could join us and come under our
care and supervision. We said we had no desire to become anything
more high ranking than civilians, but that we would do what they
wanted as far as those in the cabins above deck were concerned.
Once this arrangement was reached, we insisted they agree to stay
with it for the full trip and fully support us with the ship's crew. They
said they would not interfere as long as we did not abuse others.
Since we knew that would never be a problem, we agreed to take
charge.

The major and the five sergeants discussed the plan with the ship's
captain and his first officer and he agreed to the arrangement. We
asked what other troops would be joining the ship. To our shock, we
were told that about twenty-five hundred black quartermaster and
transportation troops would be placed in the hold below deck. We
asked if they would have their own officers, and the captain said he
thought not. His plan was to move them below decks, feed them in
a mess hall down in the hold, and lock them in, not allowing them
to come above deck until we were in Boston. We did not get to finish our conversation with the ship's captain because the black troops
arrived and he had to supervise their loading.

We discussed the captain's plan with the doctors. All concluded
that a ten- to twelve-day voyage in the stormy North Atlantic could
result in a disaster if his plan was followed. The bunks below decks
were typical for a troop transport. They were built of metal pipe that
formed stacks of bunks six high. Each soldier had to fit himself into
a canvas bunk that was paired side-by-side with another bunk from
the next stack. The stacks were about two feet apart and tied together
with pipe into a massive structure that filled much of each hold.

Each soldier had to climb as much as ten feet up the pipe structure to get to his bunk, and there were no safety belts. When a man
lay in his bunk, he was only a foot below the man above him unless
he was in the top bunk. No one could sit upright, and there were no
lights for reading. I had taken a similar ship with the same arrangements from New Jersey to Liverpool in 1944. Invariably men who
were prone to seasickness occupied the top bunks, which gave the
greatest sensation of movement. Since vomit flows downhill, everyone in the stack was sure to become sick.

Liberty ships were designed to carry heavy cargo loads, and a load
of troops was comparatively light. This meant the ship rode higher
in the water, which accentuated their tendency to roll. In a storm this
really could become wild, most uncomfortable for the troops aboard.

No matter what anyone did for them, the men in the hold would
be miserable. Even worse, unless they were given the opportunity to
go above decks for an occasional breath of fresh air and some exercise and encouraged regularly to clean up and take food and water,
some of them could die. The conditions the ship's captain sought
to impose on these men would surely lead to fights among them, and
it was possible that more serious violence might erupt. We agreed
that his plan was unacceptable. Although we did not like the idea of
taking on the additional responsibility, we went to the captain and
persuaded him to agree to allow us to assume control of all the army
troops on board while he limited his responsibilities to managing the
maneuvers of his ship. At first he objected to allowing the black
troops to come up on deck for exercise. He said he was afraid they
would riot and take over the ship. After pointing out that these men,
like us, wanted only to go home, we asked him what they, or anyone
else, would want with this rusty old bucket of bolts. He was somewhat
taken aback by our comments about the quality of his ship, but after considering our suggestions, he recognized their wisdom and that
we would consider no other alternative. He gave in and agreed to
our proposal.

Next, we asked him about the ship's medical facilities. He said it
was equipped with a two-cabin infirmary and carried a small supply
of drugs. We had the doctors inspect the facilities, and they found
them totally inadequate for the needs of the nearly three thousand

men who would be making the ten-day voyage. We asked if they had brought any medical supplies or equipment with them and found they had little to add. With Ray in the background telling them what to do, the major, two quartermaster officers, and the four doctors, went to the dockyard hospital and arranged to obtain an acceptable stock of additional medical supplies. They came back, fully prepared to treat our numbers for such ailments as seasickness and other stomach disorders, headaches, minor sprains and fractures, cuts that needed suturing, and numerous other ailments or injuries we were likely to experience. We also found more space below decks for those acute seasickness cases that became dehydrated and needed intravenous feeding and closer attention. We were also fortunate that four of the troopers in our group were combat medics and would be of great help to the doctors.

After the black troops boarded we went below to find those who were in charge of them. Although there were a number of black noncoms in their ranks, we found only six sergeants in charge of what was the equivalent of two large battalions, and they were not at all clear about their duties and responsibilities. We asked the six of them to come to our mess hall to discuss the situation. They seemed like good men, but they had always depended on their officers for guidance and were used to deferring to white people. When we asked what their major concerns were, they said seasickness and rough seas. We laughed and said that those were our main fears, too. We told them we had four doctors and four combat medics on board who were reasonably well equipped to treat most common problems. They were relieved and said they would give their men this good news. Then we told them of the agreement we had made with the ship's captain and asked if they would rather work with us or make their own arrangements with him. We left them to talk it over for a few minutes. When we returned, they said that working with us would be best for them. We had already decided to keep one cabin empty for emergencies, so we told them we had extra cabins that would take up to sixteen of their noncoms if they wanted to join us. A dozen of them accepted the offer.

We discussed the ideas we had about insisting on cleaning up, getting exercise, eating regular meals whenever they could, drinking sufficient water, and getting fresh air whenever possible. Our diet the first two days would be fresh meat and vegetables, but after that it would be limited to creamed chipped beef, boiled dried fish, soup, and fried Spam, with some additional canned goods including a few fruits and vegetables. This diet was not likely to agree with men who were at all susceptible to seasickness. We told them how we had separated our men who were prone to seasickness from the rest and how we planned to care for the sick, then suggested that they do the same thing.

They accepted our proposals and went below to explain everything to their men. They implemented the idea of separating the seasick-prone men from the rest and made up an exercise schedule. We all hoped we would be able to go outside for exercise and that storms would not keep us inside for the whole trip. They also asked that ten of us and at least two doctors tour their below-deck quarters twice a day. In view of their large numbers, this was a good idea. After discussing this request with them, all of the doctors and medics agreed to tour their area twice a day along with five of our NCOs and five of our more experienced and reliable troopers.

We left the Antwerp docks and moved slowly through the Schelde estuary in the afternoon sun. The waterway flowed through Belgium and then Holland for about thirty miles, then opened into the North Sea. Dikes lined the waterway, so we were able to look down on the surrounding land from the upper parts of the ship. There were windmills all along the dikes, and we could see colorful houses beyond them. There was little sign of the heavy fighting required to secure this waterway in 1944.

A few hundred miles out at sea we ran into a series of fierce storms that lashed us nearly all the way to Boston. The decks were soon covered with ice, and we were all imprisoned in the ship after the second day of what turned out to be a twelve-day crossing. Seven of the men below decks had broken arms, and we had one broken arm and one broken leg among the troopers in our cabins. Fortunately none of these breaks were compound fractures. There were also numerous sprains and bruises. The infirmary and the extra cabin were full of men needing attention for injuries and complications from seasickness, but everyone reached the states alive and safe.

Although it was far from a pleasure cruise, our command arrangements worked out well. The twelve black noncoms living in the cabins with us were men of intelligence and good humor and became good comrades. Two of them were tigers at poker. They did everything we suggested and performed well. It is beyond imagination how difficult that voyage would have been for all of us if we had not intervened with the captain and persuaded him to let us take charge. As it was, none of us liked riding out one storm after another in a poor ship that never stopped rolling and everyone feared would sink at any time.

I thought a lot during the voyage about how black Americans were treated in World War II. I had graduated from an integrated high school in a Cincinnati suburb in 1942. I played football and baseball with a number of blacks, and two of them were among my better friends. Both had shown high intelligence, good social skills, and were responsive to friendship. My experience with blacks in the ETO was very limited because of the army's segregation policy. Army policy resulted in only a few blacks being assigned to frontline combat units. There were a small number of segregated antiaircraft, field artillery, tank, and tank destroyer battalions, and two of the army's infantry divisions were black. However, the vast majority of blacks served in quartermaster and transportation units. The same was true of the air force, which had only one black fighter group, the famed Tuskegee airmen who fought in North Africa and Italy, and one black bomber group, which never left the states. The sea services were even worse. Only a comparative handful of blacks served aboard ships in a capacity other than as mess stewards or cooks, and those were limited to service on auxiliary ships. No blacks at all were assigned to frontline combat units in the Marine Corps.

During the Civil War, the performance of U.S. colored regiments in combat was as good as many white units. Blacks also fought with distinction on the frontier and in the Spanish-American War. Early in the twentieth century, however, the armed services made a conscious decision to strictly limit the assignment of blacks to combat units. This was a particularly bitter pill for black Americans to swallow. By denying them the opportunity to serve in combat, the services denied them full participation in what would become the most important event in their lifetime. It also kept them from receiving the credit that comes with having made sacrifices on the battlefield. Ironically, even those who did fight did not get appropriate recognition for their actions. No blacks in World War II were awarded the Medal of Honor, although a board commissioned by the army a few years ago determined that seven black heroes deserved that recognition, albeit belatedly. There was no logical reason to keep the majority of blacks from participating in combat; prejudice was the sole cause.

On one hand we resented the fact that the army kept blacks out of combat, but there was nothing we could do about it. On the other hand, the general feeling at the time was that we could not trust blacks to fight well next to us. Our experience indicated that white troops in poorly trained divisions were not trustworthy to fight next to us either. My opinion was that the level of training was the main factor in these differences, not being black or white. Of course if the army said blacks could not be trusted to fight and then did not train them or allow them to fight, this became a self-fulfilling prophecy.

My other main observation of black troops was on the ship that brought me home. The treatment planned for them was dreadful. Clearly, it would have only been meted out to those who were perceived by whites to be second-class citizens. My contact with these blacks led me to believe they did not deserve such treatment. From today's vantage point, I cannot help but wonder how much more improved race relations would be if blacks had been allowed to serve in combat on an equal basis with whites in World War II. I believe the country would now be much better off.

We arrived in Boston on 22 December, two days late. All were disappointed because Christmas was so close and we were certain that we could not possibly reach our homes in time. Reaching our discharge destinations and being processed for discharge would obviously take too long.

The 82d Airborne men were the last troops to leave the ship after the officers and the blacks. We five sergeants were pleased with what we had accomplished. We did not have to evoke the Articles of War or military police or a large command structure to gain the full cooperation of the troops on board. We had gained the total cooperation of almost three thousand men, including twelve commissioned officers and the ship's captain and crew, through the use of moral persuasion and common sense, along with the credibility our obviously superior level of past experience gave us.

This was an example of what capable, experienced, noncommissioned officers accomplished in the 82d throughout the war. We five also recognized that none did more or less than any other; ours was truly a team effort. It was particularly pleasing to have the lawyer-major and some of the other officers shake our hands and tell us we had done well and that they were pleased to have served under us. We congratulated one another for doing our last army jobs well.

25

Home at Last

My parents and I kept up a weekly correspondence throughout the time I was overseas. Their letters in late 1944 indicated that there was considerable turmoil on the home front. My father, Henry, worked for the Food Machinery Corporation (FMC), a major heavy equipment manufacturing company. He had managed a manufacturing plant that made water pumps ranging in size from huge agricultural pumps for irrigation to sump pumps for home use. Production of most pumps was suspended at the start of the war, when FMC, like most of American industry, converted to war production. My father, who had been in the water pump business throughout his prewar career, soon found himself in charge of a plant near Los Angeles that made amphibious tanks. In late 1944 he wrote that the vehicle they had been producing had become obsolete, demand was down, and that his plant would close before the end of the year.

By that time it was clear to everyone that the war would soon end and the demand for munitions and armament would slow down radically; therefore, FMC was beginning to plan for its postwar future. The company had two Midwest pump-manufacturing plants—one in Quincy, Illinois, and the other in Canton, Ohio. It also had a large Indianapolis plant that had been producing Sherman tanks throughout the war but would soon shut its production line down. Some consideration was being given to consolidating the company's eastern pump-manufacturing and other operations at the Indianapolis plant.

After the war ended in August I had written to my parents explaining that I had to tell the army where I wanted to be discharged because this was necessary for them to complete my discharge papers. Almost every state had a discharge center, but I did not want to take the chance of asking for any changes as it might delay my separation from the service. My father replied that he would soon be moving to manage one of the Midwest plants and that he might end up managing all three. In the end we decided that Camp Atterbury, Indiana, was the closest post to the three cities to which my parents might be transferred. It proved to be a good choice because they soon wrote that they were moving from Pasadena, California, to Illinois, where he would manage the Quincy plant.

After our Liberty ship docked, we went through customs and then to a nearby transient barracks. The customs inspection was a joke because all of us from the 82d had several German weapons we had taken as souvenirs, all complete with the appropriate ammunition. The transient barracks commander examined our orders, which were then given back to us. He also provided us with train tickets for the trip to our various discharge points.

The first thing I did when I had the opportunity was to telephone my parents and tell them I was back in the country. Gas rationing had ended, so my parents planned to drive from Quincy to Camp Atterbury to pick me up as soon as I was able to give them a release date. I was an only child born after my mother had suffered several miscarriages. Thus, my war service had been very difficult for my parents to cope with, and they were elated that their anxieties were at last over.

Since I was the only one from our 82d Airborne Division group going to Camp Atterbury for discharge, I said good-bye to everyone on the morning of the twenty-third and boarded my train. I was given a sleeper berth, which was enormously comfortable after my previous experiences riding in European boxcars.

The New England countryside in December was gray and dismal, not living up to any of my memories of the United States. Surely my recollections of the consistent beauty of my homeland had become exaggerated after almost two years in war-torn Europe. The appearance did not improve as the train passed through New York City and then on to Pittsburgh. We passed through Indianapolis, where several cars were switched to a train that would take them southwest to Camp Atterbury. The trip had taken two days, and I arrived there on Christmas evening.

It took all the next day for me to be processed for discharge because there were a large number of other soldiers at the camp for the same purpose. The discharge center was run by a group of army clerks who had been noncombatants throughout the war. They seemed lazy and were totally disinterested in any of the soldiers they were processing. No service records were available, and the clerks I was dealing with neither knew of nor cared anything about the 82d Airborne Division. I was told I would be discharged by noon on the twenty-seventh and that they would not be hurried. I called my parents and told them they could pick me up at the camp gates at noon the next day or that I could take a bus and meet them anywhere they suggested. I also told them that if they came they should be prepared to wait, perhaps all afternoon, while the army did things at its own slow pace.

My parents would consider no alternative other than picking me up, and they drove most of the night to make it to Camp Atterbury by noon on the twenty-seventh. I came out at 1330, which was not too bad for the army. We spent the night in an Indianapolis hotel and then drove on to Quincy the next day. For the next few weeks, my mother tried to make up for all the good meals I had missed over almost three years. After a quiet New Year's Eve celebration, we began to try to return to a normal life. It was a marvelous homecoming. My mother insisted that I do two things immediately: have a photograph taken in uniform (frontispiece), and get a facial. The idea of a facial sounded stupid to me, but I humored her. I was glad I did. Getting the European dirt thoroughly removed from my pores turned out to be a real treat.

I called the registrar's office at Purdue during the first week of January and said I wanted to enroll for the trimester that started in early March. The clerk said she would mail the necessary papers to me and assured me I would have no trouble being readmitted. With these transitional steps it became clear that my war had ended. I was ready to put the army and all its boredom, horrors, and high adventure behind me and return to civilian life.

Epilogue

The problems we faced once the war was over seemed much less difficult. Returning GIs had to find jobs or go back to college. Europe was wrecked and international commerce was limited in the aftermath of the war. Fear of future international conflicts between major powers such as World Wars I and II concentrated international thinking on means to prevent such wars. The United States developed three government-backed initiatives aimed at mitigating these problems and improving the lives of its citizens.

Contrary to its actions after World War I, when the United States failed to support the League of Nations, this country was active in organizing and supporting the United Nations (UN). The UN has not been perfect, and it is still evolving, but it has been instrumental in reducing the threat of world conflicts and the rise of power-hungry dictators such as Adolf Hitler. Although there are still too many dictators running governments in the world today, they are petty compared to those who started World War II. With all its flaws, the UN offers the greatest hope for maintaining global peace and containing minor conflicts that do flare up.

The second major initiative was the Marshall Plan. This contributed much to the rebuilding of Europe, including our former enemies. It has paid off in improved commerce and goodwill many times over and is still the basis for acceptance of the United States as a friend and world leader by Europeans.

The third initiative was the GI Bill of Rights. Under this plan, the government financed the education of a returning soldier. It was not an elite program because it encompassed all types of education—

including basic literacy, industrial training, and college programs—and it was available to all who wished to enter an educational program, not just those who hoped to continue in one. This program contributed greatly to the quality of the U.S. workforce for a generation. Secondarily, it phased the entry of returning soldiers into the workforce over several years, avoiding the dumping of millions into the workplace in a very few months. Think of the internal conflict that might have occurred if a significant number of returning soldiers had not been diverted into education programs. Furthermore, I think it is fair to say that this program has paid for itself many times over as a result of increased productivity and tax revenue from better-educated workers.

When the war in Europe ended, all feared the Soviet Union, which was dictatorial and little better than Nazi Germany. As nuclear bombs and intercontinental ballistic missiles were developed, this fear heightened. The Soviets had announced international goals of expansion and took advantage of their occupation to annex a number of eastern European countries to their empire.

My experience with the Russians in Berlin led me to a conclusion about them that was not commonly held but which I frequently voiced. Without the Great Patriotic War to motivate the average Russian, I was convinced that it would be difficult for a dictatorial regime to seriously threaten our way of life. The Soviet economic system was terribly inefficient and seemed to me incapable of both feeding its people and meeting the nation's ambitious military goals at the same time. Moreover, I thought them to be technically inept. Still, if the Soviets had fired a hundred missiles carrying nuclear warheads all aimed at the United States and ten hit us, ten hit Europe, and the rest failed and fell into the ocean or on Russia, it would have been a disaster.

The United States won the Cold War in the 1970s and 1980s by continuously inventing new and improved weapons systems. In their attempts to keep up, the Soviets overextended their limited technical ability and economic resources and bankrupted themselves. At the same time, the demand for money for technology took food from their citizens' plates. Among other things, these demands resulted in the failure of their inefficient system.

By 1990, the eastern European countries dominated by the Soviets were beginning to see opportunities to escape the Soviet Empire. I was in Czechoslovakia in 1967 and observed firsthand how much the vast majority of the citizens of that country hated the Soviets. The Soviets had previous problems in Hungary and soon were to have them in Poland and East Germany. When they embarked on an expansionist war in Afghanistan and were beaten while being unable to feed their own population, the whole Soviet system began to collapse. It turned into a "no-win" war. Body bags coming home to families from an unpopular war were the final straw. At the same time, international travel and the spread of mass media that could not be censored showed the Soviet people that life could be better and resulted in even greater dissatisfaction with the communist elite.

The United States waged its own no-win war in Vietnam. I hope it has learned that such wars are unproductive. Gallant men should not be wasted in such actions. A country should carefully evaluate its purposes, the rationality of perceived threats to its national security, and other logical factors before it decides to go to war. If it decides to do so, it should dedicate itself to achieving victory.

The attempts of Russia and the other republics that broke off from the Soviet Union to embrace democratic capitalism are encouraging. However, it will be difficult for a culture that has never known anything but a despotic form of government to progress quickly. It has taken the United States, a country born of democratic ideals, more than two hundred years to reach its present level of democracy. It is unreasonable to expect the Russians to achieve success in a significantly shorter time span. They and the rest of the world will have to be patient.

In spite of the small wars of the past half-century, this has been a far more peaceful and constructive time than any other fifty-year period for centuries. Those who fought in what may well prove to have been mankind's last global conflict, including those who dropped the atomic bombs on Japan, are largely responsible for these improved conditions. Although the world faces problems like overpopulation, I am optimistic that there is enough goodwill in the world today to continue the trend of the past fifty years.

• • •

With the help of Lt. Col. (Retired) Herman L. Alley and Starlyn Jorgensen, I have tried to trace the postwar experience of some of those who shared my experiences with me. For the most part these were men who were close and important to me. I regret that the list is only partial.

First, I will write about those who served with me in the 456th PFAB. This was a fine and diverse group of men. Unfortunately, many are dead now. However, I shall not dwell on death but will report instead on where the living are at the time I write this, if known.

Captain Alley, our battery commander, continued in the Regular Army, fought in the Korean War, and was the protocol officer at Fort Bliss, Texas, when he retired after twenty-five years of service as a lieutenant colonel. He taught school for a year, and then returned to his old job at Fort Bliss as a federal civilian employee, retiring seventeen years later. He earned a bachelor's degree in business administration at the University of Georgia. Herman has three children and lives with Gloria, his wife of fifty-three years, in Dothan, Alabama. Herman told me that his proudest moment in the army was when he participated in the New York City victory parade in January 1945. His only regret was that only one officer and seven enlisted men who had seen combat were with him. The rest of us had gone home at the first opportunity.

Lieutenant Henry J. Aust, our battery executive officer, returned to his family's financial business. He remained in the Army Reserve and retired as a colonel after thirty years.

Lieutenant William L. Cameron, one of my forward observer team chiefs, stayed in the army and fought in Korea. He later became an army missile officer and retired from the service as a major.

Lieutenant John S. Osmussen, another of our forward observer team chiefs, lost the use of an arm in Holland. After spending many months in a veterans' hospital, he returned to his home in Minneapolis.

First Sergeant Arthur V. Hazlett, our battery first sergeant in Normandy and Holland, was an Old Army man. After losing a leg in Holland, he stayed in the Regular Army and retired as a first sergeant after thirty years of service.

Staff Sergeant Russell H. Burton Jr., a section leader, forward observer, and our first sergeant in 1945, was our last casualty of the war. Russ stayed in the Regular Army and received a direct commission. He fought in Korea and retired as a lieutenant colonel after thirty years.

Staff Sergeant John J. Donahue, our supply sergeant, succeeded Russ Burton as first sergeant. Donahue went home after the war and worked in the steel mills in Gary, Indiana.

Staff Sergeant Ossie Cordell, our mess sergeant, returned to his wife and children and ran a restaurant in Arkansas.

Sergeant John G. Donohoe, who was in charge of the battery's perimeter security, returned to Brooklyn, New York, where he worked for several newspapers as a typesetter.

Sergeant John A. Price, a gunner, section chief, and later my roommate at Biarritz American University, was a foreman in a Chicago yeast plant at the time he was drafted. John used the GI Bill to attend Illinois State University, where he earned his bachelor's degree, and then graduated from Harvard Law School. He moved to Colorado, practiced law, and was appointed as a district court judge in 1972. He retired in 1992 and now lives with Caroline, his wife of fifty-four years, in Grand Junction, Colorado.

Corporal Paul Swazuk, one of our ammunition handlers, returned to Pittsburgh, married, and had four children. He worked for a company that built nuclear engines for submarines until he retired. He now lives there with his daughter.

Corporal Robert M. Gaffney, our battery clerk, leaves a sad story for such a bright and personable man. He completed college, married, had a family, and worked for Scribners Publishing Company in New York. He became an alcoholic and died homeless, on a street in Miami in the '90s.

Technician Fourth Grade Richard W. Mote, one of our gun mechanics, returned to Indianapolis, married, and taught high school history until he retired. He is still active in that state's antiabortion movement.

Technician Fifth Grade Robert Bean stayed in the service, was commissioned, and retired as a colonel after thirty years.

Private Marcel C. Four, my driver on occasion, returned to New

York where his family operated a restaurant. He eventually became manager and ran it until he retired.

Private Leonard Bell Jr. stayed in the army and retired after thirty years as a command sergeant major. He later became chief of police in Piggott, Arkansas.

Private Joseph B. Clark returned to Brooklyn, New York, where he became a detective on the police force.

Two other people in the 456th PFAB were important to me:

Lieutenant Colonel Wagner J. D'Alessio, our battalion commander, had been a lawyer in San Francisco before the war and afterward returned to his practice.

Staff Sergeant Arthur G. Frenck, who served in headquarters battery and is the father of Starlyn Jorgensen, stayed in the airborne, fought in Korea, and retired after thirty years as a chief warrant officer.

I would be remiss if I finished this list of comrades without mentioning the officers of the infantry units the 456th PFAB supported.

Colonel William B. Ekman, the 505th PIR commander, joined the outfit just before D day and remained in command throughout the war. He remained in the army, was promoted to brigadier general, and was post commander of Fort Dix, New Jersey, when he retired after thirty years of service.

A battalion commander in a parachute infantry regiment did not have a long life expectancy. Of the twenty-seven battalion commanders in the American and British Airborne Divisions dropped into Normandy, sixteen were killed in action within three days. The 505th PIR had fifteen battalion commanders during its time in the ETO from North Africa to Berlin (seven battle stars). Of these, two were promoted out of their jobs, three survived to the end of the war, and ten were killed or wounded badly enough to be withdrawn from duty.

Then there are the two generals who I met.

Lieutenant General Matthew B. Ridgway, first our division and later XVIII Airborne Corps commander, graduated from West Point in April 1917. After World War II, Ridgway served as commanding general of UN forces in Korea. He became army chief of staff after the Korean War and retired as a full general in June 1955. He served as chairman of the Mellon Institute of Industrial Research until he retired from that post in 1960.

Major General James M. Gavin, 505th RCT and then division commander, graduated from West Point in 1929 and was one of the youngest major generals in the army. Gavin retired as a lieutenant general and served as the U.S. ambassador to France. I had the pleasure of seeing him again for a pleasant half-hour visit when he was chairman of Arthur D. Little and my company was a client of that industrial research firm.

Lastly, there is General of the Army Dwight D, Eisenhower, who led the Allied armies in Europe to victory. Although I criticize General Eisenhower for his support of Field Marshal Montgomery's poorly considered Operation Market-Garden, it was one of the few mistakes he made. After the war, Eisenhower continued to give the people of the United States excellent service first as army chief of staff and then as president for two terms. He had a rare combination of military skill and political acumen that should rank him among the five great generals this country has produced.

The GI Bill helped me, too. My parents supported part of my educational needs, and the money I saved in the army helped, but the GI Bill contributed largely to the financing of my return to Purdue, where I earned a bachelor's degree in chemical engineering in 1948. It also helped to finance graduate school at the Wharton School of Finance and Commerce, where I earned a master's degree in business administration in 1950.

I had great difficulty making friends during the first three years after the war. This was a defense mechanism against survival guilt. The simple solution was for my subconscious to demand that I not make friends at all. Another postwar problem I had was making the transition from combat to college. It was difficult for me to concentrate on college subjects, which seemed trivial in comparison to the responsibilities I had been given during the war.

My marriage to Betty Anne Heidbreder in 1947 was a great step toward solving these problems. Her influence enabled me to forget many of the bad things that had happened to me in the war. Fortunately, by 1950 most of this aberration had disappeared. My marriage and all that went with it contributed to my recovering my ability to make friends and my grades improved from mediocre to honors. Having someone else to work for changed me from a student who was only going through the motions to one who was interested and highly motivated.

As of 1999, Betty and I have been married for fifty-two years. Our two children, John Jr. ("Dave") and Anne, along with our grand-children, Jaime and John III, have been the joys of our lives.

The good things that happened to me during my army service probably did as much for my subsequent business career as did my education. It taught me the value of leadership, loyalty, responsibil-ity, and teamwork in a practical way that no formal education could have. I was successful in my short army career and this led to a suc-cessful business career. It was fortunate that I joined Battery A at a time when it was being rebuilt. Because the unit was short of non-commissioned officers I was given unusual opportunities for pro-motion. My acceptance of responsibility enhanced my self-confi-dence and self-esteem, which led to quick maturation.

I worked for four companies between 1950 and 1990, when I re-tired. My experience was diverse. I held a variety of staff and execu-tive positions in twenty-three years with a chemical company. Dur-ing that time I led many merger and acquisition efforts. I moved to Colorado in 1973 to become vice president of a start-up mining com-pany, and then became executive vice president of a medical elec-tronics firm. Finally, I founded a direct marketing company, which I managed for the last ten years of my career. Since retiring I have been active as a director of several companies, and I have always been active as an investor, usually successfully.

Writing was something I had always wanted to do, and as I men-tioned in the beginning, this memoir is my second book. My primary motivation in writing it is to leave a legacy for my children and grand-children and a window through which others can view those times. Writing it has been difficult because it brought old memories to light, some of which were bad and some good. It covers my personal ex-periences, adventures, and mishaps over a 959-day period. Millions of soldiers from all the countries that fought in World War II had similar experiences. My story is not unique in general terms. As I write this in 1999, I recognize that I am fortunate to have been a good observer with a strong memory, and to some degree the book's ex-istence is the result of whatever modest writing skill I possess.

The stories of about twenty close friends I lost in the fighting will never be told, and their twenty lost stories are but a small sample of several million more untold stories. Many English memorials for soldiers killed in the two great world wars are engraved with words written during World War I by poet Laurence Binyon. Those words reflect my feelings about these lost men and their stories very well:

They shall not grow old, as we that are left grow old;
Age shall not weary them, nor the years condemn,
At the going down of the sun and in the morning,
We shall remember them.p

Bibliography

Ambrose, Stephen E. *D-Day, June 6, 1944: The Climactic Battle of World War II.* New York: Simon and Schuster, 1994.

Blair, Clay. *Ridgway's Paratroopers: The American Airborne in World War II.* New York: Dial, 1985.

Booth, Michael T. *The Life of General James M. Gavin.* New York: Simon and Schuster, 1994.

Burgett, Donald. *Seven Roads to Hell: A Screaming Eagle at Bastogne.* Novato, Calif.: Presidio, 1999.

Cole, Hugh M. *The Ardennes: Battle of the Bulge.* U.S. Army in World War II. Washington, D.C.: Center of Military History, 1965.

82d Airborne Division Association. *Saga of the All-American.* Atlanta: Albert Love, 1946.

Gavin, James M. *On to Berlin: Battles of an Airborne Commander, 1943–1946.* New York: Viking, 1978.

Harrison, Gordon A. *Cross-Channel Attack.* U.S. Army in World War II. Washington, D.C.: Office of the Chief of Military History, U.S. Army, 1951.

Laby, Hubert. *Ardennes 44 Stavelot; The Dramatic Turnaround.* Faimes, Belgium: self published, 1999.

Lee, Bruce. *Marching Orders.* New York: Crown, 1995.

MacDonald, Charles B. *A Time for Trumpets: The Untold Story of the Battle of the Bulge.* New York: Morrow, 1984.

Winterbotham, Frederick W. *The Ultra Secret.* New York: Harper and Row, 1974.